Tapping Philanthropy
for Development

D1196992

Tapping

Philanthropy for

Development

Lessons Learned from a Public-Private Partnership in Rural Uganda

Lorna Michael Butler &
Della E. McMillan, editors

 Kumarian Press

A Division of Lynne Rienner Publishers, Inc. • Boulder & London

Published in the United States of America in 2015 by
Kumarian Press
A division of Lynne Rienner Publishers, Inc.
1800 30th Street, Boulder, Colorado 80301
www.rienner.com

and in the United Kingdom by
Kumarian Press
A division of Lynne Rienner Publishers, Inc.
3 Henrietta Street, Covent Garden, London WC2E 8LU

Library of Congress Cataloging-in-Publication Data
A Cataloging-in-Publication record for this book
is available from the Library of Congress.

ISBN 978-1-62637-194-1 (hc)
ISBN 978-1-62637-195-8 (pbk)

British Cataloguing in Publication Data
A Cataloguing in Publication record for this book
is available from the British Library.

Printed and bound in the United States of America

 The paper used in this publication meets the requirements
of the American National Standard for Permanence of
Paper for Printed Library Materials Z39.48-1992.

5 4 3 2 1

Contents

Illustrations

Tables

Figures

Foreword

Gerald A. and Karen A. Kolschowsky

We are happy to have been a small part of the process that led to this book documenting some of the early history of the Center for Sustainable Rural Livelihoods (CSRL) program in Uganda. We are especially grateful to all of the experts who worked with Lorna Michael Butler and Della E. McMillan on organizing and writing the book. These primary authors of the individual chapters were the "boots on the ground" that built the program; the chapters are rooted in their experiences. Based on this firsthand knowledge, the book offers practical advice for other donors. Although the steps that the authors describe may seem obvious, that was not the case when we embarked on this new type of philanthropic endeavor.

It all started when we had some time to talk during our six-hour drive to Ames, Iowa, for the Iowa State University (ISU) Foundation meetings in fall 2000. Jerry was by then contemplating retirement, so we were doing some estate planning and beginning to think about longer-term commitments. But generally, we were pretty inexperienced in philanthropic endeavors.

Perhaps because of his agribusiness background, Jerry felt that he would like to do something in sustainable agriculture. He was aware of a new position created in the College of Agriculture and Life Sciences (CALS)—the Henry A. Wallace Endowed Chair for Sustainable Agriculture. We knew that the individual hired for this position had recently arrived on campus. Around the same time, the college had announced a graduate degree program in sustainable agriculture (the program was launched in 2001). Karen said, "We have been blessed," and she suggested that we do something for the poor. So the university seemed like a good place to start. We had donated to ISU previously, for scholarships and a building project in animal sciences, but we were never deeply involved with these gifts.

The next step involved sitting down with someone from CALS. Jerry scheduled an initial "get to know each other" meeting with the new college fund-raising officer. In the course of the conversation, Jerry told him what we were thinking—and he ran with it! That was the first step.

Over the next year, we talked with several people who were doing things internationally—ideas did not come overnight. It took time, perhaps a year and a half, before we decided to provide some initial seed money for researching and planning an international initiative. That generated more ideas—some we liked, and some we didn't. By this time, we had both decided that we wanted to benefit the poorest of the poor.

In June 2003, we took part in a "think tank" that was part of ISU's initial planning process. That think tank opened everyone's eyes, including ours, to what was being done and what more could be done. Listening to a small group of enthusiastic and experienced individuals made a huge difference. It also reinforced to us that it was a good choice to work through the university.

We solidified these ideas during our first visit to Uganda in 2004. Our exchanges with the local people, the Volunteer Efforts for Development Concerns (VEDCO), and Makerere University (MAK) staff, as well as with the ISU faculty who had lived and worked in Africa, convinced us that this effort had to be hands-on if it was to be sustainable. We became more involved over the three years that the program was being developed—as we all learned—but after the amount of funding required was determined, we knew we could not be "not involved"!

This made us realize that we could not give large sums of money without having a good understanding about what was going on and how the money was going to be spent. When you give someone a thousand dollars, that is one thing. When you give them a million dollars, that is something else. We knew that we needed to be part of the process, to become more involved. We wanted to see the development of whatever we supported. That was the next significant step in our journey.

The initial agreement that we signed with ISU was simple. While we didn't dictate what the program was supposed to look like, we did insist on a careful planning and budgeting process. The budget was initially our only "benchmark." Most of the key planning decisions were made by consensus among the partners—ISU, MAK, VEDCO, and the local communities. Our input always seemed to be appreciated, and everyone appeared comfortable in voicing their opinions.

Although we are proud to be the CSRL program's founding bene-factors, we have never wanted to be at the forefront. In the final analy-sis, getting things done in philanthropy is rather like what Jerry saw in business. Whether it be to expand into a new country, find a good part-ner, build a new plant, or set up a new production line—keeping in mind different cultures, traditions, practices, laws, work ethics, and so on—it is all about people. Find the right individuals, allow them to make a plan, authorize them to execute the plan, and then encourage them to reevaluate the plan based on what did and did not work. And of course, do all of this with the customer in mind—nothing happens until you sell something!

Bringing in ISU and MAK students to work with the program staff during the summer, starting in 2006, was one of the best decisions that we and the partners ever made. Through those students' eyes, we were forced to start focusing on the program's future. The same students became strong advocates for curriculum change in their host institu-tions, and they also attracted a number of new private donors, both large and small.

If we can offer advice to other donors about the CSRL model, it would be to approach any type of philanthropic endeavor as a journey. It doesn't always work the way you want it to—it evolves, and it improves. It is a process.

Acknowledgments

The path to this book has been meandering and long. It started with a workshop in Evanston, Illinois, that brought together many of the key individuals involved in the design, execution, and monitoring of the Center for Sustainable Rural Livelihoods (CSRL) program to reflect on lessons learned over the past ten-plus years. In the course of doing this, these individuals discovered that there were some missing data and a need for additional analyses. They also recognized that there were both strengths and weaknesses in the program experiences. Like the program itself, this led to further insights, growth, and views about the future. The book-writing process contributed to that development.

First and foremost, we thank Gerald A. and Karen A. Kolschowsky, CSRL's founding benefactors, and the many other donors who have supported the CSRL program. Without them, there would be no CSRL.

In addition to the primary chapter authors, there were many knowledgeable and committed individuals who generously contributed to particular themes, lessons learned, and recommendations. In particular, we recognize the assistance of the Volunteer Efforts for Development Concerns (VEDCO) staff who serve, or have served, in Kamuli, as well as some of the Makerere University students and faculty; these include Donald Kugonza, Bernard "Ben" Obaa, Nancy Rapando, and Phinehas Tukamuhabwa, who responded to questions and helped with historical information, data collection, and refinement.

We are grateful to many Iowa State University individuals who made a special effort to provide various types of information. We appreciate the assistance provided by Denise Bjelland, Dylan Clark, Carole

Gieseke, Melea Reicks Licht, Brian Meyer, Jodi O'Donnell, and Josie Six. We also thank Raymond Klein and Lisa Eslinger of the Iowa State University Foundation, who responded to our requests with needed information and contacts.

We acknowledge the efforts of current and past VEDCO staff who contributed their institutional knowledge of the program and their understanding of the data sets that were needed to complete the program analysis. In particular, we thank Grace Babiyre, Ronnie Balibuzani, Laura Byaruhanga, Charles Kategere, Stephen Kato, Esther Matama, Benon Musasizi, Gideon Nadiope, Jane Nakiranda, Mary Nyasimi, Patrick Sangi, John Sembera, and Jane Sempa. Joseph Bbemba, Henry Nsereko, and Annette Nakyejwe Sebulime were a great help in obtaining important historical data.

Finally, as the editors of this book, we are grateful to our editor Lynn Hurtak. She provided the external eye that we needed to distill simple lessons learned and recommendations. She hounded us from day one to think and write simply and clearly. The staff at Lynne Rienner Publishers gave us confidence, enthusiasm, and hard-core editorial savvy in refining the manuscript. We are especially grateful to Shena Redmond, Diane Foose, Alejandra Wilcox, and Lynne Rienner, as well as the three anonymous reviewers who critiqued the first draft.

Our partners, Robert Butler and David Wilson, were patient listeners and occasional section reviewers. We could not have asked for more.

—*Lorna Michael Butler &*
Della E. McMillan

Introduction:
Tapping Philanthropy for Development

Della E. McMillan and Lorna Michael Butler

Venture philanthropy is a type of institutional gift giving that is gaining importance throughout the world. With *venture philanthropy,* benefactors invest in causes that they support while maintaining a direct connection to the resulting program and playing a key role in leveraging additional support from other donors.

This type of philanthropy is diverse and growing. At one end of the continuum of venture philanthropists are well-known donors like the Bill and Melinda Gates, Carnegie, and Rockefeller Foundations. At the other end are an increasing number of smaller, family-managed private foundations and individuals who are giving or planning to give money to causes in which they believe.

This emerging class of private philanthropists expects the same high standards of entrepreneurship, drive, and accountability that drove their own businesses to success, and they often want to influence how their money is spent. Programs that wish to benefit from their support must understand these expectations and what it means in terms of program planning, communication, and reporting. This book is designed to tell the story of one such program and to share the lessons learned with individuals and organizations hoping to attempt something similar.

The story starts with two established Iowa State University (ISU) donors, Gerald A. and Karen A. Kolschowsky, who decided to push the university to get involved in a grassroots antipoverty program in the developing world. We describe how initial discussions with the Kolschowskys prompted a small group of ISU faculty and a fund-raising officer to determine how they could collaborate. Located in Ames, ISU already had a historic commitment to the Kolschowskys' goal, but US government and international support for this type of program in developing countries had dwindled. This group of faculty needed a suitable donor, and the Kolschowskys needed a suitable institution to help them advance their new philanthropic interests.

Initially, ISU required a clear idea of what the program was to accomplish; thus, two years were spent in deciding which country, partners, and activities were a good match for this type of joint partnership. Working through Ugandan partners, Volunteer Efforts for Development Concerns (VEDCO) and Makerere University (MAK) in Kampala, ISU executed a low-cost program to address some of the root causes of rural poverty in one of Uganda's poorest districts, Kamuli.[1] With support from private donors, the program—christened the Center for Sustainable Rural Livelihoods (CSRL)—grew. By 2013, CSRL had more than 208 donors, leveraging over $12 million in private gifts plus other external grants. The net impact of these activities has been a measurable increase in the standard of living for some of the most vulnerable households in Kamuli.

Based on an analysis of the CSRL story, we identified nine steps that other programs are likely to pass through in the course of developing a similar base of private donor support. Each of the first eight steps is the subject of a chapter in this book; the ninth step—which focuses on maintaining continual communication with the benefactors—is crosscutting in each of the chapters. Each chapter begins with a brief summary of the challenges that any new program is likely to encounter in dealing with the subject step, then describes the CSRL program's attempts to address those challenges, and concludes with a summary of lessons learned and recommendations based on CSRL's experience that other organizations can use to develop well-thought-out, private benefactor–funded programs.

In recent years, the growing number of donors interested in strategic or results-based philanthropy has given rise to several books and even university-based centers in the United States. Those books and centers offer practical guidance to new and existing programs and the benefactors working with them. While this book is compatible with some of the emerging guidelines on venture philanthropy,[2] it is also different because (1) it is written from the point of view of the benefactor-recipient partnership; (2) it focuses on the evolution of a single-program case study over thirteen years; and (3) it addresses new program development as a series of interlocking steps. Thus, the book should help those with new or struggling programs understand and grapple with the special challenges that they are likely to face at each step of a new or developing private benefactor–funded program. It can assist universities to think more strategically about potential partners.[3] It also illuminates some of the special strengths and weaknesses of universities as institutional homes for results-based philanthropy.

This book shows some of the challenges and results that can come from executing an innovative three-way partnership that links universities with nongovernmental organizations (NGOs). It is compatible with a number of recent books that challenge the traditional partnership models in development.[4]

For students, this book serves to provide a practical real-world perspective on the mechanics of designing and executing a domestic or international development program. This perspective is missing from most how-to guides on program design and execution, which tend to focus on processes like writing proposals and developing monitoring and evaluation plans rather than the development and management of donor support. However, more organizations are thinking about building the roots of sustainability into development programs from the start through links to local institutions. Students who have had training and experience in the design or execution of this type of grassroots private benefactor partnership will increase their market value to the NGOs or development agencies that are likely to hire them.[5]

Not least, we hope that this book will stimulate new thinking on the part of the leaders of philanthropic organizations and philanthropists, especially those considering a link with US and international universities for some part of their programs.

Notes

1. Throughout this book, when "Kamuli" is used alone it refers only to the district and "Kamuli town" refers to the town.

2. Key references include Eric Friedman, *Reinventing Philanthropy: A Framework for More Effective Giving* (Washington, DC: Potomac Books, 2013); Joel L. Fleishman, *The Foundation: How Private Wealth Is Changing the World* (New York: Public Affairs Books, 2007); Thomas J. Tierney and Joel L. Fleishman, *Give Smart: Philanthropy that Gets Results* (New York: Public Affairs Books, 2011); and Leal Brainard and Derek Chollet's *Global Development 2.0: Can Philanthropists, the Public, and the Poor Make Poverty History?* (Washington, DC: Brookings Institution, 2008). Each of these books—which are gaining wide readership among the general public as well as academics—is designed to provide a framework for more effective giving based on the review

of emerging trends and academic studies of philanthropy. The same texts propose guidelines to make philanthropic giving more effective.

3. One of the first books on this topic, which is a useful complement to this book, is Ralph Lowenstein, *Pragmatic Fundraising for College Administrators and Development Officers* (Gainesville: University of Florida Press, 1997).

4. Jennifer M. Brinkerhoff, *Partnership for International Development: Rhetoric or Results?* (Bloomfield, CT: Kumarian Press, 2002).

5. Derick W. Brinkerhoff and Jennifer M. Brinkerhoff, *Working for Change: Making a Career in International Public Service* (Bloomfield, CT: Kumarian Press, 2005).

1

Identifying Opportunities

O. Richard Bundy III

Private benefactors do not just appear. They are courted. A successful courtship needs to be carefully orchestrated and planned while leaving space for chance happenings and unexpected questions. As in any courtship, the potential donor and institution should get to know one another before making any formal commitments. First of all, is the attraction mutual? And can something worthwhile come from the relationship? This is a time when the prospective benefactor and the development institution can learn about one another's motives, interests, and capabilities.

This chapter provides a brief overview of the process that Iowa State University (ISU) used to respond to some common challenges that are likely to emerge when institutions first contemplate the value of a partnership with private benefactors:

- Establishing an organizational base—connecting key organizational staff to the fund-raising office and to potential private benefactors;
- Nurturing fledgling donor relationships in the early stages—cultivating relationships with existing and new program friends that have potential for supporting the expansion of organizational initiatives;

The author wishes to acknowledge the helpful input and contributions of David Acker, Lorna Michael Butler, Dylan G. Clark, Lisa Eslinger, Robert Mazur, Della E. McMillan, Josie Six, and Mark Westgate.

- Cultivating, stewarding, and engaging established benefactors—providing a vision of what a potential investment could accomplish and capitalizing on the experience and knowledge of the initial benefactors; and
- Widening and deepening the support base beyond the initial founders' commitments—leveraging additional support for the program.

Establishing an Organizational Base

Key Challenges

Getting to Know the Fund-Raising Office. Any donor—large or small—wants their money to be tracked and safe. This is why most philanthropic institutions or government institutions that work for the common good—be they hospitals, universities, nongovernmental organizations (NGOs), or even public school systems—have fund-raising offices, with the role of securing and managing private support from current and prospective funders. Some institutions may even route new proposals through this office to ensure compliance with the agency's fiscal rules and regulations.

A good fund-raising office is critical for building private or external support for a new program because (1) it knows which agencies have given to that institution in the past; (2) it is aware of which private donors may be planning to expand their engagement in the future; and (3) it understands the government rules, regulations, and tax laws that affect philanthropic giving and the agency's internal institutional rules for managing these funds. The office is also familiar with the organization's mission goals and priorities.

For the fund-raising office to do its job, it needs to know what type of program is envisioned, who is involved, and to which external agencies it is talking. The staff leading the new program must also be informed about the institution's rules and regulations for private sector giving and communication with donors.

If an organization does not have a fund-raising office, it might have a new business development or grant-writing office. If an organization does not have a tradition of managing private gifts, it might consider having an independent entity manage this function. This could be a short-term private consultation until the institution is able to establish the types of oversight that private benefactors expect from the institutions that they support.

Creating a Management Team. One of the keys to building new programs with donors is to create a management team, which shows that there is a nucleus of staff and outsiders who are seriously committed to the program concept. Getting too organized and official at this stage is unnecessary. A start-up management team should be informal and comprised of people who have experience in the area that is being proposed for the new program and who are committed to the new program, even if it is still quite amorphous and in the initial planning stages. This group should be thinking about general guidelines, activity time lines, and communicating with key individuals and groups. Once a prospective donor is identified, they become the go-to people for the office and the emerging face of the new program. To facilitate the fund-raising officer's informed communication with the group, it is wise to appoint a management team leader, at least on an interim basis.

The Center for Sustainable Rural Livelihoods Experience

Relationships Matter. In September 2000, ISU's Henry A. Wallace Endowed Chair for Sustainable Agriculture (hereafter Wallace Chair) Lorna Michael Butler and College of Agriculture and Life Sciences (CALS) executive director of development Richard Bundy who was responsible for the college's private fund-raising activities, were both new to the college. A preexisting fund-raising objective related to Butler's office compelled the two to meet early in their respective tenures, during which time Butler shared her extensive work experiences in Africa and her desire to potentially launch programs on the continent through her office. In this early conversation, it was clear that an open and trusting relationship might be possible between these two individuals, and that proved key to the long-term effort that followed.

Less than a month later, Bundy introduced Butler to Gerald A. "Jerry" Kolschowsky, a prominent graduate of the CALS Agricultural Business Department and the successful former chairman of the board and co–chief executive officer of a food products company based near Chicago. The ISU alumnus and his wife, Karen A., had become reconnected with the university as adults when their youngest son enrolled in the late 1980s and their active engagement with ISU grew substantially over a number of years, primarily through service on the ISU Foundation Board of Directors. They were generous donors to multiple programs on campus, had season tickets to several of the sports teams, and were regular participants in activities related to the campus museum.

From this initial conversation, however, their philanthropic relationship with ISU was about to change.

During their careers, the Kolschowskys had traveled extensively in developing nations and witnessed poverty, hunger, and disease first-hand. They had made a commitment to each other that one day they would try to improve the lives of the rural poor in developing nations and, during their initial meeting with the new director of development in October 2000, Jerry asked if ISU was doing any work in the area of sustainable agriculture in the developing world. At this early stage, the couple's vision was not fully formed—or so it seemed to their early ISU contacts. What was clear was the Kolschowskys' commitment to making a difference in developing nations and their sense that ISU was in an excellent position to help them do this. This conversation would turn out to be the start of the Center for Sustainable Rural Livelihoods (CSRL).

The Kolschowskys approached their philanthropic interests in a way that, at the time, was quite different from what most private donor managers in fund-raising offices were accustomed to. In retrospect, the Kolschowskys were on the cutting edge of an emerging trend—now called *venture philanthropy*—that was first recognized in the United States in the mid-1990s.[1] John D. Rockefeller III first used the term in 1969 to refer to "the adventurous funding of unpopular causes."[2] However, the idea began circulating in the philanthropic world following the publication of an article in the *Harvard Business Review* about what foundations could learn from venture capitalists (see Box 1.1).[3]

Building a Start-Up Management Team. At first, there was only a small nucleus of individuals interacting with the potential donors.[4] While all of its members did not become involved immediately, the group provided early guidance to the Sustainable Rural Livelihoods (SRL) initiative.

Gathering a diverse committed group. The team eventually consisted of seven faculty and staff members from six different campus units: the Colleges of Agriculture and Life Sciences; Business; Liberal Arts and Sciences; Human Sciences; the Greenlee School of Journalism; and the ISU Foundation.[5] Drawing on different disciplines and colleges proved valuable given the eventual complexity of the program. Everyone voluntarily contributed time and ideas. No extra financial compensation was involved in the planning phase.

Planning in a vacuum. Members of the management team began to formulate ideas about a potential program long before they knew if

---

Box 1.1 Definitions of Venture Philanthropy

There is general agreement around a set of core characteristics to describe venture philanthropy: venture philanthropists are deeply engaged with the organization they have chosen to support and make a long-term commitment to fund the organization, working hard to leverage their support to generate additional funding. They seek to build the capacity of the organization and its leaders to more effectively accomplish its mission, and are focused on measuring the outcomes of their support. Where in the past, donors made their gift and then trusted the recipient of the gift to do the good work to which the gift was committed, venture philanthropists are—first and foremost—characterized by a much deeper personal engagement with the nonprofit they are supporting.[6]

> Whatever traditional philanthropists were doing, the venture philanthropists concluded, wasn't working—society was still brimming with problems. Clearly, if you really wanted to save the world, you had to do more than write checks: You had to *act*. You had to find great people, help them build great social-service organizations, and then hold them accountable for their results. In other words, you had to attack social problems the way venture capitalists and entrepreneurs attacked business problems—with hands-on, we're-in-this-together, failure-isn't-an-option partnerships between *investors* and *investees*.[7]

Venture philanthropists are keenly interested in solving problems as opposed to building institutions, but they value leadership, sustainability, and capacity building that is both broad and deep within the organizations they support. They are willing to make long-term—often very large—financial commitments toward success, but with exceptionally high expectations for accountability, measurable results, and a defined exit strategy. They are champions of experimenting with new approaches to achieve bold ambitions, but risks need to be managed carefully.[8]

---

there would be any funds available. They talked enough together to gradually identify a preliminary vision, a set of values to guide the planning process, and a framework that might serve as a guide for the program. From a fairly early stage, the management team agreed that, if a program were to be launched in a developing country, the sustainable livelihoods framework (SLF) should guide the planning and implementation (see Chapter 3).

Later, when planning funds became available, the team recommended an interim director and played an active role in hiring the first program manager. Because they were a diverse group with different backgrounds and experiences, they became extremely valuable in communicating with different departments and networks, all of which helped in the partner selection process (see Chapter 2). Over the years, the majority of these individuals have continued to have some type of relationship with the program.

The preliminary proposal and budget. At the request of the initial benefactors, a draft proposal was drawn up by some of the team members in mid-2002. It described a potential start-up program in an African country, yet to be defined, and attached a budget. This proved challenging since there was no clear vision of how large a program to consider, what the central themes might be, where the program might be located, or how it would be implemented in a yet-to-be-named developing country. In the process of developing the first draft proposal, a de facto program director was also selected by the management team. However, the proposal proved to be "too much too soon," and the Kolschowskys made it clear that they wanted ISU to develop a more finely tuned plan for implementation. They proposed that there be a year to develop a carefully crafted plan. To make this happen, they provided an expendable gift of $100,000 to support planning and start-up activities (Table 1.1).

The start-up communication plan. The interim director determined there would be advantages to sharing what was happening with others, both within and outside of the organization. The management team made a great effort to interact with other faculty, staff, and students, and with external organizations. Some of this occurred through seminars, news releases, and invited presentations. These early communications proved useful in the search for execution partners (see Chapter 2) and in helping to grow the program.

Nurturing Fledgling Donor Relationships in the Early Stages

Key Challenges

Building a Bond of Trust. Once a program gets an actual grant—however small—the relationship between donor and recipient shifts to a new level of trust and accountability. Most private donors want to know how their money has been and will be spent. They must also trust that their initial generosity will not create a landslide of other requests.

Table 1.1 Time Line of Major Private-Donor Gifts for CSRL Start-Up, 2002–2004

Date	Gift Amount	What Happened as a Result
December 2002	$100,000	Stimulated a one-year planning process to clarify approach, gather information, make contacts, and begin to identify possible partners
		Enabled appointment of part-time interim director
		Established CSRL office with program assistant
		Hired graduate student assistant
		Funded reconnaissance visits by some of the management team members to Mexico, Peru, and Ghana
		Convened an external think tank to critique early plans
July–November 2003	$10,000	Reconnaissance visits by some of the management team members to Malawi, Kenya, and Uganda, including follow up visit to Uganda
December 2003	$1,000,000 (expendable)	Established CSRL at ISU Established core operating budget
November 2004	$9,000,000	Established endowment for long-term CSRL program

Source: ISU Foundation, Wallace Chair, and CSRL office records, 2002–2004.

Many well-intended "good doers" do not understand this and bombard their donors with a seemingly inexhaustible flow of new requests, which can cause donors to back away. Most donors will also want to have a role in collaborative planning. This is why one of the most important rules of effective donor engagement is for the fund-raising officer to build and retain a trusting relationship with the prospective benefactors.

Creating Opportunities for Prospective Donors to Talk with the Management Team. Not every potential benefactor will be a good match for every program and every institution. The best donors are those whose core values and expectations are aligned with those of the host institution and its leaders. This is a learning process that takes time and patience. A wise program staff will consider identifying a few activities to enable the organization and the prospective benefactors to share ideas about the potential program so as to determine if they are a good match.

The CSRL Experience

Initial Brainstorming. The direct involvement of CSRL's founding benefactors in a series of early brainstorming processes helped to outline some of the central elements of the livelihoods and food security program that they had first inquired about. These discussions also made it clear that the Kolschowskys did not want to provide undue or misinformed influence to important decisions about partners or a location. Between September 2000 and August 2002, the Kolschowskys met with the CALS faculty and staff from the ISU Foundation more than two dozen times for probing conversations about ISU's strengths and weaknesses, and various strategies that might be used to direct the college's strengths toward the establishment of a program to accomplish their philanthropic objectives. Initially, the fund-raising officer maintained a careful hold on who and how many individuals were in communication with the potential funders. The more actively engaged that the management team became, the greater their ownership in the outcome and the deeper their level of mutual understanding and trust. This continual engagement promoted a sense of optimism among members of the ISU management team.

The Think Tank. The high point of the founding benefactors' early engagement took place in June 2003, when a think tank of global development experts was convened at ISU (see Chapter 2). The Kolschowskys participated fully in this event, and it was at this gathering that some of the central themes about what would eventually become the CSRL program would be set. It also served to ramp up the benefactors' level of interest.

Additional Support for Field Visits to Facilitate Partner Selection. The think tank prompted immediate plans for several team members to visit Malawi, Kenya, and Uganda. There was little hesitation on the donors' part to add another smaller contribution to the planning grant to support the last few steps of the planning phase (Table 1.1). At the same time, the confidence they exhibited also helped to leverage additional funds for this purpose from various units in CALS. Upon return from all three of these reconnaissance visits, the findings were discussed with the management team, and there was a tentative recommendation to focus on Uganda (Figure 1.1). A follow-up visit was made to Uganda to begin to develop a short list of potential partners.

Figure 1.1 Location of Uganda in Africa

The Gift that Propelled ISU into Uganda. Even though the reconnaissance team returned with only a partner short list, the Kolschowskys expressed their confidence in the ISU team—and CALS—by pledging a gift of $1 million to get the program started (Table 1.1). It was at this juncture that the Kolschowskys began to put parameters around the use of their gifts that, to this day, guide the overall budgeting and strategic direction of CSRL. These conditions included a commitment to demonstrating impact by using standard metrics for evaluation.[9]

The Creation of CSRL to Manage the SRL Program. The initial $1 million commitment provided the impetus for the establishment of the CSRL program in CALS in December 2004. About this time, a proposal went forth to the ISU administration to establish a center. The involved faculty crafted a proposal describing the vision for CSRL, including who was to be involved, a proposed structure, and available funding. The CALS dean, Catherine Woteki, and other members of the university administration, including the president, reviewed the proposal. Once approved by the president, the proposal was sent forward to the Board of Regents for approval. The CSRL office, which was already in place, began to function under the leadership of its founding director, Robert Mazur, with backstopping from the Wallace Chair and other members of the management team. Funds received were channeled through the ISU Foundation with oversight from the CSRL director. The only other university requirement for the newly formed center was to establish an advisory board.[10]

The First Friends of CSRL Visit to Uganda. From the start, ISU was committed to the concept of showing the donors firsthand the impact of their giving. Thus, the decision was made to invite the Kolschowskys to visit the program in January 2004 to meet the new partners from Makerere University (MAK) and Volunteer Efforts for Development Concerns (VEDCO), participate in the signing of collaborative agreements with both partners, and see the work being done by VEDCO in the Luwero District. The visit would culminate with a trip to Kamuli, a region in Uganda that had enjoyed little attention from Western aid workers and was a target area for expanding the VEDCO model (Figure 1.2).

The first Friends of CSRL visit to Uganda in August 2004 was a phenomenal success and is a case study on the effectiveness of "high-touch donor cultivation."[11] This eight-day visit was a nonstop experience that strengthened the benefactors' interest in the program, deepened the bond of trust and respect that had grown between the Kolschowskys and the ISU team, and showcased the potential for even greater impact with more support.[12] Informal discussions about opportunities to enhance the program occurred throughout the course of the week and, on the final night in Kampala while waiting for the rest of the group to arrive for dinner, the Kolschowskys and the fund-raising officer had an in-depth conversation about their desire to expand the scope of the program and ensure that ISU had the resources to conduct work

Figure 1.2 District of Kamuli in Uganda

over a long period of time. That evening, they pledged $8 million to endow CSRL and an additional $1 million in current-use funding to fund the program while the endowment grew (this additional $1 million brought their total current-use commitment to $2 million).

Managing Communication with the Founding Benefactors. For the first four years of the planning process—and the first year of implementation—the fund-raising officer was the principal contact with the Kolschowskys.[13] The reason this worked was that the fund-raising officer was well informed about most administrative and program matters because he was part of the management team. He had also established a close personal relationship with the Kolschowskys. The level of professionalism that the fund-raising officer brought to the table was clearly appreciated by the Kolschowskys, and it had everything to do with the positive bond that was cultivated between them and ISU.

Cultivating, Stewarding, and Engaging Established Benefactors

Key Challenges

Today's philanthropists are often interested in solving specific problems, and may want to have some level of involvement in influencing the intervention that they are supporting. For example, global business experience may strengthen a program's management capabilities. However, it is wise to determine the level of donor engagement that is expected, and how it might be managed. For these reasons, it is prudent to listen to the ideas that may be offered from new and existing donors and to be sensitive to just how much involvement they want.

The CSRL Experience

Creating the Core CSRL Program Endowment and Additional Investment by the Founding Benefactors. The Kolschowskys' total pledge of $10 million by late 2004 was the ultimate expression of the venture philanthropists' commitment to long-term sustainable funding for their programs. This gift was a combination of outright support intended to provide annual operating funds over a five-year period, during which time the donors would also make pledge payments to establish an $8 million operating endowment, the earnings of which would start to become available in 2009–2010 and would coincide with the end of the annual support commitment (Table 1.2).

After three years, it became clear that the administrative costs to run CSRL were higher than originally expected. At the beginning of the 2008–2009 academic year, the Kolschowskys agreed to a revision of the original allocation percentages—those percentages currently stand at 75 percent for Ugandan field operations, 20 percent for ISU administrative expenses, and 5 percent for capital expenses.

Subsequent to this initial gift, the Kolschowskys have made additional one-time outright gifts or short-term multiyear commitments to launch or expand certain elements of the core CSRL program. The CSRL endowment is obviously a very personal expression of the Kolschowskys' desire for the program to always have a sustainable source of core funding and, despite the broad parameters placed around the use of endowment earnings as the core budget, there is flexibility for funds from the core to be reallocated as other sources of funding are identified to supplant the CSRL endowment support. The Kolschowskys always envisioned that there would be other funders who would come

Table 1.2 Model of the CSRL Endowment Plan (figures for illustration purposes only)

Calendar Year[a]	Endowment Total	Endowment Earnings	Annual Gift	Core Operating Budget
Year 1	$3,240,000	Reinvested	$300,000	$300,000
Year 2	$4,579,200	Reinvested	$350,000	$350,000
Year 3	$6,025,536	Reinvested	$400,000	$400,000
Year 4	$7,587,579	Reinvested	$450,000	$450,000
Year 5	$9,274,585	Reinvested	$500,000	$500,000
Year 6	$10,582,823	$513,729	0	$500,000
Year 7	$10,900,307	$529,141	0	$500,000
Year 8	$11,227,317	$545,015	0	$550,000
Year 9	$11,564,136	$561,366	0	$550,000

Source: Model prepared by Lisa Eslinger, ISU Foundation, February 12, 2014.

Notes: Illustration assumes a $10 million total gift, of which $2 million is paid in incrementally increasing current use (annual) gifts, and an $8 million gift for endowment purposes paid as $3 million in Year 1 and $1 million additional through Year 6 ($8 million total). It assumes an 8 percent endowment return and a 5 percent endowment spending rate.

a. Years are numbered for illustration purposes only. ISU's fiscal year runs from July 1–June 30.

forward with additional program support, which is one of the reasons that they chose to not have the program or center named on their behalf.

The Early Donor Communication Plan. From the onset, the fundraising officer served as the contact with the benefactors as to just how much information they wanted to share publicly; for example, whether their names were to be made public and whether the amount of the gift was to be announced. In their case, the Kolschowskys were not seeking publicity and, for the first three years of their support, their names were never publicly associated with their gifts to CSRL. The ISU Foundation and the university honored their wishes to remain anonymous. In November 2004, they agreed to let ISU announce their endowment gift in the hopes that it would inspire other donors to make similar commitments.[14]

Continuing Benefactor Involvement in Planning and Reporting. An integral part of the CSRL stewardship strategy was to continue to expose the benefactors to the program. A centerpiece of this strategy was a series of donor-focused trips that followed essentially the same schedule as the Kolschowskys' first visit in 2004.

Field trips to the program site. A total of ten prospective donors attended these semiannual trips between 2005 and 2011, and each trip resulted in significant new investments of private support. On all of these trips, senior members of the university administration—the president, provost, and various deans—were also included in an effort to expand institutional awareness and support for the program at the highest levels.

Creating the executive committee. Another expression of the Kolschowskys' unique engagement with the program was their desire to meet regularly with the organization and program leadership for strategic discussions about accomplishments and directions. As part of the agreement to fund the program, the Kolschowskys established an executive committee consisting of several faculty members from the initial management team, representatives from the ISU Foundation, and themselves. The executive committee, including the Kolschowskys, continues to meet at least twice per year, and among the key agenda topics are budget overview, program updates and assessments, and leadership development for key personnel associated with the program. This agenda has since been expanded to give attention to future directions. In recent years, some of the other donors have participated in the parts of the biannual executive committee that focuses on the field programs. This system of regular executive committee meetings has paid large dividends in terms of building new donor support and in providing constructive ideas for program improvement.

The Innovative Impact of the Founding Benefactors' Involvement in the Program. There were several points in the evolution of CSRL when it became apparent that, by gaining the attention and support of globally proficient founding benefactors, ISU would end up stronger (see Box 1.2). Some of this influence was derived in subtle ways such as a conversation over lunch. At other times, the Kolschowskys took the initiative to promote the interests of CSRL at the highest levels of the university. However, there was never a time when they insisted that CSRL be managed one way and not another. This communication between the founding benefactors and ISU was beneficial because (1) it pushed the program to embark on more rigorous planning; (2) it encouraged the program to expand its activities into more creative directions; and (3) it helped the program reach out to the worldwide community of international development experts by organizing the initial think tank, and drawing on the benefactors' personal network to bring on board various international representatives of important NGOs for the CSRL

Box 1.2 Impact of the Founding Benefactors' Active Engagement in the CSRL Program

Benefactors' Rigorous Planning

In the very early courtship phase, it was the Kolschowskys who insisted that ISU embark on a more rigorous planning process. While a detailed proposal had been presented to them, it was neither based on an identified partnership nor a well-thought-through program strategy. Neither the Kolschowskys nor the management team was entirely clear on how and where the program might proceed. The Kolschowskys must have sensed this. So they suggested that ISU consider taking a full year to more carefully investigate options and plan the details of the program. To facilitate this, they provided ISU with a gift of $100,000. Without this encouragement, the university probably would not have interacted with so many knowledgeable individuals in advance of selecting its partners, nor would the ISU administration have developed such a deep sense of ownership in the potential program. In retrospect, it appears that the planning year made sense to the prospective benefactors in that they would learn more about ISU's ability to carry out a major international global program and, perhaps, be more certain that their investment was in good hands.

Pushing for Higher Levels

About a year into the program, the partnership with VEDCO and MAK was just beginning to come together. VEDCO, with the help of the new CSRL field program manager, was focused on building a competent team of volunteer trainers who had the skills to train Kamuli farmers. In Ames, Iowa, the management team continued to interact with the CSRL director about program operations and management structure. Occasionally, some of the team met with the Kolschowskys as members of the executive committee.

Expanding the Program's Reach

During the years in which the program was evolving, the Kolschowskys laid out several big challenges for ISU but, at the same time, they provided ISU with tremendous freedom. Their own international experience provided them with the knowledge of what it takes to be the "best in class." They knew it was important to learn from others. This lesson played out in many ways for CSRL. They welcomed ISU's use of global networks in the planning phase, and they strongly endorsed the use of the

(continues)

Box 1.2 Continued

think tank for that same reason. This also came into play when we were setting up the CSRL Advisory Board. They opened their own networks to ISU and, as a result, some of the best individuals in the global development business agreed to serve on the board. Through their contacts, ISU also explored the potential of a faith-based partnership and, even though it did not materialize, this connection has proved important in other ways such as shaping the implementation approach and identifying student internship sites.

Planting the Seeds of Sustainability

The Kolschowskys' own personal philosophy about sustainability has influenced ISU in many ways. Their financial gifts established an endowment that will provide operating funds for CSRL in perpetuity. While this may not seem so innovative, there have been instances at other universities when large gifts were received and not invested in an endowed fund. As a result, some noteworthy programs were unable to continue when the funds ran out. The Kolschowskys' philosophies have prompted ISU to pay greater attention to the human resources capacity needs of CSRL's partner institutions and to look for ways to support partners' institutional development goals. In addition, it was probably the Kolschowskys' questions to the executive committee about purchasing land for an ISU headquarters facility in Uganda that moved the idea of ISU registering as a NGO in Uganda higher on the university's agenda.

Influence at the Institutional Level

After CSRL had been operating for about five years, the Kolschowskys' influence began to be noticed at both the CALS and university levels. During the development of the university's new strategic plan, they urged ISU's president to adopt the CALS 2050 challenge, a statement of commitment to the most critical global issues, as a university-wide challenge. They counseled CALS administrators to transform the college by drawing on the experience that had been developed through CSRL. The Kolschowskys, as well as other private donors to CSRL, have had a direct influence on internationalizing the CALS study abroad programs. More recently, this influence can be seen in the launching of the Global Food Security Consortium and the long-term vision projected by CALS to further expand international engagement college-wide (see Chapter 9).

Source: Lorna Michael Butler's summary, based on e-mail and personal conversations with David Acker and Richard Bundy, September 29–30, 2013.

Advisory Board. It also pushed the program to think about some added short-term actions—such as turning the initial gifts into an endowment, strengthening the partners' human resources capacity, and registering as an independent NGO in Uganda—that enhanced the program's chances for sustaining its impact and helped build ISU's internal support for the program.

Widening and Deepening the Support Base Beyond the Initial Founders' Commitments

Key Challenges

One of the hallmarks of a successful program is that it continues to grow. This means that fund-raising is never a single-time event, but something that continues over the lifetime of a program. A sophisticated benefactor knows this and will appreciate the program developing a sophisticated process for identifying new potential funding sources. This is a concept that the fund-raising communities call *leveraging*. This is not leveraging in the sense of debt leveraging, but rather using funds from one endowment or funder to attract support from other sources.

Care must be taken, however, to ensure that the founding bene-factors are involved, at least peripherally, in the fund-raising process because (1) most founding benefactors will want to ensure the integrity of their initial investment and will not want to see the pro-gram adding new funding sources that might overshadow or divert resources from their initial investment; (2) they are likely to be one of the program's best guides to new potential funding sources; and (3) their involvement can help attract greater internal support from the lead institution.

The CSRL Experience

The Kolschowskys gave ISU significant flexibility in how their funds could be utilized to advance the program, and the CSRL management team made a conscious decision to use their initial gift to incentivize other donors to give. The leveraging of the Kolschowskys' commitment evolved gradually through four distinct aggregate stages: (1) direct institutional investment; (2) institutional investment of additional donor resources; (3) direct additional donor investment; and (4) competitive funding (see Figure 1.3).

Figure 1.3 Progressive Leveraging of the Founding Benefactors' Investment in the Program Through the Addition of Other Sources of Support

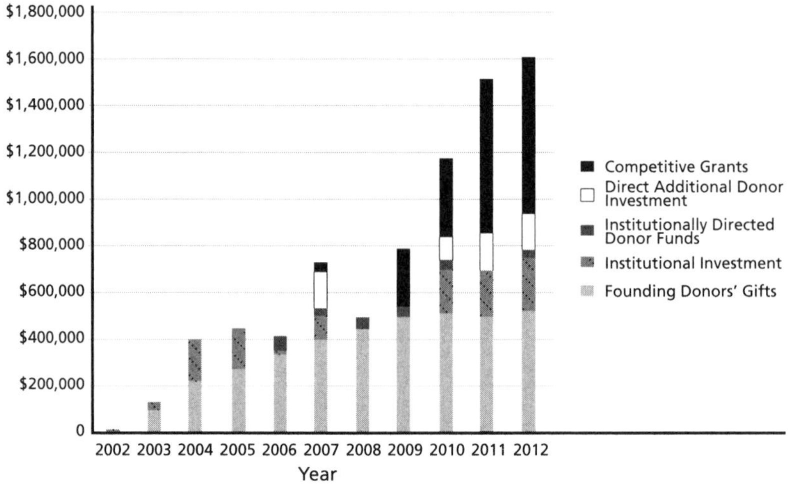

Sources: CSRL annual reports, unpublished reports from executive committee meetings, and CALS Administrative Services.

Notes: Total funding levels for 2002–2007 and 2010–2012 are precise, per CSRL annual reports and unpublished reports from executive committee meetings. Institutional investment and direct additional donor investment for 2008–2009 are estimates based on ISU Foundation and CALS Administrative Services records.

Institutional Investment. In the early years, even before ISU was assured of receiving a long-term commitment of funds, Wallace Chair Lorna Michael Butler devoted a high percentage of her time to the CSRL program. Not only did Butler use the funds provided to the holder of the Wallace Chair to visit Uganda and other potential program sites, but she worked closely with the management team and the director to define an implementation strategy and get the program started. This office made many of its resources available to the early CSRL office, and it cohosted CSRL's Ugandan partners so they could visit ISU to meet with faculty and students and explore areas of collaboration. Butler also supported early program monitoring and helped to support ISU, VEDCO, and MAK staff and students who took part in program endeavors.

Together, Butler and the CALS dean provided $20,000 for four seed grant initiatives that each had long-term ramifications for program directions and faculty and staff participation in CSRL, including:

- Documentation of Ugandan farmer case studies for program promotion and a preliminary database of potential CSRL funders and collaborators;
- Examination of the role of social capital in technology adaptation for food security in communities impacted by human immunodeficiency virus/acquired immunodeficiency syndrome (HIV/AIDS);
- Exploration of Ugandan animal breeding, production, and improvement; and
- Exploration of the potential for a Ugandan school garden program to improve children's and youths' nutritional status, academic success, agricultural production knowledge, and entrepreneurial opportunities.

The university administration also made travel grants available for faculty and staff who took part in the CSRL program. While there might have been a tendency to take this for granted, both the college and university were strongly committed to this program from the onset. They paid the salaries of faculty and staff who played a central role in the program. Other than the CRSL director (part-time), program assistant/coordinator, and graduate assistant (part-time), participating faculty and staff were funded with ISU monies (see Chapter 9).

The initial gift from the Kolschowskys in early 2003 had a nearly immediate leveraging effect within CALS. A program that had never existed before quickly began to attract the pro bono efforts of a large group of senior faculty, and would soon draw substantial internal financial resources as the program grew in stature and interest. The appointment of Robert Mazur as the interim director (until CSRL was officially established in August 2005) was the first allocation of direct institutional financial support toward the program, as CALS provided salary relief to his home department (sociology) to facilitate his active participation in the program. CALS also provided office space and partial funding for a support staff position, salaries of other involved faculty and staff, and some travel funds (Table 1.3). A substantial number of dollars was leveraged by the initial gift. Many different departments and units at ISU contributed funds in support of the program. These were used for travel, supplies, office and meeting facilities, salaries, and so forth. There was even a private scholarship that supported one of the first Ugandan student's graduate studies at ISU. This leveraging trend has continued, particularly with regard to CALS support, as well as an increased number of private gifts and competitive grants.

Table 1.3 Estimated Funds Available to SRL/CSRL in the Start-Up Years, 2002–2006

Fiscal Year	SRL Income[a]	Other Funds[b]	Total Operating Funds (estimated)	Percent SRL/CSRL	Percent Other
2002–2003	0	$9,057	$9,057	0	100
2003–2004	$100,000[c]	$29,558	$129,558	77	23
2004–2005	$225,000	$181,691	$406,691	55	45
2005–2006	$275,417	$176,852	$452,269	61	39

Sources: SRL/CSRL Annual Reports; records from Robert Mazur and Lorna Michael Butler.
Notes: Fiscal year ran from July 1 to June 31. CSRL began to develop budget statements based on the calendar year in 2009.
  a. Operating funds generated from the CSRL endowment.
  b. Estimated contributions and grants from various ISU departments and offices, including some in-kind contributions, and other designated gifts (e.g., for service learning, borehole construction, and livestock improvement).
  c. Private expendable gift for CSRL program planning and start-up.

Institutionally Directed Donor Funds. The same core endowment catalyzed other established ISU donors to support the program. During the first semester of the 2006–2007 academic year, for example, CALS was the beneficiary of a gift from the estate of Raymond and Mary Baker, which was used to establish the Raymond and Mary Baker Endowed Chair in Global Agriculture (hereafter Baker Chair). Though not required to be used for CSRL, funding has nonetheless been strategically invested by the inaugural Baker Chair to support CSRL programs.

This same approach was mirrored often in the early years of the program as graduate faculty throughout the college—largely through the original management team and their colleagues—began to direct assistantship dollars to students whose research aligned with the CSRL program. The Wallace Chair was an early champion of this approach by allocating donor funds under her control to students whose research aligned with CSRL programs. Additionally, beginning with the first service-learning cohort in 2006, the Department of Agronomy offered significant travel scholarships from their donor-funded endowment to students who participated in the CSRL program, regardless of their major in the college.

Direct Additional Donor Investment. As the program progressed, it developed a business plan that included several elements particularly attractive to other donors. As these new donors were exposed to the opportunities, they often chose component parts of the program to fund.

One donor couple who participated in multiple trips to Uganda was smitten by the service-learning program; another couple, whose daughter participated in one of the early service-learning groups, subsequently traveled to Uganda and made important gifts to establish several community boreholes and build a kitchen and girls dormitory at the Namasagali primary school. Yet another donor directed annual support to the Livestock Purchase Fund.

The combined effect of the fungible nature of the Kolschowskys' gifts was that as their money for specific projects was replaced with gifts from other donors, the Kolschowskys' support for the core central budget increased incrementally. ISU's success in raising more money from other donors for prescribed purposes already in the strategic plan meant that there were more flexible resources for core community activities.

Competitive Grants. As far back as the think tank in June 2003, the CSRL management team had been keenly aware of the importance of leveraging private gifts to secure external funding. A thread running through the discussions was the fact that the United States Agency for International Development (USAID) was "increasingly interested in identifying partners who have relationships with private donors."[15]

Over time, numerous faculty and staff made the effort to write grant proposals with the goal of bringing in external funds to support CSRL. Some of these efforts were successful; others were not. The USAID-funded Sustainable Agriculture and Natural Resource Management (SANREM) Collaborative Research Support Program (CRSP)[16] grant enabled ISU to collaborate with several other institutions in planning ways to improve livelihoods through landscape management, biodiversity conservation and improved child nutrition in Uganda, Tanzania, and Ghana. The USAID-supported Global Livestock CRSP Enhancing Child Nutrition Through Animal Source Food Management, which focused on improving child nutrition in Ghana through animal source foods, included an educational component to train Ugandans in the integration of community nutrition, extension, and animal science, and it provided support for a Ugandan graduate student to study nutrition at the University of Ghana.

Between 2005 and 2013, ISU faculty generated a total of eighteen different competitive research grant awards, all of which focused on Uganda's development problems (Box 1.3), amounting to over $4.66 million for the university.[17] Between 2013 and 2014, the CALS faculty brought in $8.8 million in external funding to investigate development in Africa.[18]

**Box 1.3 Ways CSRL Used Leveraged Funds to
Grow the Program**

- Faculty from the Department of Animal Science obtained support from the Monsanto Fund and private donors to help improve Kamuli animal breeds and farming systems for livestock production. This grant, led by ISU animal science professor Max Rothschild, trained Kamuli farmers in animal disease prevention and control, feeding, and management skills, and it enabled farmers to build livestock structures for their pigs.
- CSRL's first field program manager, Dorothy Masinde, collaborated with MAK's Department of Food Science and Technology to obtain a grant from the McKnight Foundation for promotion and production of grain amaranth for improved human nutrition and health.
- The associate dean, David Acker, was successful in obtaining a grant from the Rockefeller Foundation to train a doctoral student from Uganda in plant biotechnology. Because of the developing linkages with Uganda, talented Uganda students were often considered for scholarship opportunities. She enrolled at ISU and completed her Doctor of Philosophy (PhD) in four years.

Source: CSRL Program Records (Ames, Iowa, October 2013).

Lessons Learned and Recommendations

Major strengths of the CSRL program's system for opening the door to private benefactors included (1) ISU's early organization of a strong CSRL management team that included an officially recognized representative of the university's fund-raising office; (2) the management team's commitment to working through the university's fund-raising office to inform some of the university's existing and new donors about the new program; (3) the committee's close collaboration with the first-generation donors in the initial expansion of the program and its funding base; and (4) the strong commitment of the original benefactors and the university to using the endowment to diversify the program's funding base.

The chief weakness of the program was the length of time that it took to get the first large endowment up and running. Over the longer term, this investment was more than compensated by the fact that it created a sustainable endowment which, in turn, helped the program leverage other types of internal (i.e., university) and external (i.e., donor, foundation, and agency) support.

Establishing an Organizational Base

ISU's journey toward the identification of its first group of donors was launched by forging a strong link between the office of the newly appointed Wallace Chair and the ISU Foundation. This relationship made it possible for the ISU Foundation to connect CALS with two established donors who were thinking about committing some support to the university that might set the course for an innovative initiative. Also important was the formation of the first management team, with active involvement from both the fund-raising officer and senior ISU management.[19] As the management team evolved, it became the force that conceptualized the program, identified its initial leadership, and defined potential areas of collaboration with the first group of interested benefactors. The founding benefactors' willingness to fund a small start-up grant accelerated this planning and negotiation process. It also sent a clear message to ISU that this emerging initiative was well supported by the faculty and could actually work.

Lesson 1:
Make initial contacts with the fund-raising office of the institution that hopes to develop a new program.

Recommendations:
- Work through senior organization management to identify the most appropriate contact in the fund-raising office.
- Develop some key talking points to discuss with the fund-raising office so staff has adequate background on the prospective program's goals and potential impacts.
- Provide an overview of staff members that might potentially be involved.

Lesson 2:
Cultivate a relationship with the fund-raising officer in
case unanticipated funding opportunities emerge.

Recommendations:
- Find ways to connect the organization's fund-raising office with key members of the staff.
- Encourage discussions between the fund-raising officer and staff about new initiatives and programs that could potentially advance the organization.
- Provide regular updates on the program, suggested directions, and program justification to the fund-raising officer so that he or she can discuss these new ideas with potential benefactors.
- Allow the fund-raising officer to take the lead in exploring the opportunities, carefully and confidentially, when there seems to be a good match between a program idea and an interested donor.

Lesson 3:
Identify a core group of experienced individuals,
including the fund-raising officer, who are committed to
the program idea.

Recommendations:
- Choose a diverse team of experienced individuals in the organization to lead the planning of potential donor-supported fund-raising initiatives.
- Charge the team with developing guidelines for new fund-raising initiatives, including a preliminary program proposal and budget—knowing that this could change many times.

Lesson 4:
Work with the fund-raising office to seek some start-up
funds for planning a new initiative, including pilot tests.

Recommendations:
- Ask benefactors to consider a modest start-up gift that might be used to improve the program plan or pilot test a new initiative.

- Involve the donor with the staff in the design and assessment of the pilot activity.

Nurturing Fledgling Donor Relationships in the Early Stages

Once the potential benefactors were identified by the ISU Foundation officer, the challenge was to determine if the partners were a good match. To address this issue, the management team helped facilitate the potential benefactors' participation in a limited number of discussions with the team, even visiting the probable program site with the program's prospective partner. These joint activities helped the donors to better define their interests in relation to those of ISU's and vice versa. Although some of the team members interacted informally with the donors, most direct communication with the donors was routed through the ISU Foundation representative. This careful routing of communication was critical to building donor trust and confidentiality.

> **Lesson 5:**
> **Build a trust relationship between the interested benefactors and the organization to increase the chances for success.**

Recommendations:
- Ensure that the fund-raising officer maintains primary contact with the prospective donor in the early stages of the prospective donor's fund-raising discussions.
- Create informal opportunities for members of the management team to learn from each other and from others outside of the team, including the foundation officer and the prospective benefactors.
- Arrange for regular meetings and updates with organization leaders, including members of departments and units beyond the prospective program's immediate department or unit.

> **Lesson 6:**
> **Include potential benefactors in some of the key planning deliberations about possible directions, approaches, strategies, and partnerships.**

Recommendations:
- Facilitate meetings and discussions involving the potential bene-factors; organizational leaders; and, if the benefactors wish, some of the management team members.
- Determine whether an organization's values, goals, and mode of operation are a good match and if the organization is comfortable with the level and style of involvement that the funding partner may want.
- Allow time and patience to listen to and learn from potential benefactors.
- Involve the donor in design, oversight, and assessment of the pilot.

Cultivating, Stewarding, and Engaging Established Benefactors

Once the initial endowment was established, the focus of the donor communication strategy shifted to maintaining the trust relationship. The ISU stewardship model was committed to encouraging some lim-ited ongoing benefactor involvement in the program's day-to-day plan-ning and execution processes. The program was also committed to developing a structured model for communication with the donors that fit their expectations and desires.

Lesson 7:
Help management communicate with the rest of the organization and with the fund-raising office.

Recommendations:
- Plan ways that early activities and successes will be communi-cated across the organization.
- Have the first communication come from the administration and the fund-raising office as a legitimate statement of support for the new venture.
- Include other members of the organization in the planning process to avoid exclusivity.
- Reach out to other staff for ideas, contacts, and technical advice.
- Provide regular updates about the program to the benefactors—there should be no surprises.
- Respect the wishes of the benefactors concerning how much information about their gift to share with the public.

> **Lesson 8:**
> **Share progress with current and potential benefactors as the program advances.**

Recommendations:
- Agree on the best methods and desired frequency for maintaining communications with major benefactors.
- Plan appropriate methods for maintaining communications with other donors.
- Organize annual or biannual trips to the program site (or other program-related activities); invite a few key benefactors and, occasionally, potential donors.
- Arrange to bring execution partners and their staff members to visit the home office of the lead organization to meet and talk with benefactors and donors.
- Listen to the prospective benefactors to determine just how engaged they may want to be—for example, in the planning process, partner selection, management, financial oversight, and reviewing of outcomes.
- Benefactor engagement, at any level, needs to be clearly defined, discussed, agreed on, and documented in the gift contract.

> **Lesson 9:**
> **Be open to innovative ideas.**

Recommendations:
- Listen to, and learn from, the benefactors regarding program management, particularly if they have global experience.
- Occasionally ask the advice of benefactors, especially when there is a crisis—then there will be no surprises.
- Look to benefactors for leads about other sources of support, advice, and innovation.

Widening and Deepening the Support Base Beyond the Initial Founders' Commitments

The CSRL program was committed to diversified funding sources from the start. During the initial planning phase, the program used a wide variety of start-up grants from different established university funds. As the program grew, the founding benefactors and the fund-raising office helped the CSRL leadership widen its support base. This collaboration helped identify a few established donors who had worked with ISU for a long time and were willing to support some of CSRL's new initiatives. The same collaboration helped identify various areas—like collaborative research programs and nonuniversity foundations—where the program could access additional funds and other types of nonmonetary support to help strengthen the core program.

> **Lesson 10:**
> **Continue to foster a solid working relationship with the fund-raising office.**

Recommendations:

- Familiarize new fund-raising officers with the program background and activities.
- Consider hiring a fund-raising officer to work specifically with the program to reduce the transaction costs of training and retraining new officers.
- Minimize the impact of staff turnover on coordination by ensuring regular communication with the top management of the fund-raising office as well as with the individual fund-raising officer.

> **Lesson 11:**
> **Continue to explore new sources of support for the program.**

Recommendations:

- Try to secure large gifts as endowments to cover core costs over time, which will also facilitate fund-raising from other sources.
- Find ways to attract the interest and support of other units and departments within the organization.
- Look for creative ways to fund travel, small projects, and larger externally funded projects.
- Work through the assigned fund-raising officer to acquaint other potential donors with the program; identify further ways to communicate these activities to them.

- Plan mechanisms to communicate accomplishments to a wider audience, for example with public celebrations, a website, newsletters, presentations, site visits, and news releases.
- Emphasize the role of the endowment in covering core operating costs.

Notes

1. Social Innovator, "Venture Philanthropy" (London: Social Innovation eXchange [SIX], 2010), based on the following downloadable books, which are all in the Social Innovator Series: Ways to Design, Develop and Grow Social Innovation. Robin Murray, Julie Caulier-Grice, and Geoff Mulgan, *The Open Book of Social Innovation.* Social Innovator Series: Ways to Design, Develop and Grow Social Innovation (London: National Endowment for Science, Technology and the Arts [NESTA], 2010); Robin Murray, Julie Caulier-Grice, and Geoff Mulgan, *Social Venturing* (London: National Endowment for Science, Technology and the Arts [NESTA], 2009); Robin Murray, *Danger and Opportunity: Crisis and the New Social Economy* (London: National Endowment for Science, Technology and the Arts [NESTA], 2009). Mario Morino and Bill Shore, *High Engagement Philanthropy: A Bridge to a More Effective Social Sector,* Report No. 4 (Washington, DC: Venture Philanthropy Partners and Community Wealth Ventures, 2004), pp. 8–22; Luisa C. Bouverini, "When Venture Philanthropy Rocks the Ivory Tower: An Examination of High Impact Donors and Their Potential for Higher Education Development" (PhD diss., University of Pennsylvania, 2005); L. Brilliant, J. Wales, and J. Rodin, "The Changing Face of Philanthropy," paper presented at the Sixth Annual Global Philanthropy Forum Conference: "Financing Social Change: Leveraging Markets and Entrepreneurship," Mountain View, CA, April 2007.

2. Social Innovator, "Venture Philanthropy."

3. Christine W. Letts, William Ryan, and Allen Grossman, "Virtuous Capital: What Foundations Can Learn from Venture Capitalists," *Harvard Business Review* 75, no. 2 (1997): 38.

4. The initial group included the foundation officer, the CALS dean, the chair, and the director of global programs. Early in 2001, Butler decided to reach out to a more diverse group of faculty members, all of whom were deeply interested in various aspects of international development.

5. The initial SRL management team members were Eric Abbott (Journalism), David Acker (Agricultural Education and associate dean), Sanjeev Agarwal (Business/Marketing), Richard Bundy (ISU Foundation), Lorna Michael Butler (Anthropology/Sociology and Wallace Chair), Grace Marquis (International Nutrition), Robert Mazur (Sociology), and Ricardo Salvador (Agronomy). Later, several additional faculty members took on active leadership roles: Mark Westgate (Agronomy), Gail Nonnecke (Horticulture), Max Rothschild (Animal Science), and Dorothy Masinde (Agricultural Education/Sociology).

Many other faculty, staff, and students have contributed to the program over time.

6. Social Innovator, "Venture Philanthropy"; Tara Weiss and Hannah Clark, "'Venture Philanthropy' Is New Buzz in Business," Forbes.com, June 26, 2006.

7. Henry Blodget, "Grant Away: Why Venture Philanthropy Is Important, Even if It Sounds Ridiculous," *Slate Magazine,* November 13, 2006, www.slate.com/articles/life/philanthropy/2006/11/grant_away.html (emphasis in original).

8. Morino and Shore, *High Engagement Philanthropy,* pp. 8–22.

9. The original gift agreement required the CSRL program to use standard performance measures and to produce an annual progress report that featured a summary of the program's strategic plan and comments from the director on the accomplishments of the program toward meeting those strategic objectives (SOs). In contrast to conventional donor programs, the Kolschowskys looked to the original management team to determine what the initial metrics should be and were patient with the program leadership as they developed a set of mutually agreed on measures.

Their initial $1 million commitment, which was pledged as four annual payments of $250,000, came with an expectation that 85 percent of the funds would be used to support field operations in Uganda (including the salary of the field program manager), with another 5 percent allocated specifically for capital investments. The remaining 10 percent was allocated to administrative expenses for the ISU management team, in keeping with the venture philanthropists' understanding that core administrative expenses also needed support if one was to reasonably expect the field operations would be successful. This $250,000 annual pledge payment was called the "core funding" and was labeled as such to differentiate it from anticipated funding that might come from other sources.

10. The initial advisory board, created in early 2007, was composed of three external members and two internal member, plus five ex officio members (see Chapter 2).

11. Kim Klein, "Donor Cultivation: What It Is and What It Is Not," *Grassroots Fundraising Journal* 18, no. 5 (1999): 1–3. The phrase "high-touch donor cultivation" is a term from the author, Richard Bundy, and is an amalgam of the popular development officer concepts of "high-touch customer relations" and "donor cultivation." While the term is Bundy's, the description of donor treatment is supported by Klein.

12. The group spent three days in Kampala, meeting with MAK faculty as well as NGO and government officials, including the US ambassador. Three more days were focused on the program's relationship with VEDCO, touring its program sites in Luwero District before taking the long drive to Kamuli to explore partnership opportunities there. The contrast between families working with VEDCO in Luwero and families who had experienced little to no support in Kamuli was stark and drove home in powerful ways the impact that the CSRL program could have in these communities.

13. The same fund-raising officer served as the principal contact between the Kolschowskys and the campus for his entire tenure at ISU—from September 2000 to December 2010.

14. "Gifts of $10 Million Will Endow ISU Program that Helps Developing Nations," Iowa State University News Service, November 1, 2004, http://www .public.iastate.edu/~nscentral/news/04/nov/srl.shtml.

15. Jimmy Kolker, US ambassador to Uganda, in conversation with Richard Bundy, Gerald A. Kolschowsky, Karen A. Kolschowsky, Catherine Woteki, Robert Mazur, Lorna Michael Butler, and David Acker; along with Paul Crawford of USAID, Mike Gonzalez of USAID, and Jeff Levine of USAID, Kampala, Uganda, August 17, 2004.

16. SANREM CRSP is a US Congress initiative, supported by USAID since 1992, to support people in developing countries who are making decisions on how to improve livelihoods through sustainable agriculture and natural resource management. The program, which involves many different partner institutions, assists collaborators to improve their decisionmaking capacity through additional knowledge and information, tools, and methods of analysis. This phase of the SANREM CRSP (2009–2014) (now known as Feed the Future SANREM Innovation Lab) focuses on increasing smallholder food security through the introduction of conservation agriculture production systems. SANREM Innovation Lab, "History: Phase IV," 2014, http://www.oired.vt.edu /sanremcrsp/public/about/.

17. Special report from the ISU Office of Sponsored Programs Administration database, downloaded by Josie Six, ISU CALS Director of Budget and Finance, January 2014. Data compiled in a table titled "Competitive Research Awards for Development in Uganda for the Period 7/1/2005 through 12/10/13," attached to e-mail from David Acker, CALS associate dean, to Lorna Michael Butler, January 28, 2014.

18. Data compiled by David Acker based on data from CALS Global Programs office records. Totals have been rounded for ease of presentation. Table titled "2013–14 Success in Competing for Funding " attached to email from David Acker, CALS associate dean, to Lorna Michael Butler, January 28, 2014.

19. "The primary and initial reason we kept at it with ISU was because ISU actually responded when we asked questions—ISU's follow-up to our inquiries was among the best of any fund raising operations we have interacted with." Gerald A. Kolschowsky comments at the public announcement of the gift of $10 million to endow ISU program, ISU Foundation Governors luncheon, Ames, Iowa, November 1, 2004. See also ISU News Service, "Gifts of $10 Million Will Endow ISU Program That Helps Developing Nations," Ames, IA, November 1, 2004.

2

Courting Prospective Partners

Lorna Michael Butler and Robert Mazur

A good partnership can make it possible for institutions to work in an area far from home base. But good partnerships do not happen easily—they require ample homework, diligent networking, and many face-to-face discussions. Even when the fit seems mutual, there will be payoffs for going through a careful organizational assessment to learn about one another's motives, interests, experiences, and capabilities.

This chapter describes the process that the Center for Sustainable Rural Livelihoods (CSRL) program used to address four common challenges that most privately supported programs are likely to encounter when looking for partners:

- Getting organized to start the search-—creating an informal organization to help identify prospective partners that has high levels of institutional support from the lead institution;
- Gathering and processing planning information—learning as much as possible about potential partners and program sites;
- Making the shift from potential to actual partners—reaching agreement on the most appropriate partners and determining how the partnerships operate; and

The authors wish to acknowledge the helpful input and contributions of Dorothy Masinde and David Acker.

- Keeping the partnership alive—building the communication channels that will be needed to nurture the partnership.

Getting Organized to Start the Search

Key Challenges

When is the ideal time to gather a few experienced colleagues around a table to explore a potential development program? The earlier this happens, the better are the chances to generate needed administrative support and provide the rationale for building a more sustained dialogue with the fund-raising office. If the idea catches on, and the fund-raising officer is part of the early fervor, the momentum may provide the needed link to a prospective benefactor (see Chapter 1). This is also the group that is best suited for helping to organize the search for any new implementation partners. This informal sounding board can eventually take the form of a management team.

Three key challenges likely to emerge at this juncture are (1) determining who should be involved in this initial management team; (2) building a strong base of high-level institutional support for the management team and the program development processes that it is attempting to spearhead; and (3) leveraging initial institutional support for start-up costs such as office space, equipment, and program-related travel.

The CSRL Experience

Early Organization of the Group. During the 2001–2002 academic year, Henry A. Wallace Endowed Chair for Sustainable Agriculture (hereafter Wallace Chair) Lorna Michael Butler participated in some of the early discussions between the Iowa State University (ISU) fund-raising office and a new set of potential donors for international agriculture (see Chapter 1). During these discussions, the prospective benefactors made it clear that they were interested in funding a new program for the ISU College of Agriculture and Life Sciences (CALS) if an acceptable vision for a global development program could be devised.

To address this issue, Butler and CALS executive director of development Richard Bundy started talking with a small group of people with whom Butler already had working relationships. This loosely knit group, most of whom had global experience, gradually took on the responsibilities of a planning and management team. No one had a formal appointment and, in the beginning, there was no defined leader. And there was no assurance that their efforts would lead to anything solid. The group did not always meet together, but the discussions continued throughout the year, during which a level of trust and openness evolved as well as a consensus as to the type of program that might work for ISU and the prospective benefactors.

Identifying the First Director and Leveraging Start-Up Funds. When the funding for one year of planning became available in early 2003,[1] Robert Mazur, a sociologist with extensive African experience and whose scholarship focused on the development process, agreed to become the part-time interim director of the planning process. With help from CALS administration, a small office was established on the same floor as the dean's office, which was important because it fostered informal communication where it counted. The benefactors had the foresight to earmark funds in the planning grant for a graduate assistant at the very beginning, reflecting their commitment to providing opportunities for young people in this initiative at every level. A temporary program assistant was hired to oversee office operations such as budget, purchasing, communications, meetings, travel, and eventually staff recruitment. The fact that all members of the management team and its small staff had some type of international experience did much to energize the planning process for almost two years.

Even with a planning grant, the costs involved in visiting potential partners in developing countries were substantial. With this in mind, the management team worked to leverage other funds from various internal ISU sources to stretch the available budget. This may have sent a signal to the initial benefactors that ISU was sincerely committed to the proposed program.

Gathering and Processing Planning Information

Key Challenges

It is not an easy task to identify a prospective partner in the best of circumstances. In general, however, there is no substitute for having a personal contact because partnerships are all about trust and an organization is more likely to have confidence in an institutional contact that is referred by a trusted associate.

Three key challenges that a program is likely to encounter at this stage are (1) identifying an initial list of qualities that the management team would like to see in new partners; (2) getting as much information as possible about potential partners; and (3) conducting follow-up visits to obtain a more in-depth appreciation of the strengths, capacities, and core values that the partner would likely bring to the new partnership.

The CSRL Experience

Identifying the Initial List of Essential Partner Qualities. The early management team knew that the program would need partners who would be a good fit with ISU's values and goals, which included the early vision to start with the local people and use the livelihoods framework as a guide. There was recognition that the university was a long distance away from a developing country, but ISU would not be happy being a contractor—the team wanted a partner with qualities that complemented its own, and one that was located close to the ground.

While this did not need to rule out an international nongovernmental organization (NGO) or globally proficient university, there were some excellent reasons for considering developing country partners. The management team's reasoning was that developing country partners would be more likely to know the country's politics, policies, and cultures, and would be known within their own country. They would also be more likely to have in-country networks and, if the program did not go well, they would have to answer to their own associates. Since ISU was committed to building a sustainable outcome, the management team felt there was much to be said for collaborating with an in-country organization and, over time, helping to strengthen that organization's capacity.

Internal Networking and Information Gathering. By using literature reviews, student gatherings, staff interviews, networking, phone calls to international colleagues, visits to other universities doing similar work, and eventually a few targeted country visits, the management team gathered most of the information available about developing countries, organizations, and programs that might lead ISU to the right partners. As information was assembled, it was shared with the team. Briefs were compiled on selected countries that outlined human development, economic data, development projections, external linkages, cultural history, unique programs, potential partner organizations or institutions, and so forth. The first countries that the team looked closely at were those with which ISU had some level of knowledge through collaborative projects, research experience, student links, or resident alumni.

Initial Site Visits. Once this information was gathered, various members of the management team made visits—often in pairs—to countries that it thought could be partnership possibilities, including Peru, southern Mexico, and Ghana, which were the sites of existing university projects. Questions were asked, field projects were visited, and meetings were held so the team could learn from aid officials and other organizations with field-based programs. Each member of the management team attempted to learn how a potential partner would want to proceed if given an opportunity to partner with ISU in a sustainable livelihoods (SL) program with a rural community focus. The team was also concerned about previous partnership experience, attitudes on having a partner versus a contractor, and the level of transparency that seemed evident.

The Think Tank. To widen the search, the management team organized an external think tank at ISU in July 2003. The two-and-a-half-day workshop brought together outside expertise in designing and executing community development and hunger alleviation projects in developing countries.[2]

The think tank forum was a major turning point in the CSRL program's evolution because it enabled the management team and founding benefactors to reach consensus on the type of partner to consider and in what part of the world to start looking (see Box 2.1). Sub-Saharan Africa was moved to the top of the list. The same think tank helped the management team identify several important institutional contacts in the African countries under consideration for the program.

The think tank's recommendation for targeting an African country made sense since several members of the management team had experience in the region, and the degree of poverty and food insecurity in African countries was clear. Exploratory visits were soon made to Malawi, Kenya, and Uganda, followed by a tentative recommendation that the program should begin in Uganda.

In retrospect, it was probably selection of the right partners that became more important than selection of the actual country. However, the team started out thinking in terms of country selection.

The Second Round of Site Visits. The think tank was followed by a second round of visits from August to December 2003 to three additional countries in East and Southern Africa, a region that the program was most serious about as a potential program site. After almost three years of planning, Uganda was selected. Uganda exhibited significant

---

Box 2.1 Key Think Tank Recommendations

- Plan in advance for the permanent things you will leave behind.
- Move Africa to the top of your list; South Asia is also appropriate.
- Look for a "rising star"—a country that is moving forward.
- Look for an existing program, organization, or partner that has shown evidence of success and commitment.
- Go where no one else is working—not a country or region inundated with development programs.
- Consider partners that bring strengths not available at ISU—this may not be a university.
- Look for conducive government policies and initiatives.
- Take into account that a set of interventions will be more useful than one major focus.
- Look for program leadership from the selected country or region; have someone on the ground who can listen to the community.

Source: Lorna Michael Butler, "SRL Think Tank Forum: Summary of Highlights," SRL Internal Document, ISU, 2003.

---

signs of poverty, food insecurity, and malnutrition, and its overall human development was among the lowest in the world.[3] Discussions with NGOs, government agencies, and Uganda's Makerere University (MAK) leaders suggested that there were good prospects for realization of rural development and food security goals. Agricultural research programs had technologies that were ready to go, and there were comparable programs on the ground from which to learn. Uganda's location in the East African region offered potential for future regional expansion and collaboration.

A fortunate recommendation from one of the think tank members led the management team to meet with the dean of the MAK Faculty of Agriculture during the site visit in Uganda. Through the dean's initial introductions and the help of his energetic young staff, the team met numerous individuals and organizations who shared ISU's interests and who allowed the team members to talk with their staff and visit project sites (see Box 2.2). Without this generous assistance, getting acquainted in Uganda would have been much more difficult. During the same visit, the team also received considerable assistance from the International Center for Tropical Agriculture (CIAT) and World Agroforestry Centre

---

**Box 2.2 Case Study of Personal Relationships:
Opening Doors During One of the Initial
Reconnaissance Missions to Uganda**

"Our initial meeting in Uganda was with [MAK] Dean Mateete Bekunda—which was based on a personal recommendation from one of our think tank participants—and it proved interesting. He said, 'because Cheryl and I are friends, I am welcoming you to my office and I am going to help you. But it is very interesting that you have arrived at the same time as Jeffry Sachs and his team from Earth Institute. . . . They are setting up community-based programs throughout Africa. That team has asked me to assist them in making helpful contacts at the very top to help jumpstart a Uganda program, and they want to begin with the president and other top-level government officials that could help facilitate the start-up of a Millennium Development Project in Uganda.' [This project did begin in Ruhiira, southwest Uganda, in Isingiro District, through high-level political contacts.] Mateete said, 'So I am going to help you to connect with all the grassroots NGOs. [laughing] It is going to be very interesting for me to look back in 10–12 years to see which one is the right approach.'"

Source: Lorna Michael Butler in conversation with Della E. McMillan, North Saanich, British Columbia, January 16, 2012.

(ICRAF) staff, based on previous working relationships with management team members. In almost every case, it was a personal relationship with someone on the management team or someone who had attended the think tank that opened the right doors.[4]

Making the Shift from Potential to Actual Partners

Key Challenges

Once a team has identified a pool of suitable partner candidates, the next challenge is narrowing the search. Although this step looks like the previous one, it actually is quite different. This is because it requires the management team to use the information from the previous step to develop a more finely tuned list of partner criteria and conduct a more in-depth discussion with potential partners about shared goals and interests.

One of the most critical steps in a partnership is the moment when the relationship shifts from potential to actual partners. It is during this transition that the partners determine how they will work together and coordinate joint planning, accounting, and reporting.

Once partners are identified and the relationship is confirmed, the final partnership decision must be communicated to all of the organizations that were considered but not picked. These early contacts may be valuable at a later time. Following this, regular and continuing discussions and communications with the partners that have been chosen need to be arranged to begin working out the details of the formal partnership agreement. It is at this juncture that the partners are able to get serious about outlining their formal and informal expectations for the partnership.

A final step involves developing the formal partnership agreement. The best partnership agreements are usually those that outline certain formal mechanisms for managing the partnership in very general terms, including clarifying each partner's expectations for their roles within the partnership and for financial accounting and reporting. The same agreements should specify the initial coordinating mechanisms.

The CSRL Experience

Developing a Finely Tuned List of Essential Partner Characteristics. The decision to initiate ISU's program in Uganda was made following several further site visits, during which management team members held more targeted discussions with a short list of potential partners. At the same time, they convened an informal seminar about the SL approach at MAK. But the most helpful gathering was a planning workshop for representatives of eight different NGOs and MAK staff from various disciplines. In this setting, the team learned a great deal about these organizations and their suggested approaches for how and where to begin a livelihoods program in Uganda. The group also speculated about the expertise that would be needed to implement a livelihoods program in Uganda and about available Ugandan resources. Some of the questions that shaped the workshop were:

- What are the core values and areas of expertise within your organization?
- Would one or more of the workshop participants be a good fit with the vision and mission of CSRL?
- What might the responsibilities be of a local partner and of ISU?

- Who could ISU work with as an equitable partner, even though it was bringing financial resources?

Choosing the Partners. Following this workshop, the management team narrowed the list of potential partners to three or four strong organizations in Uganda that it felt could be viable partners for the type of program being planned. The final decision was not made until after the field program manager Dorothy Masinde arrived in June 2004 since the management team wanted her to play a role in the final decision.

Volunteer Efforts for Development Concerns. One of many Ugandan organizations contacted by ISU in the search for appropriate partners was Volunteer Efforts for Development Concerns (VEDCO). The members of the management team who conducted the initial site visits to Uganda were impressed with the way VEDCO used a farmer-to-farmer approach to assist farmer groups to improve farming and marketing technologies.[5] VEDCO also had a plan in place to expand to a new region in southeast Uganda. This was particularly appealing since it was thought that it would be an advantage for both organizations to start fresh in a new setting. As the organizations got to know each other, it became clear that VEDCO welcomed ISU as a working partner, rather than solely as a donor with funds to allocate. This convinced ISU that both organizations could become stronger together, learning from shared experiences, collaborative problem solving, and continual reflection and improvement. These attributes were noted on a standard form that the management team developed to summarize their reviews of each partner's pluses and minuses (Table 2.1). When the team first became acquainted with VEDCO, the executive director was anticipating an expansion to Kamuli. Local government and community leaders welcomed ISU. VEDCO staff expressed enthusiasm for the opportunity to partner with ISU and willingly sat down with the team to craft a start-up program and budget.[6]

This initial visit was followed up by a series of site visits to Kamuli. The residents of Kamuli expressed enthusiasm about VEDCO's and ISU's involvement in their communities since they were greatly in need of agricultural and other support. There were few NGOs working in this district when the program began. An additional consideration for ISU was that Kamuli was a reasonable distance from the capital of Kampala—only 143 kilometers (89 miles), a three- to four-hour drive given the road and traffic conditions at the time.

Makerere University. At the same time as it was getting to know VEDCO, ISU hoped to identify a second partner with the necessary

Table 2.1 **Factors Used for Selecting VEDCO as a Partner**

Factors	Attributes
Extension and farmer engagement	Experience with livelihood components—food security, crop and animal production, health and sanitation, leadership development and capacity development, marketing
	Commitment to gender and policy issues
	Knowledge of participatory methods
	Proven method of farmer outreach and training
Administrative headquarters	Uganda (Kampala)
	Active and reputable board of directors
History and reputation	Over twenty-five years of experience with rural communities
	Track record at improving farmers' livelihoods
	Long-term funders who have stayed with the organization
Organizational competencies	Strong and committed leadership that is welcoming
	Transparency and accountability
	Interest in collaborative learning
	Competent headquarters staff
Field staff expertise	Recruitment through volunteerism, especially students from Makerere University
	Diploma- and certificate-level training
Target community	Moving in to a new district (Kamuli) where there had been little NGO involvement
	Sufficiently rural, but not excessively far from Entebbe Airport (a three- to four-hour drive)
	Documented evidence of community need
Learning organization	Receptive to a partnership based on a learning relationship
	Collaborative outlook

Source: Data from CSRL archives, 2012.

qualities for becoming a learning organization.[7] The ISU management team was impressed by the key role that MAK faculty and staff played in helping to expand ISU's Uganda network, critiquing and contributing to the CSRL program design, helping think through the meaning of a true partnership, and providing technical expertise.

As it became better acquainted with MAK—particularly the Faculty of Agriculture, now called the College of Agricultural and Environmental Sciences (CAES)—ISU learned about the extensive resources of this faculty as well as its the desire to increase farmer education capabilities and to involve its students in practical field learning experiences (Table 2.2). Clearly, the Faculty of Agriculture was looking for ways that it could extend its reach to rural communities with practical information, applied research, and student learning. This was an emerging institutional concern that fit well with the type of program that ISU was proposing. Based on this commitment to extension and farmer engagement and the other institutional factors that the ISU management team had identified as essential partner characteristics, MAK's Faculty of Agriculture became ISU's second partner (Table 2.2).

Signing the Initial Partnership Agreements. Once the final partner decision was made, one of the field program manager's first jobs was sending formal letters to the other Ugandan partners that were not chosen. The director also sent letters about the decision to other organizations with whom ISU had visited.

The ISU-VEDCO partnership began in September 2004, after four years of intensive preplanning. It might not have occurred so quickly on the ground if the farmers in Kamuli had not been preparing their land for planting in anticipation of the long rains from September to November.

Table 2.2 Factors Used for Selecting Makerere University as a Partner

Factors	Attributes
Extension and farmer engagement	Farmer Training Institute (Kabanyolo)
	Department of Agricultural Extension and Innovations in the College of Agricultural and Environmental Sciences
	Undergraduate student internship requirement with plans for expansion
	Potential for links to academic departments related to agriculture, food security, and nutrition as well as the School of Public Health and others
Compatibility with ISU	Large teaching and research program, including commitment to farmer education
	Commitment to student learning
History and reputation	One of the oldest (1922) and most reputable universities in Africa
Learning organization	Receptive to a partnership based on a learning relationship
	Collaborative outlook
Organizational competencies	Strong and committed leadership that is welcoming
	Transparency and accountability
	Interest in learning and collaboration
	Competent and well-trained personnel

Source: Data from CSRL archives, 2012.

Five-year collaborative agreements were signed by ISU with both VEDCO and MAK in August 2004. The five-year collaborative agreement with VEDCO was for services. VEDCO, being the primary partner in the field, was expected to carry out a continuing field-based program in Kamuli. A contract was drafted that outlined ISU's expectations for services. With the contract was a strategic plan and budget, both of which were ultimately agreed on by ISU and VEDCO. During the first few years, budgets were developed annually (see Chapters 3 and 4).

Where MAK was concerned, ISU had no expectation of a continuing annual contract. MAK was a different type of partner than VEDCO. Specific contracts were developed with MAK when there was a need for technical support, student supervision, or faculty consultation (see Chapter 3).

Keeping the Partnership Alive

Key Challenges

There is no such thing as too much communication in a partnership. This is especially true if the program to be executed is located far from the lead institution. Although technology now makes this type of inter-partner coordination easier, there is no substitute for face-to-face contact. The problem is especially serious if the new program is located in an area where the Internet and power are less predictable than at the lead institution. It is wise to think of other mechanisms for keeping in touch on a regular basis by developing a pattern of informal communication between the program director at the lead institution and the partner representatives, and determining whether or not some sort of advisory board is needed to link the partners for strategic planning and advice.

The CSRL Experience

Informal Communication Channels. During the first few years of the CSRL program, most communication with the partners was facilitated through the field program manager who was informally designated as the link between the partners. No clear plan for interpartner communication was ever defined. Perhaps this was because the director traveled to Uganda frequently, and he also maintained active e-mail and phone communications with the field program manager.

In addition, the management team and a few faculty members communicated directly with VEDCO and MAK staff for specific technical initiatives. This communication—which was routed through the CSRL director—included arrangements for personal visits to Uganda and planning of particular field initiatives. A third important communication node involved bringing the chief executive officers (CEOs), staff, and eventually even students to ISU for special training and meetings.[8]

Early Working Groups in Uganda. Initially, there was an informal MAK working group composed of five or six representatives from different departments, including Food Science and Technology, Agricultural Extension, Crop Science, and Agricultural Economics. This group gathered when the director and other ISU management team members happened to be in Uganda.

Lessons Learned and Recommendations

CSRL helped identify partners that had similar values and commitment by (1) using the same CSRL management committee that encompassed a wide cross-section of staff, as well as one representative of the university's fund-raising office, to organize the search, and (2) organizing a series of events and field visits that helped the management committee identify new potential partners and key personal contacts within those institutions.

Since there was no preconceived program plan, each partner signed a flexible collaborative agreement with ISU instead of a fixed contract, which made it easier for the program to build on what VEDCO was already doing in Kamuli and to scale it up at a later time.

The chief weakness of the CSRL partner courtship was that it took a long preplanning period to sort through the different partnership options and locations. In retrospect, the process of choosing its overseas partners might have been quicker and less risky if CSRL had opted to carry out a series of short-term projects with prospective partners.

Good communication was critical to working through any kinks. Especially important, all of the partners committed to a system of annual partner meetings and regular communication between the director and the each partner's lead representative.

Getting Organized to Start the Search

There are two requirements for a successful search: good information and strong institutional support from the lead institution that is dispensing the funds. One of the best ways to get good information is to build the search on the professional networks of the management team members. Each person in the group will have firsthand knowledge of potential partners and their relative strengths and weaknesses. This is the type of information that you cannot obtain from a Web search or a project proposal. One of the best ways to get good institutional support from the lead institution is to have its head appoint a representative to serve on the search committee. It is equally important to include an appointed representative of the fund-raising office so that perspective donors can be kept in the loop.

Lesson 1:
Identify a small, informal management team to guide the early planning process.

Recommendations:
- Develop a loosely knit management team to take the lead in conceptualizing the program and planning the early steps.
- Identify someone to take on interim leadership of the start-up phase who has experience with similar projects, who understands financial management, and who is a good communicator.

Lesson 2:
Maintain continual communication with the top leadership and other members of the organization.

Recommendations:
- Arrange for regular meetings and personal updates with leaders and administrators of the organization—the more actively engaged this group is, the greater will be the ownership in the outcome and the deeper will be the level of mutual understanding and trust.
- Include the foundation officer in these discussions and, where possible, the prospective benefactors.
- Involve administrators from beyond the unit where appropriate to institutionalize ownership.

Lesson 3:
Involve potential financial benefactors in selected
key planning deliberations, including the search for
execution partners.

Recommendations:
- Promote as much joint learning as possible between potential benefactors and the management team.
- Listen to and learn from potential benefactors as much as possible.
- Invite potential benefactors to see firsthand what the proposed partners are doing and, later, what is being done together.

Lesson 4:
Leverage support from the lead institution to cover some
of the start-up costs.

Recommendations:
- Establish a small planning office somewhere near administrative headquarters to maintain continual communications and visibility—an office sends a signal that the effort is serious and adds to everyone's confidence.
- Ask the lead institution to provide some start-up staff support as well as office and travel support.

Gathering and Processing Planning Information

One strategy for broadening a network-based search is to constitute a think tank of knowledgeable experts in the area where the program hopes to intervene. Once a preliminary group of partners has been identified, it can be useful to organize various events and site visits to the prospective partners' offices and programs to help them become better acquainted. For all of these reasons, it is important for new programs to have a preplanning budget. In many cases, a prospective donor may be willing to finance this budget as part of their own joint planning process with the lead institution.

Lesson 5:
Gather as much pertinent information as possible about potential partner organizations and implementation sites.

Recommendations:
- Make this information available, in summary form, to the management team.
- Involve staff in gathering knowledge and information for decisionmaking.
- Use the information gathered to help with decisionmaking, but also look to the firsthand knowledge gained from site visits, personal interviews, and field observations.

Lesson 6:
Tap the knowledge and expertise of both internal and external experts before firming up plans.

Recommendations:
- Surround the management team with individuals who have on-the-ground project experience.
- Think about convening a one- to two-day think tank to learn from external experts and facilitate a dialogue between these individuals and potential benefactors, management team members, and other key actors.
- Make contact with organizations that have similar projects supported by private benefactors and learn from their experiences; look for models that exhibit long-term partnerships and sustainable outcomes.
- Follow up on leads identified by the group and share this information with the management committee.

Lesson 7:
As the search narrows, set up a variety of joint activities and field visits with some of the potential partners.

Recommendations:
- Ensure that the planning budget allows for management team members to visit some of the most promising partner organizations and sites where the program might potentially be launched.

- Make field visits to communities where the prospective partners have operated.
- Based on these initial field visits, fine-tune the initial list of essential partner qualities.

Making the Shift from Potential to Actual Partners

Once the search has been narrowed down, carry out a series of short-term projects with prospective partners to test how the partners might work together. This makes it easier to pilot test some of the proposed systems for financial accounting, training, and monitoring before scaling up.

Prior to and in conjunction with the pilot tests, develop an informal collaborative agreement with each institution that spells out the global expectations for the partnership from each partner's perspective and the communication channels that will be used to manage the partnership. The partnership agreement should also outline a core set of partnership principles for financial reporting and strategic planning.

Lesson 8:
Once the search has been narrowed, fund a series of short-term, time-restricted projects with this smaller group of prospective partners.

Recommendations:

- Launch a time-restricted pilot project with the prospective partner to examine staff capabilities, community outreach strategies, methods used to measure success, and so forth.
- Look for opportunities to bring any potential partners and their staff to visit the lead institution to build greater interinstitutional trust and encourage frank exchanges about partner goals and expectations.
- Involve the program manager in making the final decision about partner selection.
- Communicate the partnership decision to all of the organizations that were considered but not picked.
- Avoid trying to change a new partner's way of doing things—allow time for mutual learning and trust building.
- Draft the early partnership agreements in a flexible manner to clarify all partners' expectations, including the expected systems for financial management and coordination.

Keeping the Partnership Alive

One of the single most important factors that contributed to the survival of CSRL was its early commitment to developing a conscious, but informal, model of communication among the partners and between the partnership and the major benefactors. This communication built trust among the partners and made the individual partners more willing to work out problems when they emerged. Good communication builds trust, and trust builds good partnerships. When the partnerships are right, problems can usually be worked out when mistakes are made.

Lesson 9:
Develop a communication strategy to be used among all partners.

Recommendations:
- Agree on the best methods for maintaining regular communication with partners.
- Establish a fairly regular time and method for talking person-to-person with individuals responsible for the program at both the field and upper management levels.
- Keep a paper trail of these conversations and share them back and forth to be certain there are no misunderstandings about decisions.
- Maintain an annual calendar that includes important dates for all partners, and then use this for planning the best times to talk together.
- Arrange for the director, management team members, and other involved staff to visit the program site as frequently as possible.
- Arrange for the program manager to visit the organization's headquarters several times a year.
- Build a communications network within the partnership, rather than relying on one specific individual as a contact.

Notes

1. This is the initial gift of $100,000. See Table 1.1 in Chapter 1.
2. External participants in the think tank included: Merry Fredrick, executive director, Self Help International; Claude Nankam, director, Agriculture Program at World Vision; Dennis Johnson, professor of dairy science at the University of Minnesota and hunger coordinator for the Southwest Minnesota Synod of the Evangelical Lutheran Church of America; Kathleen DeWalt, director, Center for Latin American Studies, University of Pittsburgh; Jenny

Borden, chair of the Intermediate Technology Development Group in London; Mike Mtika, professor and development expert, Eastern University in Philadelphia; Cheryl Palm, senior research scientist, Columbia University's Earth Institute; and Katharine Pearson, Ford Foundation. (Organizational affiliations are those that were current at the time of the think tank.)

3. In 2000, Uganda's Human Development Index (HDI) was .392 (HDI for sub-Saharan Africa, .421; Canada, .867; and the United States, .883). United Nations Development Programme (UNDP), "Human Development Reports," Table 2: Human Development Index Trends, 1980–2013, http://hdr.undp.org/en /content/table-2-human-development-index-trends-1980-2013. The HDI is a composite index that measures whether individuals are leading a long and healthy life, attaining knowledge, and experiencing a decent standard of living, and, therefore, it provides a comparative reference for socioeconomic development that is not based on economic growth alone. United Nations Development Programme (UNDP), "Human Development Reports, Frequently Asked Questions—Human Development Index (HDI)," 2014, http://hdrstats.undp.org/en /countries/profiles/UGA.html.

4. One especially helpful colleague was an individual who one of the team members had worked with in Tanzania ten years earlier. He and his wife, both with a long history of African development work, knew about many Ugandan organizations and their management reputations. Another valuable connection came through an African graduate student at ISU who had once been a star employee at a regional international agricultural research center. Most of the Ugandan NGO introductions came from two junior MAK faculty members who had a valuable rapport with an impressive number of young Ugandan NGO staff. Some contacts were also provided by United States Agency for International Development (USAID) mission colleagues who a team member had known while working on projects in other African countries.

5. Resembling a farmer-led knowledge process as described by R. E. Rhoades and R. H. Booth, "A Model for Generating Acceptable Agricultural Technology," *Agricultural Administration* 11, no. 2 (1982): 127–137. Other like concepts are "farmer research circles," participatory action research, and participatory technology development. See D'Arcy Davis Case, *The Community's Toolbox: The Idea, Methods, and Tools for Participatory Assessment, Monitoring and Evaluation in Community Forestry.* Volume 2 of Community Forestry Field Manual (Bangkok, Thailand: FAO Regional Wood Energy Development Programme in Asia, Food and Agriculture Organization of the United Nations, 1990); C. Wettasinha, L. van Veldhuizen, and A. Waters-Bayer (eds.), *Advancing Participatory Technology Development: Case Studies on Integration into Agricultural Research, Extension and Education* (Silang, Cavite, Philippines: International Institute of Rural Reconstruction, ETC Ecoculture, ACP-EU Technical Centre for Agricultural and Rural Cooperation, 2003). See also Robert Chambers and B. P. Ghildyal, "Agricultural Research for Resource-Poor Farmers: The Farmer-First-and-Last Model," *Agricultural Administration* 20, no. 1 (1985): 1–30; Jacqueline A. Ashby, "Methodology for the Participation of Small Farmers in the Design of On-Farm Trials," *Agricultural Administration* 22, no. 1 (1986): 1–19; S. D. Biggs, Resource-Poor Farmers Participation in

Research: A Synthesis of Experiences from Nine National Agricultural Research Systems, On-Farm Client-Oriented Research Comparative Study Paper No. 3 (The Hague: the International Service for National Agricultural Research, 1989).

6. For example, in August 2004, three of the VEDCO headquarters staff (the grants officer, monitoring and evaluation officer, and operations manager) spent a full day with the field program manager and the Wallace Chair to carefully plan out a detailed start-up budget for the first fifteen months of fieldwork using the VEDCO model. Even though the staff did not know either of the ISU representatives well, they exhibited complete openness in estimating costs and considering alternative activities that could be included. The first strategic plan and sixteen-month budget of 30,778,000 Ugandan shillings (UGX 30,778,000, about US$12,000) was based on this work session.

7. Peter Senge, *The Fifth Discipline: The Art and Practice of the Learning Organization* (New York: Doubleday, 1990): 5–13. Senge coined the concept of learning organizations, encouraging organizations to shift to interconnected or systems thinking whereby a shared vision is achieved through dialogue, discussion, and team learning. To achieve this, individuals must grow and learn and, as a result, the total organization learns. The assumption is that, in situations of change, only organizations that are flexible or adaptive and able to tap individuals' commitment to creating a future will do well.

8. This began by inviting the CEOs of each partner organization for special get-acquainted seminars as well as occasional visits to the annual World Food Prize Norman E. Borlaug International Symposium in Des Moines, Iowa. Gradually, a wider range of VEDCO staff was brought to ISU each year to enhance their job skills and become better acquainted with the program and the resources of the university. Visits also included MAK staff and students, some of whom came for specialized internships and advanced degrees.

3

Getting Started

Dorothy Masinde, Lorna Michael Butler,
and Robert Mazur

Having decided to embark on an innovative philanthropic partnership, we found that the next challenges were determining how to run it—and who to place at the helm. Whether developing a domestic or overseas program, the first program manager is the most important position to fill. The way that this person operates, how he or she is contracted, and where he or she is located all are important factors that can be overlooked or undervalued in an initial program design.

Four start-up challenges that a new multipartner program with private benefactor funding is likely to encounter during the start-up phase are:

- Identifying and hiring the first program manager—selecting the right person to lead the initial program start-up phase;
- Establishing the first program office—exploring various options for setting up the type of office that the manager needs to be fully operational;
- Defining the role of the program manager—creating a leadership model to guide the start-up processes in the partnership; and
- Institutionalizing the program manager position within the partnership—defining a pathway for including the manager's position in the partnership and the lead institution's structure.

The authors wish to acknowledge the helpful input and contributions of Della E. McMillan and Gail Nonnecke.

Identifying and Hiring the First Program Manager

Key Challenges

Ideally, every program has a manager who oversees or manages the operations on behalf of the lead institution. Selection of the right individual for this role may be one of the most important decisions to be made in the start-up phase.

The first step, which is often overlooked, is to draft a position description and discuss it with the management team. This document may be more detailed than what is used to advertise the position. The management team will want to agree on the most important personal, experiential, and academic qualifications necessary for the responsibilities anticipated. If the program is in a foreign country, management experience in developing countries will be valuable, particularly in areas of budget oversight, country procedures, reporting, monitoring and evaluation (M&E), and communications.

Assuming that an operational model or implementation approach has been selected, the preferred individual should be familiar with its methodology and be able to apply it in the field. Since the particular partnership is probably a new experience for all concerned, the program manager's ability to listen to and learn from partners will go a long way in forging new relationships in a way that builds a true partnership. The program manager should command the needed respect to develop a smooth working relationship among partners and local stakeholders.

The CSRL Experience

Developing the Job Description. Once the country for program implementation had been identified, the Center for Sustainable Rural Livelihoods (CSRL) management team embarked on identifying the qualities that it wanted to see in its program manager, whose title was field program manager. Iowa State University (ISU) began advertising for a program coordinator in November 2003, with a deadline for applications in January 2004.[1] The job description, which was disseminated worldwide, emphasized the critical importance of hiring an individual with extensive multidisciplinary field experience in development and solid management experience, and required the candidate to have a general background in the two central program areas: food security and nutrition (see Box 3.1). The management team began interviewing candidates in March 2004, and an offer was made to Dorothy Masinde, the first CSRL field program manager, on May 12, 2004.

Box 3.1 General Job Requirements Cited in the Field Program Manager's Position Announcement

---

- Develop, implement, and manage a community-based program in one or more developing countries, starting in Africa, to increase household food security and improve health in impoverished rural communities;
- Focal areas: sustainable agriculture and natural resource management; human nutrition and health; marketing and small business development; local credit systems and microfinance; human resources development and community capacity strengthening;
- Liaise with country program directors and partners as well as the management team and faculty at ISU;
- Oversee planning and implementation of training activities;
- Extensive travel expected; and
- Ability to work and make decisions relatively independently.

Source: ISU position announcement for Sustainable Rural Livelihoods Program: "Program Coordinator," November 21, 2003.

An African (Kenyan) herself, Masinde brought to the position valuable practical experience in overseeing African field programs. She had an interdisciplinary educational background and had worked with many kinds of stakeholders, from the poorest female farmers to the highest government officials. She had also proved that she could multitask and maintain flexibility.

An African development program can be one of the least predictable work environments, particularly where there are several types of partners—each having a very different culture—and a wide range of individuals involved. And the livelihoods model, if taken literally, is hard to put one's arms around (see Box 3.2).

The biggest challenge is how to focus the program so that it becomes manageable. Masinde's background was perfect for carrying out a livelihood program—she was trained and had worked in a holistic manner. With this background, the interviewers felt that she could see the connections between the main program components—nutrition, livestock, crops, water, community development, education, and gender.

Box 3.2 Use of the Sustainable Livelihoods Approach as a Guide

The sustainable livelihoods (SL) approach served as a guide for the CSRL management team's thinking and planning. The SL framework, first proposed by the United Kingdom's Department for International Development (DFID) and others in the 1990s, places the poor and their assets at the center of the development equation. An individual's livelihood is made up of all the capabilities and capitals that enable her or him to make a life—wealth, food, land, physical and mental health, knowledge, skills, attitudes, and networks—with the different tangible and intangible resources that are at a person's or family's disposal. A livelihood is sustainable when assets are maintained or multiplied; when there is the ability to manage or exhibit resilience—bounce back—in response to stresses and shocks; and when it is possible to contribute to the needs of the next generation (e.g., by protecting the natural resource base or managing the water supply for everyone's access).

Livelihood assets consist of various interconnected capitals: human, social, political, natural, built, financial, and cultural. Under the right conditions (e.g., adequate rainfall, labor, family support, and markets), a farmer may be able to overcome poverty, deal with a crop failure, or cope with the illness of a child, thereby maintaining a satisfactory livelihood. With additional knowledge, a strong social network, or supportive national policies, the same farmer may be able to improve his or her livelihood situation. With the help of partners, the CSRL initiative hoped to identify ways to improve the livelihoods of small landholders in rural communities of a developing country.

Sources: Robert Chambers and G. R. Conway. 1992. "Sustainable Rural Livelihoods: Practical Concepts for the 21st Century," Discussion Paper No. 296 (Institute of Development Studies, Brighton, UK, 1991). See also DFID, Sustainable Livelihoods Guidance Sheets (DFID, London, October 2001).

Note: Some of the other organizations that have incorporated the SL model in their development approaches include the United Nations Development Programme (UNDP), Food and Agriculture Organization of the United Nations (FAO), World Food Programme (WFP), Oxfam International (Oxfam), Cooperative for Assistance and Relief Everywhere (CARE), and Institute of Development Studies (IDS).

As a Kenyan, she brought a fresh perspective to Uganda.[2] As Masinde notes later, there were advantages to being an outsider (see Box 3.3).

One of the original expectations was that the field program manager should be located at ISU in Ames. But as soon as the CSRL management team started to interview candidates with African experience, its ideas on this began to change. Masinde, in particular, questioned this aspect of the position. Her previous experience suggested that it would be smarter to have the program manager on-site, at least for the first year. As it happened, this was exactly what occurred.

Involving the Manager in Early Partner Selection. To employ the first field program manager as quickly as possible, ISU put Masinde on a short-term contract from May 30, 2004, to June 30, 2004,[3] which enabled her to be in Uganda during the visit of the management team representatives who would be making the final recommendations on the CSRL partners. It was important that the new field program manager be a part of that decision.

Establishing the First Program Office

Key Challenges

Even the best manager cannot operate without an operating budget and office. This means setting up a system where that person can access the funds, equipment, and office space needed to operate on a daily basis. Far from being simple, these details can have a powerful impact on how a new program is established and run.

The CSRL Experience

Determining Where to Locate the CSRL Field Program Manager. Masinde's first two-year contract outlined a program management

---

Box 3.3 Dorothy Masinde Reflects on Her Position in the Community

"In this case, being an outsider—not being a local person—meant I [was] not part of one particular community. I am going to the lowest level. I am going to the highest. I have no baggage. I was an outsider, yet I was a friend. I like to say I had to know how to trade my heels for my 'akalsas' [the simple shoes that women villagers wear] and then do the reverse—sometimes in the same day."

Source: Dorothy Masinde in conversation with Della E. McMillan, Evanston, IL, July 28, 2012.

model in which she would reside in Uganda during the first year and make trips back to ISU, perhaps relocating to Ames in the second year and making multiple trips to Uganda to oversee the field program.

It did not take long for the management team to conclude that the field program manager should be located in Uganda and not half a world away in Iowa. However, there was still some debate as to whether it was better for Masinde to be housed close to the field program (i.e., to live and work in Kamuli) or to be housed in Uganda's capital city of Kampala where it would be easier to stay in contact with the partners, Makerere University (MAK) and Volunteer Efforts for Development Concerns (VEDCO), as well as with other organizations that might become partners for CSRL in the future. Initially, the management team chose to base Masinde in Kampala.

Establishing the Field Office. Next, the field program manager needed an office. The CSRL management team debated where to place Masinde's office: in an independent office in Kampala; in an office at MAK; or in an office at VEDCO, the organization responsible for carrying out the field program. The first option explored was one in the facilities of an international nongovernmental organization (NGO) with which CSRL had no partnership. The organization was willing to provide office space and other basic support at a modest fee. This sounded promising until VEDCO's executive director brought up the possibility of utilizing a vacant office inside VEDCO's secure compound at its Kampala headquarters. There already had been many start-up issues that arose simply because ISU lacked the experience of operating in Uganda. ISU needed a secure location for a program vehicle once purchased, a driver, communications and printing facilities, a way to manage local accounts, and a means of obtaining a work permit for Masinde, all of which could be facilitated by VEDCO. Consequently, ISU decided to set up an office for the field program manager in VEDCO's headquarters in Kampala.

Because the program was in its infancy, Masinde made weekly visits to Kamuli, which was approximately a four-hour drive from Kampala on poorly maintained roadways. She stayed in the field for three or four days and worked in Kampala for the remaining one or two days of the week so that she could attend meetings and keep up with office work. This arrangement provided an opportunity for Masinde to interact with senior personnel at both of the partner organizations and to get acquainted with other Kampala organizations. However, these conditions proved hectic, and a lot of time was wasted traveling back and forth. Masinde's interactions with the community and the field staff were also limited by this; she was viewed as a visitor and not part of the program. Therefore, after four years, Masinde relocated to Kamuli to be closer to the program area.

Sharing VEDCO's office facilities had some obvious advantages for the field program manager, but there were also trade-offs (Table 3.1). Given that CSRL's budget for field operations was modest, sharing resources as a way to save money was a sensible plan. But being located within the program implementation partner's office proved to be a delicate balance. It was easy to be seen as a supervisor of that partner's activities and, by being so close to one partner, it was easy to neglect the other partner. In retrospect, the arrangement should have been examined after the first year to ensure that it was working well for all concerned.

Table 3.1 Pros and Cons of Placing the CSRL Field Program Manager's Office in the Headquarters of Primary Partner VEDCO

Pros	Cons
Provided cost savings for CSRL, particularly in the start-up phase.	Being too close to a partner means running the risk of getting involved in the partner's internal politics—hard to remain objective.
Enabled the field program manager to get to know the primary field partner fairly quickly, including its strengths and weaknesses.	Danger of neglecting the other partner simply because more time is spent with one partner, potentially causing resentment.
Made it possible for a rapid program start-up—no need to search out facilities, equipment, security, and so forth; and easy to get advice when needed.	There may be less chance for the field program manager to get to know other potential partners, learn about other strategies and programs in other organizations, and so forth.
Offered a way for ISU to meet the legal requirements within Uganda and still get the program up and running promptly.	Even though the field program manager represented ISU, her identity was frequently tied to VEDCO.
Facilitated important logistical arrangements for working in the country such as vehicle security, work permit for field program manager, office space, and communications.	Created a potential dependency relationship with one partner.

Source: Notes from the CSRL archives summarized in table format, 2012.

Making Funds Available for Field Operations. Setting up operations anywhere requires funds to carry out the program. Because ISU was initiating various start-up activities (e.g., informal surveys, community meetings, demonstration sites, and farmer training) but was not officially registered to conduct business in Uganda at the onset, establishing an ISU bank account in Uganda was not an option. VEDCO needed funds to operate the agreed-on activities according to the detailed work plan and budget that ISU had approved.

Thus, operating funds for VEDCO were wired by ISU directly to the VEDCO account. The first funds remitted for the period of September 1 to December 31, 2004, were disbursed based on the established trust and understanding between ISU and VEDCO that the funds would be used according to the agreed-on contract. From that point, once the receipts were received by ISU, another disbursement of funds was sent.[4]

Providing the field program manager with operating funds proved to be more complicated. In the end, ISU asked Masinde if she would agree to open a personal bank account to which her own operating funds could be wired. This system—highly unorthodox, but fitting for the constraints faced—worked well enough. Like any other ISU employee or contractor, Masinde was expected to account to ISU for these expenditures.

Defining the Role of the Program Manager

Key Challenges

When a manager is hired by the lead institution to oversee program implementation at the same time as the program's partners are selected, the manager's success is greatly dependent on the level of trust that exists among the partners, and between the lead institution and the manager. If the lead institution places ample trust in the manager to carve out an appropriate niche for management responsibilities with the partners, the situation can work well. But this success is highly dependent on transparency and a desire to consult before acting.

The manager represents the lead institution and is responsible for both financial and program accountability. How should the manager exercise leadership in a way to ensure respect and positive working relationships among partners and their staff? How does the manager serve as a liaison between the partners, the partners' field staff, the program beneficiaries, and the lead institution while remaining neutral?

This role is complex. It calls for the ability to recognize when outside knowledge and expertise is needed and, occasionally, to allow experiments to move forward without interference so that they can serve as a learning experience. Unplanned activities often arise, sometimes interfering with scheduled activities, and unexpected visitors may stretch resources and staff. The ability to listen to staff can lead to greater awareness of partners' capacities and priorities.

Six challenges that a newly hired manager is likely to confront during the first year of program implementation are:

- Getting to know the principle partners and their expectations for the partnership;
- Developing new networks to identify resources for the program;
- Linking the program to the lead partner and funders;
- Protecting the program's core mission from well-intended, but potentially incompatible, new projects;
- Opening the partners' eyes to new opportunities and constraints that could impact the program; and
- Backstopping program management without directing.

The CSRL Experience

Getting to Know VEDCO and Its Expectations for the Partnership. When the new field program manager arrived on the job in Uganda, she had to hit the ground running since VEDCO was already gearing up the first phase of its original strategic plan for Kamuli.[5]

A baseline study had been conducted by the VEDCO staff, which was used to select the initial subcounties of Namasagali and Butansi. It was at this point that ISU began to work with VEDCO in Kamuli.[6] The program had not been officially launched, although all of the official paperwork with the government offices had been completed and an office space had been identified. The field program manager joined the VEDCO team that had been tasked with starting the program.

Prior to ISU and VEDCO signing a collaborative agreement in August 2004,[7] Masinde participated with the VEDCO team in the final selection of parishes and target farmers and the identification of local groups. This gave her an opportunity to get acquainted with the program areas, community members, and VEDCO field staff. A budget for the start-up program was developed and agreed on, including initial arrangements for office accommodation and logistical support. However, agreement had not been reached among the partners concerning the field program manager's roles and responsibilities for the program, and how she was to coordinate with the VEDCO staff.

The Manager's Earliest Priorities. Masinde felt that one of her earliest priorities was to focus on building the ISU-VEDCO partnership. The field program manager and ISU needed to know what VEDCO was doing to achieve their goals and how it was doing so. But this was going to take time. Another wrinkle was that neither organization had ever discussed the responsibilities of the field program manager in terms of VEDCO's contract for carrying out the program or MAK's involvement in providing technical advice and support.

Learning from the Local Partners. This process was complicated by that fact that the CSRL office at ISU had no traditional program document or scope of work to guide the program start-up (see Box 3.4). What the program did have was VEDCO's three-year strategic plan for Kamuli[8] and a management team document that spelled out the approach, philosophy, and principles for the CSRL program as well as a preliminary program strategy, activities, and thematic foci.

VEDCO's strategic plan tasked the Kamuli team with executing the CSRL program using the farmer-to-farmer approach that it had used successfully in previous work in Luwero District. This farmer-to-farmer model involved training a few local farmers in improved technologies, who could then serve as farmer trainers in their own communities. These farmer trainers were not paid for their roles; rather, their farms served as demonstration farms for improved agricultural methods and they received tools to help them carry out their jobs.

Box 3.4 The Challenges of Not Having an Identifiable Program Document

"All of a sudden, we were signing a [collaborative agreement] with an organization that we barely knew. I watched this with fear at every stage ... everyone was excited except me, because I knew that once they put down their pens, the hard work starts. I was used to managing programs that had a program document—usually a proposal—that detailed the program's objectives and expected outputs. After the excitement of getting the job wore off, I asked for the program document. There was no program document. There was only a clean table."

Source: Dorothy Masinde in conversation with Della E. McMillan, Evanston, IL, July 28, 2012.

A CSRL program document emphasized the need to address livelihood strategies by focusing on the different resources available to program participants. To enhance resiliency, the ISU team hoped that
VEDCO would encourage households to build on their asset base (e.g.,
skills, knowledge, health, social networks, and farmland); improve the
natural resource base; and focus on household food security and children's and mothers' nutrition and health. To address these issues, the
CSRL management team recommended that VEDCO consider employ-
ing some field personnel who had training and experience in human
nutrition and natural resource management.

ISU's CSRL director and members of the management team spent
time with Masinde to discuss the general goals of the program, the livelihoods approach, the related philosophy about supporting VEDCO's work
with farmers, and the reasons for the partnership. Otherwise, the field
program manager had complete freedom to begin in any way that she
felt would work. She had to learn quickly about how to reconcile what
ISU expected with what VEDCO was already doing on the ground.
Since VEDCO was moving ahead in Kamuli, Masinde was determined
to learn from VEDCO by observing, asking questions, listening to the
staff, and spending time with the staff in the field.

This approach created challenges with the staff on the ground
because they did not fully understand Masinde's role in the VEDCO
structure. Having a full-time donor representative in the field was not
the norm. Masinde discussed this particular challenge with VEDCO's
executive director Henry Kizito Musoke and, eventually, they developed a system through which she could communicate her input on the
program to him during monthly meetings. Musoke then communicated
these matters to the field program team. The fact that the scope of work
for the first field program manager was flexible facilitated this type of
negotiations (see Box 3.5).

*Developing New Networks to Identify Other Resources and Build
Social Capital in Local Communities.* Prior to program implementation in Kamuli, the CSRL management team felt that it needed to know
more about existing Ugandan innovations that might be useful to the
program. Rather than establish an in-country advisory board in the early
phases, CSRL implemented a state-of-the-art review of innovations in
Uganda led by MAK. To facilitate this review, MAK's dean of the Faculty of Agriculture facilitated the creation of a technical advisory committee for the program (see Box 3.6).

Box 3.5 The Importance of a Flexible Scope of Work for the First Program Manager

"Building flexibility into your program design and execution has nuts-and-bolts implications for your operation on the ground. The scope of work for the program manager has to be flexible. The contract officer who is managing the partnership has to be flexible and be willing to accommodate creativity . . . within limits. You must work through the administrative layers that bring together a partnership management team."

Source: Dorothy Masinde in conversation with Della E. McMillan, Evanston, IL, July 28, 2012.

Through her association with MAK, Masinde was able to establish relationships within the National Agricultural Research Organisation (NARO) such as one with a previous acquaintance who later became a partner in several grant-supported programs with which CSRL collaborated. The most valuable program collaborators usually emerged through personal networks—the partners' associations, the management team's connections, or networks established by the field program manager. Although there was not a clear-cut plan for how to seek out and engage outside technical support, Masinde drew on personal contacts made by her immediate colleagues.

Masinde made deliberate efforts to interact with local government officials such as the National Agricultural Advisory Services (NAADS)

Box 3.6 The Initial Responsibilities Proposed for the Technical Committee

The field program manager visited MAK departments to identify potential faculty and students to participate in the review of innovations. It was this pool of faculty that Masinde drew on when later establishing a technical committee. Through this early exercise, the MAK faculty and students developed an understanding of the CSRL program, and Masinde uncovered useful information—and gained the goodwill of the dean.

(continues)

Box 3.6 Continued

In October 2004, Masinde, VEDCO's executive director, and MAK's dean of the Faculty of Agriculture visited the ISU campus. During the visit, the dean observed that most of the reports he had seen were based on individual Ugandan partners' inputs into the program, which to him signaled the three partners were not working together as a team. By the end of the visit, Masinde started to work on ways to bring all of the partners together. At the same time, there had been discussions of establishing some sort of technical committee to play a local advisory role to the Kamuli program. This committee was formed toward the end of the first fiscal year (in June 2005). The executive director of VEDCO and MAK's dean of the Faculty of Agriculture drafted the initial objectives for the committee, which included:

- Monitoring the technical aspects of the CSRL program and proposing modifications therein;
- Reviewing annual work plans and budgets and recommending technical and budget adjustments;
- Reviewing the recommendations of the M&E team and external evaluators, and recommending adjustments if appropriate;
- Reviewing annual reports relative to the technical progress being made;
- Providing advice to the program management on operational issues relative to the programs; and
- Identifying areas of intervention and advising on potential resource people or partners for proposal development.

While built on good intentions, this committee met only a few times. Reasons for this may have been that there were mixed understandings concerning the committee's purpose; the committee may have been premature in its formation; or the committee may not have been legitimized appropriately at administrative and budget levels. If it had been formed around a more narrow function, such as improving the technical agriculture training of the field staff, there might have been greater chances for the group's continuity and usefulness.

Sources: Dorothy Masinde, Robert Mazur, and Lorna M. Butler, "Technical Committee," unpublished document, Kampala, SRL office, October 2004; Dorothy Masinde, "Minutes of Meeting with Makerere University Staff," unpublished document, Kampala, SRL office, November 19, 2004; Dorothy Masinde, "Minutes of the First Technical Committee (TC) Meeting of the SRL Program held at VEDCO Boardroom," unpublished document, Kampala, December 3, 2004.

coordinator; members of parliament and the deputy speaker of parliament who later became speaker; the local council chairperson (LC V chair);[9] and ministry representatives such as the district agriculture officer, district education officer, and district director of medical services. Local and central government officials continued to provide other forms of support, including facilitation of program training sessions, contributions of technical support, and mobilization of wider community support.[10]

Linking the Program to the Lead Institution and Benefactors. The field program manager was the only employed representative of CSRL in Uganda during the first fiscal year (July 2004–June 2005). Initially, Masinde's role was to provide program guidance and oversight; training and capacity building for the field staff when needed; budgetary monitoring and accountability for funds; and communications to and from CSRL. Once program implementation began, she was also charged with developing an acceptable management structure for the program.

From the start, Masinde was the primary liaison between both of the Ugandan partners and ISU. She also realized that, out of necessity, she was the key individual to bring the Ugandan partners together for program planning and implementation activities. This was a major insight because little thought had been given to the importance of interpartner planning before the program started.

Quickly, Masinde became the point person for everyone—for all of the ISU and MAK faculty, students, and visitors who came to Kamuli and anyone who had a question about the CSRL program. Through Masinde's participation in meetings on the ISU campus, her reports and presentations, and her answers to questions, there was little doubt that she had an influence on how everyone involved—including CSRL benefactors—saw the program.

Determining if a Local Advisory Board Is Needed. Even before the field program manager was hired, there was discussion among the management team members about whether the required CSRL Advisory Board should be formed in Uganda, in the United States, or in both places. While there was an attempt to form an early technical advisory committee (see Box 3.6), it seemed more useful to draw on the advice of the partners, their staff, and the local community in an informal way. This flexible method and the priority put on soliciting advice from partners and stakeholders seemed to help to build ownership in the program. Later, as the program matured, it became increasingly valuable to involve Ugandans in a more formal way and to meet with them on their own turf (see Chapter 4).

Protecting the Program's Core Mission from Well-Intended, but Potentially Incompatible, New Projects. As the program expanded, the ISU community became more interested in program activities in Uganda. In addition, the CSRL director and management team sought out new collaborators that might make a contribution to the program, which resulted in new actors, program components, and activities that required management, supervision, and incorporation into existing field activities. These new opportunities brought logistical and resource requirements that had not been factored in the initial plans. It was a continual struggle to identify ways in which the new undertakings could fit in the main program and budget; some did not, and it was sometimes Masinde who made this call.

By late 2006, it became apparent that the field program manager needed a local assistant to help with some of the logistics that resulted from the addition of program components, including the influx of ISU visitors. This was around the same time that a team began to explore the potential for a school garden program, which evolved into what is now a well-established service-learning program. The assistant who was selected divided her time between helping with logistics for the service-learning program, arranging logistics for CSRL, and assisting with financial accountability.

Opening the Partners' Eyes to New Opportunities and Constraints. During the first year of the program when CSRL sought to enhance its nutrition and health program, Masinde made extensive visits to various institutions and organizations engaged in nutrition and health activities. Through these early contacts, and those previously made by the management team, she was able to identify resource people who were either trained in a nutrition-related field or had direct community nutrition experience.

As program implementation progressed, Masinde began to identify technical gaps in the program and hold discussions about these gaps with VEDCO's executive director and the CSRL director, which led to VEDCO boosting the caliber of staff that they recruited for Kamuli. The new staff, who began to arrive in late 2005, brought higher qualifications and valuable experience that were a better match for program needs. This motivated existing staff to seek further training to enhance their skills, some with support from CSRL or its affiliates. The capacity-building effort, although not spelled out in the beginning, fit well with CSRL's goals and objectives. Strengthening the capacity of CSRL's partners gradually became an important program component and one much appreciated by private benefactors.

Backstopping Program Management Without Directing. Masinde chose not to act as program supervisor since the team leader for VEDCO's Eastern Region (Kamuli) officially played that role. However there were times when the VEDCO staff found it difficult to differentiate the role of the field program manager from that of supervisor or watchdog versus that of mentor and enabler.[11]

With VEDCO. Masinde soon learned to step back from some of the daily activities in Kamuli, such as staff meetings and spending time in VEDCO's Kamuli office, and to interact with the field staff only when absolutely necessary. Most of her communications with the field staff went through VEDCO's Kamuli team leader. Since she was responsible for the entire program in Uganda and not just the activities being routed through VEDCO in Kamuli, Masinde deliberately chose to locate the new office she created in February 2008 in Kamuli town, slightly removed from the VEDCO field office, to maintain the needed social distance and to create a sense of independence. In addition, she made a greater effort to gain the professional confidence of the field staff through more firmness and less friendship.

With MAK. Working with MAK was less challenging because Masinde's office was not directly located within the institution. However, she had to determine how to entice faculty and staff to participate in program activities since (1) the program was located four hours away from MAK by car; (2) faculty already had large classes to teach; (3) faculty needed to generate external research funds; and (4) MAK had no funding allocation for faculty to conduct outreach programs, the only exception being oversight of student internships.

This process required ingenuity to encourage the professionalism and expertise of faculty and staff without raising expectations that they might be compensated by ISU for contributions before reaching any mutual agreements on what might be needed. Because the field program manager's relationship with MAK had not been clearly defined, the faculty and staff were not able to determine the level at which they should communicate. In time, Masinde chose to work through the dean of the Faculty of Agriculture or the CSRL director. However, she eventually realized that, to create a collegial relationship with the faculty and staff, it was also important to develop a working relationship with them. This played out nicely by interacting first with various department heads, then working through to a faculty member with whom she could develop a collaborative program, some of which produced grant-related research opportunities for the program. This proved to be a good strategy, and one that contributed to Masinde's professional development as well.

Institutionalizing the Program Manager's Position Within the Partnership

Key Challenges

From the beginning, all partners should anticipate the importance of institutionalizing the program manager's role within the partnership. Having no blueprint for this role in the partnership can be an opportunity to innovate. However, a flexible start comes with long-term obligations. The manager should be encouraged to begin to shape a template for all future managers to follow—documenting procedures and policies that impact the program and ways to manage them for the benefit of all partners. Even with ample time to agree on this person's role within the partnership, there are likely to be bumps along the road before full agreement is reached as to what policies and procedures that the manager should oversee and how this should be done.

Another important aspect of institutionalization concerns the establishment of procedures for replacing the manager, either for a short-term absence or for the long term. While this issue may seem premature, especially in the start-up of a new program, anticipating how this situation should be handled will help the partnership survive future management changes.

The lead institution will also want to examine ways to integrate the position within its own human resources system. Once the manager's role is institutionalized, it becomes easier for those that follow in the manager's footsteps to smoothly assume the same responsibilities.

The CSRL Experience

Helping to Harmonize Human Resources Policies. The human resources policies of the three partners were very different. Because there had been no early attempt to learn about each other's policies, Masinde was sometimes confronted with a problem that impacted everyday activities on the ground (see Box 3.7). However, many of these issues could have been avoided if there had been an early sharing session among all partners so that everyone understood each other's human resources policies from the beginning.

Integrating the Program Manager into the Structure of the Lead Institution. ISU arranged for the required visa for Masinde before she relocated to Kampala as an employee of ISU on a two-year contract. At the completion of the first contract, the university's human resources office was unable to continue her employment by using the same type of arrangement. Therefore, Masinde was employed as a private contractor to the university. This new arrangement meant that she could not take advantage of ISU's staff benefits package and the recognition normally received by university employees. She continued to work for ISU as a private contractor for five more years.

Anticipating Future Staff Changes. When Masinde was hired, ISU was anxious to have her located in Uganda to manage the program start-up. The first few years were extremely busy, and little thought was given to planning for a potential absence of the field program manager or for the possibility that she might choose to move on to another posi-

---

Box 3.7 VEDCO's Early Human Resources Policies on Volunteers' Pay

"Some of the volunteers worked very, very hard. . . . I discovered this by going through staff reports. . . . Many of the VEDCO workers who were working very late in the evening were volunteers. I started asking where are these people who are writing reports. I asked how are they coming to work and how are they paid? . . . I learned . . . you are a volunteer and you get nothing. I said, 'You have to get something in the budget for the volunteers. You have to have an allowance that goes to these people.' In 2005, we [CSRL] started building pay for volunteers into the budget system. VEDCO had to have a policy on how to compensate volunteers. They had people working but they didn't have a policy on how to compensate their volunteers."

Source: Dorothy Masinde in conversation with Della E. McMillan, Evanston, IL, July 28, 2012.

tion. Any change of staff, including that of the CSRL director, was probably not on anyone's mind. However, change is inevitable.

Even short-term staff absences function more smoothly if there is a plan for backstopping the work that is being done. During Masinde's tenure as field program manager, there were several periods when she spent two or three months in Ames. During these absences, the CSRL office was tasked with identifying a person to assume her responsibilities in Uganda. This would have gone smoother if plans had been in place for what was, in hindsight, a foreseeable situation.

Lessons Learned and Recommendations

Some of the CSRL program's principal start-up weaknesses were also major strengths. There was no precise field plan for the initial program start-up, and this gave the manager great flexibility. However, almost every decision related to the day-to-day start-up operation of the program in Uganda—from work permits for the field program manager to determining where she lived and worked—had to be researched and negotiated. This type of unregimented program start-up could have been disastrous if the program had not been built on a year of interinstitutional networking between the partners, a solid system of communication and trust between the partners that included multiple visits during the first two years, and an experienced field program manager who had the complete trust of an experienced director and management team.

Identifying and Hiring the First Program Manager

The CSRL management team wisely decided to recruit a full-time program manager who was attached to the lead institution and had more than a decade of experience administering similar types of programs. The fact that Masinde was familiar with the Uganda culture, able to exercise considerable autonomy, operate independently with the full trust of her employer, and had the respect of the Ugandan partners made a huge difference to a successful start-up.

Lesson 1:
Determine the most important qualities and qualifications desired in a program manager.

Recommendations:

- Identify the most important personal and academic qualities needed to carry out the specified duties; look for an interdisciplinary academic background and varied work experience.
- Anticipate the type of credentials that will be acceptable to the leaders of partner organizations.
- Identify a candidate who is able to interact with the type of clientele that the program is assisting as well as other community and public leaders and high-level officials.
- Choose a candidate who is able to operate independently with a minimum of supervision.
- Identify a person who is familiar with the region or country of operation.
- Look for a candidate who has management experience with the type of program being developed.
- Identify an individual with strong interpersonal skills—for example, flexible yet decisive—and good listening skills.
- Consider where and under what conditions this individual will be hired by the lead institution for the program.

Establishing the First Program Office

The original CSRL concept paper paid little attention to practical problems such as determining how the program would operate on a daily basis. This was, in large part, a reflection of the program's nontraditional (from a US point of view) relationship with its local partners. While CSRL's unwritten commitment to reinforcing local capacity was laudable, it created a host of downstream problems for the program as it started to grow. Especially important, the program's "marriage of convenience" to its local NGO partner VEDCO for an administrative office and essential infrastructure made it more difficult to establish an autonomous CSRL program office. In retrospect, all of the partners now realize that more attention should have been focused on registering ISU as an independent NGO in Uganda early in the process rather than waiting until the tenth year.

Lesson 2:
Identify a way to legally and independently get the program up and running while exploring requirements for long-term operation.

Recommendations:
- At the earliest opportunity, identify appropriate contacts concerning the legal requirements for operating within the area.
- Investigate terms and conditions for legal operation in the area of operation.
- Determine what is required either for short-term or long-term operation in the area; for example, work permits, taxes, payroll obligations, banking procedures, procurement policies, and insurance requirements.

Lesson 3:
Determine where to locate the program office.

Recommendations:
- Give serious consideration to locating a program manager in the area of operation, at least for the first few start-up years.
- Consider the pros and cons of various options before deciding where to set up a headquarters.

Defining the Role of the Program Manager

Since the CSRL program was just beginning, the partners were willing to cut the first program manager a great deal of slack. While she was able to make the program work, it might have been easier to get the program up and running if there had been an initial policy paper and collaborative agreement that clarified the program manager's role in relation to each partner, explained the general approach or model that had been selected to guide the program's implementation, and anticipated the need for each partner to participate in an interpartner coordinating body as one of the preconditions of their participation.

Lesson 4:
Come to a clear understanding about the program manager's responsibilities with regard to each partner and staff member.

Recommendations:
- Make sure that all partners and staff understand the program manager's roles and responsibilities within the partnership and on behalf of the lead institution.

- Develop a written description of the program manager's responsibilities with the partners and share it with them; review this annually and update as needed.
- Clarify and discuss the program manager's roles and responsibilities with key program staff, particularly those responsible for the field program, as well as those who may provide technical support.
- Ensure that all partners and staff understand the approach or model that is to guide program implementation.
- Encourage the program manager to devise her or his own system of program management; at the same time, encourage the manager to follow the partners' lead before attempting major changes.
- Until working relationships and lines of communication are established, the program manager should follow each partner organization's expected protocol in interacting with its staff.

Lesson 5:
Determine whether there is a need for a local advisory system, when it might be needed, and what it should look like.

Recommendations:
- Learn from the partners, particularly from the partner who is expected to take the lead for program implementation.
- Draw on partners for knowledge of the communities where the program intervenes for contacts and cultural insights.
- Go slow in setting up any type of local advisory system, at least until it becomes clear as to what type of advice is needed.
- Create a more formal local advisory structure after the first year; make it one of the preconditions of the partnership in the collaborative agreements signed with each partner.
- Develop procedures for accessing technical or other support if it should be needed.

Institutionalizing the Program Manager Position Within the Partnership

The best time to think about how the program manager will fit into the lead institution's human resources system is before hiring. By establishing an understood and accepted role for the manager within the organization's human resources system, the manager will enjoy all the employer's system benefits. This arrangement is also likely to establish the loyalty that is needed if the manager is stationed overseas.

As time progresses some of the initial components of the program, or even new additions, may evolve into independent entities. This may occur due to finding further funding sources, increasing partner interests, or changing local conditions. The partners may want to consider whether these new developments will change the responsibilities of the program manager in any way.

Lesson 6:
Develop orientation materials describing the primary managerial functions and policies that the program manager is expected to oversee within the partnership.

Recommendations:
- Involve the new program manager in the drafting of orientation materials as soon as the program starts, and update him or her regularly with input from the partners and staff.
- Facilitate sharing sessions among the partners as soon as the program manager comes on board to learn about each partner's policies and procedures that could impact the program.
- Make the management orientation handbook available to any short-term or new management staff associated with the partnership.

Lesson 7:
Establish a legitimate structure that integrates the program manager with the program management unit of the lead institution.

Recommendations:
- Develop a flexible start-up contract that will move toward integration of the first program manager—and those that follow—into the lead institution's employment structure.
- Be prepared with the best employment package possible for hiring a program manager regardless of the candidate's nationality or location.
- Anticipate that other employment options may become more suitable once the program is more established.

> **Lesson 8:**
> **Work with the partnership to outline a succession plan for the program manager's position.**

Recommendations:

- Have a written plan in place to minimize any short- or long-term disruption to the program should there be changes in management or program staff.
- When a staff change is imminent, share information about the expected change with leaders of the partnership so that everyone will know what is happening and how the responsibilities are to be handled with minimal disruption in the program.

Notes

1. The position was first called "program coordinator" for the purposes of advertisement. In this book, the individual who managed CSRL's field program in Uganda is referred to as the "field program manager." The title of this position was changed several times, eventually becoming "associate director of field programs."

2. "Years later, as we have thought about the particular qualities that made this particular program manager effective, when starting up a rather unclear pathway, it may have been her unflappable and flexible nature, her long-term vision of where she was going, and her knowledge of participatory development methods. These are qualities that are difficult to screen for in a position advertisement." Lorna Michael Butler in Skype conversation with Della McMillan, February 6, 2014.

3. Masinde's first short-term contract was followed by a two-year contract with ISU (July 1, 2004, to June 30, 2006).

4. Quarterly payments of approximately $15,200 each were wire transferred to VEDCO on the first of January, April, July, and October 2005. These quarterly disbursements continued, sometimes irregularly due to the need for documentation of expenditures, some of which proved challenging to locate.

The director and other ISU faculty made frequent visits to Uganda every year. Each time a visit was made, extra cash was carried to cover travelers' individual expenses—vehicle fuel, repairs, overtime wages for a driver, occasional rental of a non-ISU vehicle, and some supplies. Larger items, like computers and printers (often recycled from ISU faculty), were hand-carried. Because the management team members were ISU faculty, it was possible for them to get a cash advance from ISU and, on return, the expenses were documented and the funds were withdrawn from the CSRL account in Ames.

5. Estimated to have a population of close to 500,000 people as of 2012, Kamuli is 80 percent dependent on agriculture as the source of livelihood. Kamuli District Planning Unit, "District Development Plan for 2010/11–2014/15" (Kamuli, Uganda: Kamuli District Local Government, May 2011).

6. By the time that ISU decided VEDCO would be an ideal partner, VEDCO had already made the decision to start a sustainable agriculture program in Kamuli, a choice based on the low Human Development Indicators recorded in the district at the time and its low NGO coverage. Kamuli was identified as a poor district in terms of both food security and household sanitation.

7. Five-year Memorandums of Understanding (MoU) were signed between ISU and VEDCO, and between ISU and MAK, around the same time in 2004. A five-year Memorandum of Agreement, which included more details about the cooperative alliance, was signed between ISU and VEDCO in August 2009.

8. VEDCO's strategic plan was to serve as a program document for implementation, that is, as a guide for implementing CSRL's programs in Kamuli. The field program manager discussed this strategic plan with VEDCO's management team, consisting of the operations manager and the M&E and grants officers, and they agreed to adapt it for the CSRL program. The procedure for adapting VEDCO's strategic plan to match the interests of ISU's program was not spelled out in writing.

9. "The local government is divided into five levels, the lowest being the zone or village, which is level one, followed by the parish (level two), subcounty (level three), county (level four), and the district (level five [V]). All levels have a committee that is led by a chairperson. All the leaders of the local government are elected every five years . . . [and] are affiliated with political parties. . . . The local council five chairperson (LC V chairperson) heads the Kamuli District Local Government, and there is only one in the district." Dorothy Masinde, e-mail message to Lorna Michael Butler, October 28, 2014.

10. These early networks later became important in gaining approval of building plans for school structures to which CSRL contributed support.

11. Often when caught in this situation, the field program manager would try to diffuse the confusion by explaining her responsibilities to the field staff and by having a direct discussion about this with the team leader. The VEDCO policy may also have added to the confusion since VEDCO's field staff were not expected to communicate directly with a donor (and ISU was perceived as a donor).

4

Building Trust Through Accounting and Accountability

Mark E. Westgate

Partnerships are about building trust. But building trust between institutions is never easy. When links cross cultural boundaries and vastly different types of institutions, partnering is even more complex. Three common challenges for developing trusting partnerships are:

- Building partnership capital—developing a shared vision of the partnership that is in tune with each individual partner's values and priorities;[1]
- Managing people and money—facilitating partner agreement concerning a common set of accounting, personnel, and risk management procedures that comply with the standards required by the lead institution and major benefactors; and
- Shepherding joint planning and reporting—reaching a common agreement among all partners on program priorities, the program implementation approach, a common set of standard indicators to monitor progress toward the partnership's collective goals and objectives, and a system of reporting.

The authors wish to acknowledge the helpful input and contributions of Denise Bjelland, Lorna Michael Butler, Tami Corcoran, Francis Kizito, Dorothy Masinde, Della E. McMillan, Henry Kizito Musoke, Isabel Reinert, and Josie Six.

Building Partnership Capital

Key Challenges

A partnership, like a friendship, evolves over time. Sometimes the partners have known each other for many years, so they know what is at stake and what might be gained from a relationship. Under other circumstances, perhaps a mutual acquaintance has brought individuals or organizations together to explore partnership opportunities. In yet another case, careful research may have pointed out common or complimentary qualities and needs suggesting partnership potential.

Depending on what has led to a partnership relationship, knowing something about each other and agreeing on the big goals is important. If there has been no previous shared experience for building mutual trust, this is a good place to start. Joint planning is an excellent way to acquire knowledge of each other, and the shared experience of learning together and reaching common agreement is a worthwhile investment. Private benefactor funding can provide the flexible support that partners need to build social capital.

The CSRL Experience

Iowa State University (ISU) selected two Ugandan organizations as partners primarily because of their knowledge of the country and the clientele to whom the program was committed. Although ISU was not well acquainted with Volunteer Efforts for Development Concerns (VEDCO), it seemed that this respected Ugandan nongovernmental organization (NGO) with a good track record would bring very different competencies than ISU and its other partner Makerere University (MAK). VEDCO had experience working in the field with the rural poor of Uganda and could deliver improved skills and technologies to smallholder farmers. MAK brought a long history of Ugandan experience in the field of education and research, a wide range of technical expertise, and a commitment to preparing students to work in Ugandan communities with farmers, local officials, and small businesses. From the onset, all of the partners knew that they each brought different competencies, goals, and priorities where the partnership was concerned and, even early in the exploratory discussions, it felt easy to foster the personal relationships needed to move the partnership to a higher level.

A critical mechanism for building partnership capital at this juncture involved many informal discussions—over meals, social engagements, field activities, exchange visits, planning meetings, coordinating discussions, board meetings, and strategic planning sessions (Table 4.1).

Table 4.1 Key Mechanisms for Building Partnership Capital in the CSRL Program, 2004–Present

Variable	Phase One: 2004–2008	Phase Two: 2009–2013	Phase Three: 2014–Future
Program foci	Survey local situation Refine outreach model Increase food crop production Increase access to clean water Identify and support vulnerable groups Initiate student involvement (service-learning program)	Organize joint partner planning Scale up activities Add new funding streams Increase number of beneficiaries Strengthen local capacity Improve local training processes	Develop sustainable partnerships Increase private sector and local institutional involvement Integrate program components Sustain community leadership Grow private support
Building partnership capital			
Exchange visits	Administrative exchange visits; faculty and student exchanges; director, management team, and donor visits to the field		
Student and faculty exchanges	Applied research, service learning, technical assistance		
Joint planning meetings	In the United States	In Uganda	In Uganda
Advisory board	Primarily ISU faculty, administrators, and US experts in international development	More inclusive participation; ISU and MAK faculty, Ugandan and other regional experts, and VEDCO staff	
Midterm evaluation and first-year strategic plan		Midterm evaluation and first collaborative five-year plan	

Source: Mark Westgate, Lorna Michael Butler, and Della McMillan, Collaborative e-mail correspondence and Skype discussions for table development and refinement, February 1–20, 2014.

Multilevel Exchange Visits. Exchange visits between the Ugandan partners and ISU played a critical role in developing personal relationships and, therefore, protected the partnership. The visits also enabled participants to get acquainted with the culture and resources of each institution. Starting in the first year, the program supported an array of administrative exchange visits. During the first decade:

- Two deans of the ISU College of Agriculture and Life Sciences (CALS) and two ISU university presidents visited the Center for Sustainable Rural Livelihoods (CSRL) field activities;
- Two deans of the MAK College of Agricultural and Environmental Sciences (CAES) visited the United States to participate in various CSRL activities and to get to know ISU;
- The VEDCO executive director visited ISU for periods ranging from one week to over a month almost every year;
- Numerous ISU accountants and program coordinators visited Uganda to work with their VEDCO counterparts on accounts training and reporting; and
- Several VEDCO accountants visited the United States to work with their ISU counterparts for periods ranging from one to three weeks.

A glimpse into the various exchange activities illustrates how much these experiences contributed to partnership development. For example, when VEDCO's executive director and MAK's dean of the Faculty of Agriculture visited ISU, a daily schedule was arranged to facilitate meetings with faculty whose backgrounds coincided with some of the needs of their own institutions as well as those of the CSRL program in Kamuli. They also met with administrative personnel; took part in CSRL executive committee meetings; and, if CSRL benefactors were available, spent time with them. Seminars were presented for students and the public; meetings were held with students from Uganda; farm tours were conducted to highlight small-scale farm equipment and small animal production; and visits to value-added agricultural business operations were made. Many of the visits to Iowa took place in the fall to allow visitors to attend the annual World Food Prize Norman E. Borlaug International Symposium in Des Moines.

Similarly, when ISU personnel visited Uganda, they spent time with MAK administrators, faculty, and students; offered seminars and workshops; and visited MAK's Continuing Agricultural Education Center (CAEC) at Kabanyolo, national and international research centers, and other districts where VEDCO operates, such as Apac, Lira, and Luwero. Most of the ISU personnel spent time in Kamuli—visiting local farmers, observing farmer training, attending field days, participating in the service-learning program, taking part in planning workshops, or training VEDCO staff. Externally funded initiatives enabled Iowa farmers to visit Uganda to share knowledge with VEDCO staff and Kamuli farmers about crop production and marketing. Research grants enabled ISU researchers and students to spend time with Kamuli farmers, VEDCO staff, and other Uganda collaborators. All of these experiences strength-ened personal and institutional relationships and, simultaneously, deep-ened the partnership.

First-Year Participatory Rural Appraisals. During the start-up year, the program facilitated a series of participatory rural appraisals (PRAs) and joint planning activities to help the partners better understand the field situation in Kamuli. Armed with this knowledge, the partners were able to develop their first joint annual planning budget at the end of the ini-tial fiscal year. Several unanticipated activities were added that had not been in VEDCO's original plan (see Chapter 5).

Exchange Visits. The first CSRL director traveled to Uganda at least twice a year, sometimes more often. Since the program began in 2004, the ability to communicate by e-mail and Skype has improved greatly, but current CSRL director Mark Westgate travels to Uganda several times each year. He makes a point of inviting VEDCO and MAK administrators, and sometimes middle-management staff and MAK fac-ulty, to ISU each year. During these visits, the partners review program activities and resolve any personnel and funding issues. The combina-tion of face-to-face meetings and regular communications has helped minimize misunderstandings, accelerate program delays, and resolve human resources concerns. In between these visits, the CSRL program and its partners organize occasional staff and stakeholder forums, staff workshops, community field days, and planning meetings in Uganda.

Faculty and Student Involvement. Another contribution to the social fabric of the partnership was the care that was given to ensuring that an equivalent number of MAK and ISU faculty and students were sup-ported by the program. The exchange visits helped everyone at all three institutions come to know and understand each other better. Especially important, the partners learned that each institution had inherently dif-ferent ways of operating and of investing personnel time in the program, and that resources and technical capacities between the institutions var-ied greatly. This increased awareness about the factors underlying each institution's priorities for the program.

The CSRL Advisory Board. Following the formation of CSRL, ISU required that a CSRL Advisory Board be established. The five founding members were appointed in 2007. The role of the board was to advise the director and, through their vast international experience, help CSRL be a catalyst for change. Early on, the board made a pivotal observation: institutional change for all of the partner organizations had been omitted as a principle program goal. Based on a recommendation from the CSRL midterm evaluation, which was completed in January 2009, the program leadership decided to increase the local partners' representation on the board and to relocate its annual meetings from Iowa to Uganda (see Chapter 2). At this juncture, the CSRL Advisory Board was renamed the Partner Planning and Advisory Board (PPAB). Guidance from this board played a defining role in shaping the trajectory and focus of the CSRL program.[2]

Annual Meetings. Beginning in 2010, the PPAB was reconstituted into a working group more suited to visionary local program planning and assessment. It now has a stronger representation of partners and East African development experts. While the group meets annually, members are on call for timely advice. Annual meetings of partner and board members now provide the principal forum for informally reviewing the program's activities of the preceding year and proposing priorities for the coming year. The PPAB, which usually meets in Kampala, has been a powerful force for focusing CSRL's program, and has helped the management group narrow program directions to conform to available funds and monitoring and evaluation (M&E) findings.

Partnership Team Building. The CSRL program's initial concept of partnership team building focused on exchange visits.[3] By 2009, it was clear that a more formal mechanism for collaborative planning was needed. The first formal interpartner planning workshop took place near Jinja in March 2009. In addition to some of the ISU team members and key MAK faculty, VEDCO staff from most levels also participated. While billed as a program planning activity, the timing was right to foster the needed openness and sharing across the partnership, all of which helped participants understand and appreciate each other's situations and priorities. For VEDCO and MAK, this may have been the first real commitment to becoming a team in spite of having very different missions and cultures. The environment and structure of the activities did a lot to build the partnership as well as a consensus on CSRL's priorities. From that point on, there was a concerted effort to structure specific workshops and meetings to ensure greater staff participation in the planning and priority-setting process (see Chapter 6).

Managing People and Money

Key Challenges

Institutions with a long history and well-established procedures rarely have enough flexibility to accommodate the changes required to develop different institutional standards for accounts and contract management. This takes considerable time, patience, creativity, and the goodwill of organizational leaders. ISU had a long history of working with United States Agency for International Development (USAID) contracts through faculty experience with development projects as well as a good track record for managing research grant contracts supported by the US government and the private sector, but almost no experience in contracting with or partnering with an African NGO. This was new territory.

The CSRL Experience

Early Trade-Offs. Prior to recruiting the field program manager, the CSRL management team had begun to investigate the legal requirements of operating in Uganda. The program leadership quickly realized it was not possible for ISU to arrange to operate as an independent entity when it had no track record in the country. The option of registering as an independent NGO would take considerable time and expertise, and would delay the start-up of the program. Although this remained a long-term goal, ISU chose to begin to work immediately through its Ugandan partners (Table 4.2).

In practical terms, this meant that ISU could not hire personnel, initiate contracts, or open a local bank account—it was entirely dependent on its local partners to conduct its business in country. The field programs were developed in cooperation with ISU's Ugandan partners and could be funded and managed only through the local entities, VEDCO and MAK.

After some consideration, ISU's partners agreed to provide the logistical support required to operate in the country. VEDCO provided an office, facilitated a work permit for the field program manager, and helped purchase capital items and materials for in-country program implementation. MAK was ISU's Ugandan facilitator for technical expertise and research-related activities. Although the MAK faculty were heavily involved in all of the surveys and technical backup, as

Table 4.2 Key Mechanisms for Managing People and Money in the CSRL Program, 2004–Present

Variable	Phase One: 2004–2008	Phase Two: 2009–2013	Phase Three: 2014–Future
Program foci	Program start-up Increase agricultural crop production Increase access to clean water Identify vulnerable groups Initiate service-learning programs	Organize joint partner planning Scale up activities Add new funding streams Increase number of beneficiaries Strengthen local capacity	Develop sustainable partnerships Increase private sector and local institutional involvement Diversify activities and add beneficiaries Sustain community leadership Grow private support
Managing people and money			
Legal framework for the program operating in Uganda	CSRL program routes funding for field activities through VEDCO because they have no legal presence in Uganda	CSRL executes all programs through VEDCO CSRL forgoes a public identity in Uganda	CSRL becomes an independent NGO in Uganda to more independently manage current and new partnerships
CSRL accounting and management systems	ISU reporting systems are required and managed by the field program manager as ISU's representative in Uganda Selected subcontracts arranged with MAK, whose systems were more compatible with ISU's systems	CSRL helps VEDCO strengthen its financial systems to be more compatible with the ISU systems ISU and VEDCO build mutual understanding of each other's contracting and accounting cultures	VEDCO builds on lessons learned from the partnership to start restructuring its own internal systems ISU's registration as a foreign NGO creates new opportunities
CSRL human resources management systems	All local CSRL staff hired by VEDCO and managed by an ISU-paid CSRL employee (the field program manager), whose work permit was negotiated by VEDCO and lodged in the VEDCO office	Gradual increase in influence over management of the CSRL program with support from VEDCO	CSRL's new status as an independent NGO in Uganda provides greater influence over CSRL staff and their compensation

Source: Mark Westgate, Lorna Michael Butler, and Della E. McMillan, collaborative e-mail correspondence and Skype discussions for table development and refinement, February 1–20, 2014.

well as student training, these activities were negotiated on a case-by-case basis.

ISU's decision to subcontract most of the field activities through VEDCO helped the program get up and running, but it also meant that ISU lost some of its independence. The same subcontracting process meant that, when ISU needed additional administrative support in the field, the hiring process was obliged to follow VEDCO's personnel and remuneration policies.

When CSRL needed capital items like vehicles, or premises to accommodate staff, it relied on its partners. In retrospect, the lack of a registered status made it difficult for ISU to consider other partners or pursue other funding independently. Except for externally funded research projects, ISU's early operations were almost completely dependent on its partnerships with VEDCO and MAK.

While being associated with VEDCO had advantages, it also came at a cost. Since ISU had no public identity in Uganda, it was often perceived as a donor or benefactor as opposed to a true partner by the local governments and members of the Kamuli communities. Even the field program manager was often mistakenly perceived to be a VEDCO staff member. The communities that benefited from the CSRL program rarely associated the source of their achievements with ISU. As the program progressed, the need for ISU to officially register as a foreign NGO became more compelling. While this was recognized by CSRL management from the onset, the potential offered by the original partnerships made up for many of the challenges, and there was always the knowledge that the experiences gained would serve the university well when future registration was appropriate.

Accounting: Searching for Common Ground. When CSRL began in September 2004, there was one principal benefactor (the founding benefactors, Gerald A. and Karen A. Kolschowsky). Not surprisingly, the initial focus of the accounting system was on providing simple straightforward accounts to that funder, through the ISU Foundation and the CSRL executive committee, on what was being done with these early start-up funds. Little effort was put forward to learn about the partners' different types of accounting systems (Table 4.3).

None of the initial CSRL partnership agreements made mention of what accounting procedures would be used to satisfy the program accountability needs of ISU and the founding benefactors.[4] For example, the initial contractual agreements between ISU and its partners specified accounting procedures for the transfer of program funds from

Table 4.3 Initial Differences and Changes Between the VEDCO and ISU Accounting Systems

Characteristic	ISU	VEDCO
Reporting method	Fully computerized system administered by ISU accounting office	Paper based
Accounts and statements	Single program accounts and one program statement	Multiple program accounts and statements
Reporting deadlines	Deadlines for reporting consistent for all accounts, based on ISU-wide system for monthly account reconciliation	Variable for each donor project Contractual agreement to adhere to CSRL deadlines for reporting to ISU accounting office
Budgeting	Established annual program budget based on estimated line-item costs distributed among management, field operations, and capital expenditures VEDCO budgeted as a line item in field operations. Details specified in VEDCO budget	Early field budgets were developed by headquarters staff, then disseminated to Kamuli; later, field staff participated in the budget planning process Line item budget for field operations submitted by management team for CSRL approval (included 10% administrative fee) Reallocation of funds between line items; major adjustments requested in writing
Contracts for services	Fixed-price contract for established contractors, acceptable to ISU purchasing department and accounting office Oversight by CSRL office to ensure funds were allocated as intended. CSRL policy enacted to ensure all fund expenditures per quarter are accounted for in advance of new disbursement	2004–2009: Five-year contract for services. ISU accounting office required original receipts for all expenses to reconcile the account 2010: ISU purchasing office changed format to a fixed-price contract. After this, VEDCO funds received quarterly (treated as an advance from ISU). Reconciliation of accounts shifted to CSRL
Staff salaries	Salaries set by the university's human resources office in negotiation with college and department leadership (did not pertain to VEDCO staff)	Paid from a pool of funds. Wages established by VEDCO board Conform to Ugandan laws
Funding sources	ISU and external grants	Private donors of many kinds, each supporting a different program component
Policy formation	Established by the ISU administration under guidelines established by the Iowa Board of Regents Procedures specific to CSRL outlined in Memorandum of Understanding with primary partners	VEDCO Board of Directors (executed by the executive director)

Source: Mark Westgate, Lorna Michael Butler, and Della E. McMillan, collaborative e-mail correspondence and Skype discussions for table development and refinement, February 1–20, 2014.

ISU to VEDCO or MAK as well as the general contractual rules and regulations that ISU had established.[5] This created a new dynamic in which each partner had to work with the other partners through the use of its own internal accounting system.

When contracting for services with the partners, ISU provided funds up front and, for accountability purposes, requested original receipts in return. Expenditures were reconciled against budgeted lines and available funds. VEDCO had no such mechanism. It relied on donor funds that were designated for specific projects, and this sometimes led to the comingling of different funds. That policy was completely contrary to ISU's accounting procedures, which expected its program funds be kept completely separate from other VEDCO's donor funds, especially when US federal funds were involved.

Other problems occurred because the time line of the two accounting systems did not mesh. The ISU system required funds be spent during the quarter for which they were programmed, or else explained. The VEDCO system was more flexible, given the fact that a particular activity might be moved up or moved back due to some unforeseen constraint or opportunity.

Budgeting for staff also had differences. ISU had a system of line items for specific staff members, and expected the partner to budget for a particular staff member and then report that it had paid that person for the work. But VEDCO had a tradition of pooling the funds for different categories, and then billing for them once they were spent. This provided VEDCO with a way of billing some of the costs of its administration to the grant since it had little experience with charging and using contract overhead funds. ISU understood overhead; it did not understand billing labor from a pool.

Each organization sought to harmonize key aspects of their accounting systems to accommodate both of their primary accounting requirements. Reaching this point has taken considerable effort and understanding from the partners.

VEDCO was advanced funds as agreed on each quarter for personnel salaries, field activities, and program administration specified in its five-year contract with ISU. CSRL required monthly receipts from VEDCO for internal monitoring of personnel and program expense allocations. But distance and differences in basic accounting systems rendered timely reporting of expenses a perennial challenge. The primary consequence has been the delay in reconciling accounts at ISU—a prerequisite established for sending the next quarter's funds. Since

VEDCO relies entirely on external funding to pay employees and conduct its work, ongoing programs were interrupted and personnel went unpaid until funds arrived. This situation was not acceptable to CSRL. A compromise was worked out with the VEDCO Board of Directors allowing CSRL online access to the VEDCO bank accounts associated with CSRL's field operations.

Personnel and Risk Management: Finding Common Ground. Resolving personnel and financial issues from a distance has been the most challenging issue for the CSRL management office.

Personnel in Ames. Since its inception, the CRSL office at ISU has employed a part-time faculty member as its director. During the first five years of CSRL's operation, CSRL operating funds—generated by the endowment—bought out nine months of the director's salary, enabling his department to hire another person to teach his classes and pay him a summer salary. In December 2009, a new director came on board. In this case, his home department was willing to donate his base salary—a cost savings to CSRL—and CALS contributed a 15 percent administrative stipend, which is standard procedure for faculty who take on additional responsibilities such as directing a center.

In 2009, the program added a full-time program coordinator,[6] whose primary responsibility is ensuring that financial reporting of field operations and associated research projects are managed according to ISU requirements. It proved highly beneficial that CSRL's program coordinator had both accounting and master of business administration (MBA) degrees as well as considerable experience working with ISU's financial systems. The ISU Foundation provides funding for CSRL programs through twelve unique accounts, and associated USAID-funded research projects involve subcontracts to nine cooperators in three African countries and three US institutions. Each has its unique way of processing funds and managing accounts. The complexity of accounts management has changed greatly since the program began, and this has been reflected in the type of staff required for this responsibility.

Field personnel. Currently, all field personnel (with the exception of the field program manager) are hired and paid by VEDCO through funds provided from and managed by CSRL. VEDCO assumed responsibility for managing all of the human resources and payroll requirements associated with personnel. CSRL has been able to provide direct input on personnel issues through its positive working relationship with VEDCO's administration.

Employee compensation. VEDCO was built on the premise of volunteerism, which was appropriate in the context of post–civil war reconstruction in Luwero—where VEDCO was born—due to the large number of skilled young people who had their education disrupted and were desperate to get back on track through any kind of short-term employment. As the university system was rebuilt in the 1990s, more new graduates took these positions in the hope that the volunteer positions—essentially internships—would turn into permanent jobs.

When the CSRL program began in Kamuli, there were three VEDCO employees on the ground, one of whom was considered to be a volunteer. Volunteers were entitled to a small compensation unless they were part of a special donor-funded study. Almost immediately, CSRL began working with VEDCO management staff to develop new personnel guidelines to ensure that all employees, including volunteers, would be paid. Soon after, the CSRL field program manager worked with VEDCO to ensure that the Kamuli staff and their family members received health benefits through the CSRL contract.

Risk management. When CSRL started partnering with VEDCO, all VEDCO vehicles carried comprehensive insurance, which is what CSRL purchased for the CSRL-funded vehicle. As the field program manager became acquainted with VEDCO policies, she recommended some type of workers' compensation to cover on-the-job injuries. The first step was to ensure that all staff had valid driving (or riding) permits to validate the insurance. Any staff member hired by VEDCO was required to have a valid driving (or riding) permit before he or she was allowed to ride the program motorcycles. At CSRL's request, VEDCO now purchases basic life and safety insurance for employees when they drive the organization's vehicles and motorcycles.

Human resources. VEDCO's initial human resources reforms, combined with the increased emphasis on training field staff, helped catalyze a major rise in the quality of staff that the program was able to recruit. In 2008, CSRL and VEDCO agreed to institute additional employee incentives to retain staff in Kamuli. VEDCO's executive director introduced new employee benefits, including payment of an additional month of salary in December (the thirteenth-month salary) and a monthly contribution of 5 percent of salary to the employee's severance pay.

These reforms, in combination with the growing reputation of the program as being a smart place to start one's career, contributed to a dramatic increase in staff quality, measured by an increase in the number of staff with advanced degrees and a decreased reliance on volunteers.

Balancing Different Accounting Systems. As mentioned above, VEDCO and ISU had accounting systems that differed greatly, and their requirements for accounts management were not the same. From the beginning, each organization made a great effort to learn exactly what was needed to make the partnership work, including sharing detailed information about ISU's accounting requirements. Part of the field program manager's job was to provide local oversight for the accounts reporting process. It soon became apparent that ISU and VEDCO should have initially invested more time and effort in developing the needed accounting capabilities within VEDCO to keep the system on track with ISU's requirements. In addition, it would have helped if the two partners had agreed on a common set of indicators with which to track program execution. Without this tool, it was difficult to determine how much money was being spent to achieve program subcomponent objectives and whether the subcomponents were being implemented successfully.

Based on the knowledge and experience of its administrative and accounting personnel, each partner believed that it was following the correct procedures in accounting for funds allocated and spent. ISU expected to receive original receipts in return for funds that were advanced, and VEDCO was committed to following this procedure. But over time, there was an increasing time lag on VEDCO's part in sending the required receipts to the CSRL office at ISU. It often was difficult to obtain original receipts, and sometimes they were not even available. VEDCO's accounting system was not highly computerized and it became challenging to maintain detailed expenditure records in the manner expected. Eventually the ISU Accounting Office was unable to advance further funding until the receipts were received.

This accounting challenge was openly shared with the founding benefactors during the program's scheduled executive committee meetings. Far from being upset, the benefactors encouraged the CSRL director and the ISU accounting personnel to work it out. In the Kolschowskys' long experience of working in other countries, cultures, and management situations, this type of management crisis was far from unusual.

The field program manager proposed that ISU administrators and account managers visit Uganda to resolve this short-term problem. During the visit in July 2008, they were able to experience the financial environment in Uganda firsthand. Many financial transactions common in Uganda had been difficult to explain to ISU contract managers and accountants on the other side of the world. While it is easy to obtain a receipt for just about everything in the United States, it is not always so easy in Uganda. And though it may be easy in the United States to requisition an item from the same vendor every time, this is not the case in Uganda.

During the same visit to Uganda, the ISU administrators and account managers assisted the VEDCO staff in updating the financial records as required, provided practical training, and put forth a better understanding of ISU accounting procedures. Together, the ISU and VEDCO staff assessed the needs for improved account reporting and further training that would be needed to improve the account reporting systems. In January 2009, CSRL hired a new program coordinator with accounting expertise. One of the program coordinator's first tasks was to travel to Uganda to learn about the VEDCO accounting system.

Between July 2008 and January 2014, there was a series of ISU staff visits to Uganda to address accounting issues and provide hands-on training. VEDCO's accounting staff and the Kamuli team leader traveled to ISU in 2008 for accounts training and to gain a better understanding of the ISU system. Since that time there have been additional visits by VEDCO and MAK staff to ISU, for example six Ugandans visited ISU to take part in the September 2014 symposium to mark ten years of the CSRL program in Uganda. Some of this time was devoted to training associated with ISU's change of status to a Ugandan NGO.

Once the new staff training and accounts support program were initiated, the entire management system began to operate more efficiently and conflicts over accounting procedures decreased considerably.

Recognizing the Parameters of Each Partner's Systems. As the CSRL partnerships developed, the key players came to understand that each had inherently different ways of operating, investing personnel time, committing resources, and establishing priorities. Time has brought a greater acceptance of these differences and a genuine willingness on the part of everyone concerned to make the partnerships work.

This flexibility and collaborative spirit has been seen often among the partners. For example, during both short- and long-term absences of the field program manager, VEDCO reassigned staff members to take on additional responsibilities. When CSRL initiated the service-learning program, MAK identified faculty members to join that CSRL team. VEDCO's Board of Directors willingly cooperated with the ISU administration to make staff salaries more competitive.

The Lead Institution's Move to Independence. To reduce the bureaucratic complexity of dealing with each partner's internal accounting systems, in October 2011 ISU began to explore the idea of registering as an independent NGO in Uganda.

With permission from the Iowa Board of Regents, ISU applied to the Ugandan Office of Internal Affairs to register as an NGO called the Iowa State University–Uganda Program. The application included documentation on the proposed NGO constitution, bylaws, board of directors, in-country operating principles, and a host of letters of support from local government officials and current operating partners. Approval to operate as an NGO in Uganda was granted by the Republic of Uganda in November 2013.

How will ISU's independence impact the partnership? The answer will be found in how ISU exercises its new role in Uganda, and whether it is able to develop a partnership model that again places priority on the goals of the partnership versus those of any one institution. As in the first ten years of the program, there must be a commitment to an equitable partnership in which each institution feels that it will be stronger together than alone. This will require the partnership to create a new shared vision and goal, and to place a priority on open communications and trust—all of which are essential to partnership capital.

Shepherding Joint Planning and Reporting

Key Challenges

Signed agreements are only the start-up volley in facilitating the complex game of a multipartner-managed program. Contracts and budgets need to be linked to deliverables that can be tracked with indicators to facilitate joint planning and accountability by the partners. Signed agreements do not guarantee a successful working relationship; that requires time, patience, and flexibility.

The partners need to agree on specific deliverables, procedures for attaining the expected outcomes, and methods to monitor progress toward these achievements. A capacity-building plan is also an essential component, whether the partners remain the same or change. Adequate discussion and agreement on all of these components will help to ensure that program disbursements are linked to achievements and that all partners are gaining from the relationship.

The CSRL Experience

Now that CSRL is able to operate as an independent NGO, the hope is that it will be easier for its Uganda partners to follow the new mutually agreed-on accounting and management procedures.

Interpartner and Stakeholder Strategic Planning. Although the concept of joint planning was implicit in the original CSRL partner agreements, none of the original documents ever outlined a formal strategic planning process. Because the partnership was built around a learning model, there was an informal understanding among the partners that there would be continual partner discussions, working groups, committees, and informal workshops to guide the program, set priorities, and define work plans. The VEDCO staff, working with the field program manager, also facilitated a number of participatory appraisal meetings and surveys to establish program priorities at the community level (see Chapter 5). In the early years, these informal consultations and VEDCO's own strategic plan served as the basis for the VEDCO contracts for services, followed by quarterly disbursements of funds. Contracts with MAK faculty also contributed to the priority-setting process.

The first formal interpartner and stakeholder strategic planning meetings took place in Uganda in March 2009. These meetings, which involved a range of regional organizational representatives as well as staff from each partner organization, did much to build esprit de corps. These were executed in conjunction with the program's first external midterm evaluation (see Table 4.4) as part of a four-step planning process that set CSRL's directions for the next three years.[7]

This multistep process did more than set the course for the CSRL program in Kamuli in Phase Two. By now, there was a unified recognition of the importance of capacity building within each of the Ugandan partner institutions. This diverse planning process probably did more to increase the partners' understanding of the resources to which each institution had access, and how these resources might be directed to address program priorities and to strengthen the partnership (see Chapter 6).

The Original Monitoring and Evaluation System. In large part because the original agreements with the donors included the requirement that the program be monitored using international evaluation standards, the initial M&E activities (see Chapter 8) included (1) internal tracking with periodic documentation by field M&E staff on field activities and (2) external evaluations with major periodic assessments of general program impacts every year or two by a MAK consultant in cooperation with an ISU faculty member.

The former reports, prepared by the VEDCO field staff and sent quarterly to the CSRL office, summarized progress on field activities. As such, these reports generally were designed to account for how the

Table 4.4 Key Mechanisms for Shepherding Joint Planning and Reporting in the CSRL Program, 2004–Present

Variable	Phase One: 2004–2008	Phase Two: 2009–2013	Phase Three: 2014–Future
Program foci	Survey local situation Refine outreach model Increase food crop production Increase access to clean water Identify and support vulnerable groups; initiate student involvement (service-learning program)	Organize joint partner planning Scale up activities Add new funding streams Increase number of beneficiaries Strengthen local capacity	Develop sustainable partnerships Increase private sector and local institutional involvement Integrate program components Sustain community leadership Grow private support
Shepherding joint planning and reporting			
Interpartner and stakeholder strategic planning	Used VEDCO's strategic plan Integrated community and staff feedback into plan through informal discussions, working groups, and workshops	Facilitated multistep strategic planning process involving stakeholders and partners Achieved consensus among partners on program and partner priorities	Continue advisory board, stakeholder, and partner planning processes Aim for maximum impact by targeting, innovating, and planning for exit strategy
Reporting	Conducted periodic internal documentation and assessments Prepared to conduct five-year assessment	Used standard set of indicators for tracking program execution and impact	Summarize indicators into tracking tables to facilitate strategic planning
Integrating M&E for strategic planning	Executed annual community-, subparish-, and subdistrict-level participatory rural appraisals (PRAs) Identified the internal indicators that the technical teams (e.g., nutrition, agriculture, livestock, and microfinance) needed to monitor and track their activities External evaluation team identified international impact indicators, tracked through surveys Separate yearly reports are generated by the technical teams and external evaluation teams with some cross-referencing	Trained VEDCO staff in basic principles of M&E Developed a smaller number of monitoring and impact indicators with which to track each activity group Prepared a retroactive analysis of the indicators used by the program to date and described it in the program's first summative M&E report Continued reporting on monitoring and impact indicators separately	Better integration of M&E into CSRL strategic planning Strengthen the use and dissemination of M&E findings Train and retrain CSRL staff and partners in results-based M&E and strategic planning

Source: Mark Westgate, Lorna Michael Butler, and Della E. McMillan, collaborative e-mail correspondence and Skype discussions for table development and refinement, February 1–20, 2014.

team spent its time in the field (e.g., number of farmer trainings, number of women attending workshops, and number of latrines constructed). There was little evaluation of the impact of these activities, the sustainability of the interventions, or needed program adjustments. In contrast, the external evaluation assessments focused on measuring CSRL's impacts on household food security, measuring its impacts on economic stability, and identifying program adjustments.

The two approaches to M&E were not functionally connected because the results of the external evaluation assessments were almost never incorporated into the quarterly and annual reports that were based primarily on the internal tacking assessments and individual case studies.

Shift to Use of Tracking Tables for Reporting. In early 2012, CSRL trained VEDCO field staff in developing key monitoring indicators and tracking tables for documenting progress toward achieving key strategic objectives (SOs). This training, led by an external consultant, stressed the importance of linking program objectives, deliverables (intermediate results as the project develops), and monitoring indicators that provide quantitative evidence of progress. During this training session, the VEDCO field staff focused all of their field activities around four primary program objectives, identified a set of deliverables for each, and listed key indicators to be used to document progress toward them. Then, they divided into four working groups that produced a summative chapter review on each of the program's major activity groups since the activities started.[8] This advanced approach to M&E now innervates all field activities (see Chapter 7).

Special Challenges Integrating Monitoring and Evaluation with Strategic Planning. Part of the delay that the program had in developing and monitoring its strategic plan was the weak link between program management and M&E. The new emphasis on using tracking tables to identify program targets and track each partner's progress toward the achievement of these targets has facilitated program planning and coordination.

CSRL is in the process of developing a single strategic planning table—indicator performance tracking table (IPTT)—that outlines the major targets for the next five years and which group of partners or subcontractors will be responsible for each activity. It is a process that is still under way, but one that is greatly appreciated by the local staff as well as the PPAB and executive committee.

Lessons Learned and Recommendations

Like most successful partnerships, CSRL's management of accountability has evolved and continues to do so. During this ten-year period, the learning partnership has become much more skilled at building partnership capital, managing people and money, and shepherding joint planning and reporting.

Phase One (2004–2008) focused on figuring out how CSRL would become better acquainted with its Uganda partners. The learning process involved building trusted working relationships, understanding institutional cultures, and discovering components of the systems that were compatible and those that were not. In Phase Two (2009–2013), there was a deep enough relationship among and between the partners—as well as sufficient compatibility and tolerance—to allow field programs to expand. While operating systems were different, compromises and creative problem solving became possible. Through this growth process, CSRL gained enormous knowledge from the partnership and valuable experience in Uganda and is now poised to expand its field programs in Phase Three (2014–Future) as a registered NGO. This new status should help CSRL to refine its current partnerships and develop new ones.

The strength of the CSRL start-up accountability systems was their flexibility and the quality of personal relationships that enabled problem solving when it was needed. Unlike most traditional development programs that respond to a particular set of donor guidelines for design as well as for accountability, the three partners set up housekeeping with no preconceived model of how they would work together. This lack of a proposal and donor-imposed standards for accountability allowed CSRL and its partners to be creative. The same flexibility encouraged a high social commitment to the partnership. The partners were there because they wanted to work together and trusted one another. When problems arose, they sat down and worked them out.

Building Partnership Capital

The CSRL partnership model was committed to building the social capital between the partners as well as the management systems. In the short, medium, and long term, it was these social relationships that created the willingness and ability to iron out the other problems.

Lesson 1:
Take time to identify a core vision for the partnership that builds on partner strengths and the social capital that exists between individuals in each organization.

Recommendations:
- Encourage exchange visits, informal discussions, and social interaction.
- Share documents and plans from the different partner institutions.
- Encourage frequent open-ended discussions that contribute to a common vision of the program.
- Document the main outcomes of these discussions and follow-up on any agreed-to activities.
- Reach an initial consensus on the program vision and how it relates to the different partners' goals and missions in conjunction with the final preplanning of the program.
- Regularly update the core partnership vision as the individual partners change and grow, and as new partners and activities are added to the program.
- Openly share points of pride as well as ongoing challenges with benefactors.
- Keep everything transparent to both partners and benefactors.
- Encourage the lead benefactors to contribute to routine meetings that discuss the partnerships and program directions.

Lesson 2:
Share credit for success.

Recommendations:
- Ensure an equitable reporting of partner success stories that highlight the contribution of different partners and team members toward the achievement of program goals.
- Train all partners on a system of report writing that "writes to results" so that each partner's contribution to the results can be duly noted.
- Encourage all individuals involved to coauthor progress reports, research papers, and other documents.

- Build partner capacity to document, analyze, and write their contributions to the program.
- Encourage the development of Web-based documents to profile different roles played by different partners.
- Be generous with credit and recognition.

Lesson 3:
Anticipate accountability problems and the tools needed to navigate them as the partnership evolves.

Recommendations:
- Anticipate growth and changing methods of communication needed to resolve problems as they arise.
- Encourage an open dialogue with private benefactors and partners about accountability issues, and solicit their input.
- Recognize the critical importance of investing in getting to know one another's institutions during the good times.

Managing People and Money

The development of CSRL's accounting and personnel systems was complicated by the fact that the program was forced to subcontract many of its most crucial activities, each of which had its own accounting and management system. In the course of working through this, the partners came to recognize the logic behind each other's management and accounting systems. In the end, it was ISU that was responsible for the accounting of program funds, so its methods prevailed.

Although ISU's partners now understand these systems and appreciate some of the value added to their own systems as a result, they remain constrained by their own institutions' accounting requirements. Now that the program has become registered as an independent NGO in Uganda, the funds are routed through that NGO. This is beginning to reduce the conflicts with the partner institutions' management systems.

Lesson 4:
Identify a way to legally and independently get the program up and running while exploring the requirements for long-term operation.

Recommendations:
- Identify appropriate contacts to help clarify the legal require-ments for operating within the area at the earliest opportunity.
- Investigate terms and conditions for legal operation in the area and determine what is required for longer-term operation such as work permits, tax and payroll obligations, banking procedures, procurement policies, and insurance requirements.
- Continue to investigate terms and condition under which the lead institution can operate legally in a medium- to long-term time frame.

Lesson 5:
Work with partners to develop a harmonized system of accounting, management, and personnel policies, and review this from time to time.

Recommendations:
- Start the program with a clear set of financial guidelines that is agreeable to all the partners, and anticipate the need and time frame for adjusting these.
- Before you sign any protocol or joint budget, be aware of each partner's policies on salaries, social benefits, insurance, and risk management procedures (including policies regarding honorari-ums and vehicle and equipment maintenance).
- Develop a core set of principles to guide personnel issues in the partnership, including promotion and career advancement proce-dures and what (if any) provisions will be made for in-house and distance learning to build staff capacity.
- Agree on a set of insurance and risk management guidelines for the partnership.
- Ensure that all of the basic principles and guidelines for the start-up phase are spelled out in every partnership agreement.
- Ensure that all management personnel understand and accept responsibility for their role in accountability to the partnership.
- Ensure that program managers understand this role and are ade-quately trained and mentored on core accounting and accounta-bility systems.
- Anticipate the need for basic training and retraining of managers and accountants within the partner institutions.

- Involve management and accounting personnel from each partner institution in the training processes.
- Document all training sessions to ensure harmonization.

Lesson 6:
Recruit an experienced program manager to represent the lead institution's interests and to liaise with the partners responsible for program start-up.

Recommendations:
- Ensure that the program manager and director (or management team) are in regular communication during the start-up phase.
- Consult with the director before speaking on behalf of the lead partner. Once a trust relationship has been built, allow ample freedom to the managers to develop their own management approach.
- Rely on field managers to facilitate, not enforce, the harmonization of the accounting and accountability systems.
- Clarify the role of the field managers in harmonizing the accounting and accountability systems in their contracts.
- Ensure that the field managers understand this role and are adequately trained.

Shepherding Joint Planning and Reporting

Despite a strong M&E system, CSRL's M&E data were underutilized in the program's strategic planning. This began to change when the program staff was trained in results-based programming and the use of the program's preexisting databases to track the execution and impact of specific groups of activities.

Lesson 7:
Develop management systems that link strategic planning and budget processes to deliverables from the start.

Recommendations:
- Work with partners to agree on a common set of indicators with which to track progress toward the achievement of the different

components of a program, and update these periodically as part of the annual joint planning process for the program.

- Link all disbursements to the achievement of concrete progress on the jointly agreed-on indicators.
- Ensure that the concept of joint indicators and regular tracking of these indicators is incorporated into every signed partnership agreement.
- Develop a plan for storing and sharing the impacts of the program.

Lesson 8:
Build and track each partner's capacity in the core management and accounting systems required to manage the partnership.

Recommendations:

- Make partner capacity building an SO of the program.
- Identify indicators to track core capacities and incorporate them into the partnership agreements.
- Ensure that all management personnel understand and accept responsibility for their role in accountability to the partnership.
- Train and retrain all staff in the core tracking and reporting systems.
- Train and mentor staff on how to access and use the knowledge that has been obtained through the impact tracking process.

Notes

1. Partnership capital occurs after individual partners' interests begin to merge into a "sense of shared norms that guide the venture." The strength of the individuals' relationships becomes the strength that moves the connection into one of collaboration based on trust, shared knowledge, and visions for what can be done together. This creates a capacity that probably would not occur alone. Pamela L. Eddy, *Partnerships and Collaborations in Higher Education,* Association for the Study of Higher Education Report (Hoboken, NJ: Wiley, 2010), pp. 49–50.

2. The founding Advisory Board had five members: Lorna Michael Butler, professor emeritus and former Henry A. Wallace Chair for Sustainable Agriculture, Iowa State University; Matthew Liebman, Henry A. Wallace Chair for Sustainable Agriculture, Iowa State University; Reverend David Beckmann, president, Bread for the World, and World Food Prize Laureate 2011; Daniel Karanja, executive director, Partnership to Cut Hunger and Poverty in Africa;

and Catherine Woteki, global director of scientific affairs, Mars, Inc., and former dean, College of Agriculture, Iowa State University. In 2010, Woteki
became undersecretary for the US Department of Agriculture's Research, Education and Economics mission, and the department's chief scientist. Members
were appointed for terms of two and three years.

The first Advisory Board met in Ames, Iowa, in October 2007. The purpose was to tap the group's knowledge and experience to help CSRL become an
effective catalyst for change for the rural households and its partners. The board
suggested a gradual deepening of priorities and more attention to capacity
development strategies to enable farmers to take greater responsibility in providing extension services and in engaging with local officials. The second
board meeting took place in Washington, DC, in October 2008, with the purposes of reviewing CSRL's progress, examining ways to promote lessons
learned, and assessing ways to promote transformation in Uganda. Institutional
development was again stressed. Recommendations included the need to
convene workshops in Uganda to share lessons learned and to learn from
other organizations, to give attention to capacity development of the community volunteer trainers, and to draw on knowledgeable Ugandans to review
the program.

3. Collaborative partner planning was also facilitated when VEDCO's
executive director and the dean of CAES visited ISU. During their visits to
Kamuli, the CSRL director and other team members always met with the
VEDCO staff. Time was usually devoted to critiquing and planning field activities and to visiting the field.

4. This excludes the original gift agreement between the founding benefactors and the ISU Foundation, which required CSRL to use standard performance measures and to produce an annual progress report that featured a summary of the program's strategic plan and comments from the director on the
accomplishments of the program toward meeting those strategic objectives (see
Chapter 1).

5. These rules included specifying that a contract for services supported by
a Memorandum of Understanding and an annual budget had to be in place for
the services that VEDCO provided to the program in Kamuli. CSRL's requests
for purchases of large capital equipment had to be approved by the ISU Purchasing Department. This office had to approve a similar contract accompanied
by multiple bids before funds could be wired to Uganda.

6. The program coordinator is responsible for monitoring accounts, administrative reporting, and temporary student help. Until the end of Phase One
(mid-2008), the CSRL office employed a program assistant who was not
required to have accounting credentials. CSRL also employed a field program
manager on contract who provided administrative and financial oversight for
field activities in Uganda for over seven years (see Chapter 3).

7. Together with the partners and advisors, CSRL established the following
program priorities for the VEDCO strategic plan period 2009–2014: (1) a
school lunch program and Nutrition Education Centers (NECs) for young mothers and vulnerable infants; (2) food and animal production and marketing for

household food security and better nutrition; (3) capacity development of community-based trainers to improve their effectiveness and to enhance their own livelihoods; and (4) increasing household food security and economic stability of Kamuli farmers by optimizing land use.

8. Della E. McMillan, ed., *Sustainable Rural Livelihoods Program: Summative Monitoring and Evaluation (M&E) Report: 2005–2012,* Draft Report (Ames: Center for Sustainable Rural Livelihoods, Iowa State University, 2012).

5

Starting
Where the People Are

Dorothy Masinde and Della E. McMillan

A well-run, privately funded philanthropic program gives the development agencies running it greater flexibility in starting where the people are. This is in complete contrast to more traditional types of international agency–funded programs where monthly activities are outlined in a project document with little, if any, flexibility for creative adjustments. While this flexibility is a major strength, it is not without its special challenges, including:

- Program start-up—designing and executing the program so that it is not imposed (i.e., so that the local people own both the product and the process);
- Participatory monitoring and evaluation—developing a process for participatory review of the program's progress and adjusting plans for the next phase;
- Targeting household vulnerability—identifying vulnerable households and developing special interventions to target their needs;
- Capacity strengthening—strengthening the technical and organizational capacity of the communities and households targeted to sustain the supported activities once the program ends; and
- Program exit strategy—anticipating (from the onset) the models, partnerships, and links that communities and institutions will

The authors wish to acknowledge the helpful input and contributions of Laura Byaruhanga, Robert Mazur, and Gail Nonnecke.

need to sustain successful interventions when outside funding diminishes.

Program Start-Up

Key Challenges

People should be the principal focus of a development program—not technology. The introduction of improved technologies is often combined with the development of new skills or the introduction of knowledge. But listening to and learning from the people should be the highest priority. For a program to mainstream this idea, the technology development process must be as important as the product. In aid programs, practitioners tend to focus on knowledge, technology, and changes attributed to these and often forget about the people with whom they work. One must understand where the people are, why they want to improve, and what will motivate them to want to do more.

The process of getting people to adopt, or adapt to, the changes being presented to them is critical—and it can be challenging. It is important that any new activities build on local people's own knowledge and experiences. Thus, the program's strategy for listening to and learning from local people is of central importance. This local knowledge and practice defines the level at which the local community is currently operating. It also has the advantage of being tested under local conditions.

The CSRL Experience

Involving the Community in Early Planning. The Center for Sustainable Rural Livelihoods (CSRL) used participatory and qualitative methods to collect information and conduct joint planning with the community. The target clientele for CSRL was farmers who had small- to medium-sized land holdings. The program chose to work with farmers in small groups; hence, the entry point was existing groups that were located in the selected program areas. Once identified, one or more representatives from these groups were invited to a series of informal, relatively unstructured participatory rural appraisal (PRA) meetings in late 2004.[1] CSRL's idea was to speak to these representatives to better understand the local people, their needs, the environment in which they operated, the opportunities and resources already available to them, and their livelihood options.[2] Since the program was addressing issues of hunger, malnutrition, and poverty, CSRL was looking toward under-standing the people's current activities in relation to these aspects of their lives. CSRL also did a strengths, weaknesses, opportunities, and threats (SWOT) analysis to find out what the people already were doing: strengths they felt they had to build on, major weaknesses and problems, available opportunities, and what they perceived to be the major threats to their livelihood strategies.[3] This analysis gave CSRL an opportunity to better understand all aspects of the people's livelihoods.

While the initial PRA was a helpful first contact with the commu-nity, it soon became apparent that the results were too general. In partic-ular, the appraisal did not provide detailed data on the composition of the communities in relation to their current food security, wealth, and nutrition situations. Especially important, the appraisal did not clearly identify the vulnerable households that the CSRL programming was tar-geting as its top priority.

A second, more rigorously designed baseline appraisal was con-ducted a few months after the first one. Especially important, it used a variety of PRA-specific tools[4] to help the local people conduct a partic-ipatory analysis of their food insecurity issues, including a detailed look at (1) the percentage of households at each level of food insecurity in the community, (2) the constraints and opportunities of each of these groups classified by their level of food insecurity, and (3) major health and nutrition constraints of the different groups (see Chapter 5 Appen-dix Table, p. 141). Based on this appraisal, the CSRL program extension officers helped each community to develop an action plan for the first year of the program.[5] These community action plans provided the basis for parish action plans. Based on these initial exercises, CSRL field pro-gram manager Dorothy Masinde and monitoring and evaluation (M&E) specialist Haroon Sseguya developed a detailed participatory monitor-ing and evaluation (PM&E) plan that outlined how the program would continue to update the baseline appraisals and action plans each year.

The baseline PRAs provided a forum for the local people—working with the CSRL field team—to define the components of the program. The same appraisals produced a list of indicators that the communities felt would help them track their progress. Especially important, the appraisal used a standard baseline indicator—a qualitative version of the Months of Adequate Household Food Provisioning (MAHFP) indi-cator of food access—to profile the community on three dimensions: food insecurity, wealth, and nutrition and health.[6] The same profile pro-vided a mechanism for identifying the special constraints and opportu-nities of the most vulnerable households and on-site training in PM&E.

Although the general impact of the exercise was useful, certain weaknesses became more apparent over the long term. Since the first PRA did not include the quantitative needs assessment indicators, the program had to repeat the exercise in June 2006. This meant that, by the time the CSRL baseline PRA was conducted, it was not really a baseline since the program was already working with most of the target farmers.

Another weakness was that the program's initial M&E plan in 2006 did not anticipate the need to reconduct the same participatory reviews that produced the baseline vulnerability assessments. Instead, the program introduced a new methodology for assessing household vulnerability in the first follow-up survey in June 2007 based on the questions asked in the first quantitative survey.[7] The same quantitative methodology was used to track household vulnerability in each of the subsequent surveys in 2008, 2009, and 2011. This discrepancy was a missed opportunity since it meant that the CSRL program did not have consistent data against which to measure its achievements in the three areas tracked by the baseline: food insecurity, wealth, and nutrition and health.

Incorporating Indigenous Knowledge and Technology. The baseline PRA collected a wide variety of existing knowledge and practices connected with crop, livestock, sanitation, nutrition, and health practices. Trend analyses helped to identify changes in agricultural practices over time. The reasons for the existing trends in production and consumption of agricultural products were discussed during the baseline PRA meetings and helped inform the initial decisions on enterprise selection for demonstrations and training.

The program's commitment to building on a solid base of indigenous knowledge helped identify promising new technologies—like introducing new banana varieties—that had a major impact. The same attention to learning from farmers helped guide the program in the choice of certain crops that were widely adopted such as grain amaranth (see Box 5.1).

Conversely, the program's failure to incorporate indigenous knowledge on certain program activities, such as the kitchen gardens, was a contributing factor to nonadoption. Over time, it also became evident that not all farmers were operating at the same knowledge level, so using the same teaching modules for every farmer meant that some of the farmers were not interested in participating. There also were farmers who did not participate in groups (e.g., the most vulnerable), so they were easily overlooked. The community-based trainers who took part in the practitioners' workshop in 2012 recognized that different training modules were needed for farmers who had varying levels of experience.

After 2009, the program began to build its experiences in articulating indigenous knowledge of crop production practices into a wider spectrum of activities, including rural credit and marketing that had not heretofore been a major focus of analysis.

Building Local Ownership. From the start, the CSRL program was committed to building community ownership into its interventions. This con-

---

Box 5.1 How CSRL's Consideration of Indigenous Knowledge and Practice Influenced Technology Update

Banana Production

When CSRL began in Kamuli, banana (*matooke*) production had almost ground to a halt due to pests and diseases. Although the crop was a delicacy in the area, the high prices had reduced consumption. The local community—including organizations working in the area—believed the crop could not perform well. Current banana production practices were identified and evaluated and, through testing and use of resistant and tolerant varieties, the CSRL program was able reintroduce banana production in the area. Now, households that produce bananas consider it to be of high value and it is one of the income-generating crops in the area.

Grain Amaranth

Another illustration of this principle was the introduction of grain amaranth in the program area. Grain amaranth, an ancient crop that dates back to the Incas, is nutritionally dense, high yielding, and short cycle (i.e., short growing period), and can tolerate diverse climatic conditions. The crop was introduced in the program in 2005. The goal was to increase protein consumption, which was limited in local diets because of its high cost. Leafy amaranth, which is in the same family and genus as the grain amaranth, is the most commonly consumed vegetable in Kamuli. Given that the community was already producing leafy amaranth, the program built on this knowledge to introduce what was seen as new crop. The result was positive.

(continues)

Box 5.1 Continued

Kitchen Gardens
On the other hand, ignoring existing knowledge and practice led to discontinuation of what was seen as a technology that could have led to an increase in production and consumption of vegetables. CSRL introduced kitchen and sack gardens in the program area based on the success of the same technology in Uganda's central region. Within the first year, there was an enthusiastic adoption of the gardens. But by the second year, farmers had started to abandon their gardens. Seven years down the line, there is little evidence of the kitchen or sack gardens in this area. Although a study has not been done to establish the actual reason for discontinuation, a rapid appraisal of the technology found that the technology was not relevant in this area since land was not a major limiting factor for vegetable production.

Source: CSRL reports.

---

cept was reflected in the program-supported systems for community-based educators, cost sharing of start-up materials and local construction projects, start-up livestock with pass-on obligations, community-based training workshops, microfinance, and marketing.

Community-based educators. The first thirty-six community-based educators, which CSRL called rural development extensionists, were chosen by the beneficiaries in one of the plenary sessions connected with the baseline appraisals. Each extensionist was provided with access to new crop and livestock technologies. In return, he or she was expected to provide demonstrations to the wider community. By 2008, there were ninety-two extensionists and community nutrition and health workers. The nutrition and health workers, who were brought on soon after the extensionists, were responsible for nutrition and sanitation education in the communities. This proved to be one of the best ways to solidify local ownership. In 2010, CSRL shifted to a system of salaried trainers,[8] but continued to call on the unpaid volunteers to conduct the community-based demonstrations of promising crop and livestock technologies. Each year, the community volunteers (rural development extensionists, community nutrition and health workers, and later the community-based trainers)—who were the principal extension arm of the program—were evaluated by the communities in which they served during the biannual PRA public meetings.[9]

Cost sharing of start-up materials. The extensionists, nutrition and health workers, and a few model farmers received a free start-up toolkit that included seed and basic tools for growing food crops. Farmer groups received planting materials, which they multiplied and shared. Farmers who liked a technology and wanted to try it on their own farm often paid for the technology; however, payment was not a requirement. An example was when bananas were introduced into the community; farmers purchased planting materials from farmers who had established their own banana gardens.

Given the weak asset base of most farmers, the program implemented a system of cost sharing for farmer groups whereby the program absorbed a percentage of the costs or the beneficiaries were permitted to pay the cost of the inputs through an in-kind reimbursement after harvest. This encouraged farmers to try new technologies and innovations. Since the extensionists were expected to provide on-farm demonstrations of new technologies, they continued to receive start-up materials for the crops and tree varieties that they were using for their demonstration plots. All group members who managed these "multiplication gardens" benefited from them. However, some of the poorest farmers were unable to benefit from the gardens because they were not group members.

Start-up livestock with pass-on obligations. Beginning in 2004–2005, the program provided the extensionists and nutrition and health workers with start-up stock of improved livestock varieties and some limited technical assistance through subsidies to lower the initial costs of purchasing and feeding the animals, constructing improved livestock housing, and providing improved veterinarian services (see Chapter 6). Once the animals reproduced, the volunteers were expected to pass on a portion of the animals to other vulnerable households and to mentor the people who received the animals in using the techniques that the volunteers had learned.[10]

Community-based workshops. The CSRL program considered workshops to be a personal investment decision. The program chose not to imitate many other nongovernmental organizations (NGOs) by providing food or cash per diem to encourage the local beneficiaries (farmers) to attend its workshops because it found that people would come for the giveaway and not necessarily the information.

Microfinance. In 2007, the program introduced a small microfinance project. To be eligible for a loan, a candidate had to be an active member of one of the CSRL-affiliated farmer groups, be able to form a credit group of five trusted members, be considered food secure, and be capable of repaying the loan. Each group was responsible for approving its members' loan applications as well as the repayment of the loan. Once a savings group was recognized by the program, it was eligible to receive special training from the CSRL microfinance officer designed to build the individual member's capacity to develop profitable income-generating activities (IGAs). The training sessions were conducted using standard CSRL training modules on savings and credit, enterprise selection, planning and management, farming as a business, financial recordkeeping, and collective marketing.

Marketing. A major impact of the program was the increase of crop and livestock yields, which not only reduced household food insecurity but also created a surplus of these products by the third and fourth implementation years. One output of the program's midterm assessment exercise in 2009 was a series of recommendations for how the CSRL program could strengthen the capacity of the local farmers' associations to market their products. In the interest of building community ownership, the program provided limited assistance with the creation of storage and bulking centers and the development of marketing cooperatives. Groups were also helped to understand and access various new technologies for downloading price information to sell their products for higher prices at more distant markets.[11]

Early Evidence of Impact

There is clear qualitative and quantitative evidence that CSRL's commitment to participatory approaches in program implementation has encouraged high levels of local ownership. These high levels of ownership are reflected in the biannual PRAs and the steady growth in the capacity and activities of the local groups, associations, and cooperatives.

However, CSRL's participatory way of doing business sometimes led the program to undervalue certain key activities—such as livestock—which were not as evident to local people since they were not a major part of their customary livelihood system. The same highly participatory processes sometimes caused the program to add new activities—such as the microfinance program, water conservation technologies, or short-term collaborative research grant activities—that ended up being more opportunistic than practical.

Participatory Monitoring and Evaluation

Key Challenges

For a program to remain people centered, it needs a people-centered process for strategic planning and review. This process is frequently referred to as PM&E (see Box 5.2).

The CSRL Experience

CSRL's PM&E system started with the baseline appraisals described earlier, which produced an action plan for each of the farmer groups and communities (Table 5.1). Each action plan included a series of focused, practical, and tangible targets such as moving livestock ownership from one cow to three cows, increasing the per hectare productivity of a crop from five bags to ten bags, or having at least 50 percent of the seedlings received still alive after a certain period of time.

To ensure high levels of beneficiary engagement, the program organized a biannual review of each group and community's action plan, during which they reviewed the previous year's experience and set new targets for the coming year (Table 5.1). These written and verbal presentations and plans—including a record of the major points covered in the debates—were then consolidated by the CSRL staff into a biannual parish report and planning document that was publicly reviewed and discussed at the parish level twice a year. The program staff organized a larger subcounty-level meeting once a year to review the consolidated reports and plan for the next year. The information was complemented by periodic external M&E evaluations (Table 5.1).

Early Evidence of Impact

The CSRL PM&E system created a mechanism for farmers' voices to be heard (see Box 5.3). It created a means for the program staff to plan based on what they heard from the community. Anecdotal information shows that the PM&E system enhances the program impact by (1) making the CSRL program more transparent to local people and their leaders; (2) improving the performance of the community-based volunteer extensionists and trainers because there was someone watching what was going on; and (3) building the capacity of the local communities to demand more accountability from their leaders. An example of this was when one of the CSRL-targeted communities confronted a corrupt schoolmaster and asked him to resign.

Box 5.2 Definitions of Participatory Monitoring and Evaluation

What Is Participatory Monitoring and Evaluation?

PM&E is a process through which stakeholders at various levels engage in monitoring or evaluating a particular project, program, or policy; share control over the content, process, and results of the M&E activity; and engage in taking or identifying corrective actions. PM&E focuses on the active engagement of primary stakeholders.

Why Is Participatory Monitoring and Evaluation Important?

Participation is increasingly recognized as being integral to the M&E process since it offers new ways of assessing and learning from changes that are more inclusive and responsive to the needs and aspirations of those most directly affected. PM&E is not only geared toward measuring the effectiveness of a project, but also toward building ownership and empowering beneficiaries, building accountability and transparency, and taking corrective actions to improve performance and outcomes.

What Are the Principles of Participatory Monitoring and Evaluation?

Conventionally, M&E has involved outside experts who come in to measure performance against preset indicators, using standardized procedures and tools. PM&E differs from more conventional approaches in that it seeks to engage key project stakeholders more actively in reflecting and assessing the progress of their project and, particularly, the achievement of results. Core principles of PM&E are:

- Primary stakeholders are active participants—not just sources of information;
- Building capacity of local people to analyze, reflect, and take action;
- Joint learning of stakeholders at various levels; and
- Catalyzing commitment to taking corrective actions.

Source: World Bank, Participation and Civic Engagement (Washington, DC: World Bank, 2013).

Table 5.1 Core Components of the CSRL Planning and Participatory Monitoring and Evaluation Model

Core Component	Person Responsible	Output	Impact on Project Management	Areas to Strengthen in Next Phase of CSRL
Participatory monitoring and evaluation system				
Baseline PRA and action plans	Facilitation and data collection and consolidation by CSRL extension officers	*Written document summarizing:* • Identification with the local community of definitions of poverty, nutrition, and food security • Identification of the number of households in each category • Community and group target for the first cropping season	Helped the CSRL program identify the most important elements of its program	Conduct a second PRA to elicit: (1) local perspectives on how the project has affected poverty, nutrition, and food security; (2) a number of simple core indicators that community leaders can agree to monitor along with the community M&E monitors
Biannual review and revision of each group and community-level action plans	Facilitation and data collection and consolidation by the community-based monitoring agents and the extension staff	*Written document summarizing:* • A participatory review of the community and group action plans, targets, and performance of extension staff • The revised targets for the next cropping year	Helped identify new constraints and opportunities Helped adjust the CSRL program to new constraints and opportunities Provided a forum for communities to review staff performance	Identify a small number of core indicators for each objective that can be reported on to complement the qualitative information
Biannual parish and annual subcounty review and planning meetings	Data collection and reporting by designated community leaders with reports written up by CSRL extension workers	Biannual group, parish, and subdistrict reports on planning Participatory visioning (planning)	Provided feedback to the CSRL leadership on activities as a basis for planning	Identify indicators that can be measured by community-based monitoring agents Strengthen community's use of PM&E to strengthen local access to government and private sector services

(continues)

Table 5.1 Continued

Core Component	Person Responsible	Output	Impact on Project Management	Areas to Strengthen in Next Phase of CSRL
External CSRL evaluations				
External evaluation survey	Data collection by independent enumerators hired and supervised by the CSRL evaluation specialist	Longitudinal tracking of a core number of indicators via a quantitative survey	Provided longitudinal data on household and community-level assets	Shift focus of the external evaluation survey from tracking indicators based on a survey to the analysis of indicators being collected by the monitoring agents Better integration of the evaluation's quantitative data with the information collected by the PRAs Help the CSRL staff and community think about indicators for sustainability that will help them to better plan and manage the program's exit strategy

Source: Mark Westgate, Lorna Michael Butler, and Della E. McMillan, collaborative e-mail correspondence and Skype discussions for table development and refinement, February 1–20, 2014.

Box 5.3 The Role of Participatory Rural Appraisals in Putting People First

"It is important that the local people—as well as the researchers—be involved in conceptualizing and monitoring a rural development program. If reducing poverty and income inequality is what the project focuses on, then the program beneficiaries need to have a role in defining the problem as well as finding new ways to address it. When we talk about livelihoods, we are talking about a very expansive concept. Where do we start?

"Look at what we did. Some of it worked very well; some of it did not. First, we worked with the local communities to define a poor household. We asked them, 'What does a household where there is inadequate nutrition look like?' Based on that, we were able to work with them to develop a set of activities.

"Once we have conceptualized this we can start working with them. We say, 'What are the targets?' This is my road map. On the road map you work with the communities to identify a number the obstacles that we have to cover to reach the goals they have identified for a specific set of activities. This is an exercise that empowers the local community to define its problems and to make decisions on what they want to do to improve themselves.

"If you involve them in defining what they see as poverty and hunger, then it is not me saying this, it is them. I am not saying that international standards are not important. They are important. Both kinds of information are needed for different audiences. It is critical for a development project to have a mechanism for listening to the farmer's own self-analysis of the situation. A typical dialogue might go:

'If you are not food secure, what can you do to change that?'

'I am not able to take two meals a day.'

'What can you do to increase the number of meals you eat?'

'I only have two small fields. I need to increase my production from five to ten bags a day.'

"This type of straightforward [participatory rural appraisal] analysis can then open the door to a frank and open discussion of the new technologies that the project is promoting in a language they understand."

Source: Dorothy Masinde in conversation with Della E. McMillan, Evanston, IL, July 28, 2012.

Most of the CSRL PM&E program data was not analyzed or reported on in a way that it could be understood by upper management or the program's major partners. Specifically, that was because (1) most of the PM&E reports focused the results achieved during a single year and (2) there was almost no cross-fertilization of data between the quantitative data collected by the CSRL external evaluations and the PM&E reports.

In the next phase of the program, CSRL will try to better integrate the PM&E system and the different types of quantitative data on activities that the communities are collecting with the results of the program's external evaluation surveys (see Table 5.1). This information should help both the communities and the partners get a better grasp of overall trends. In September 2012, the CSRL staff identified a list of indicators that the communities and CSRL M&E officers are currently tracking. Based on this list, the program developed a draft indicator performance tracking table (IPTT) that listed all of these internal indicators as well as the external impact indicators that CSRL had measured through its external evaluations. The program's M&E officer is currently working with the staff to simplify this list of indicators into a shorter, more concise table for each strategic objective (SO) of the program. Once this is done, the program will update its M&E manual to describe this new, more integrated PM&E system.

Targeting Household Vulnerability

Key Challenges

The concept of targeting vulnerable households and the most vulnerable individuals within a given population is central to food security and livelihood systems research and development in sub-Saharan Africa. In any population, there is a group of households that can be classified as extremely food and income insecure, which is vulnerable to recurring risks. The livelihoods approach places priority on the poor and most vulnerable households. These are typically households that, because of age, gender, illness, disability, or some other constraint like ethnicity, do not have access to the basic resources that they need to participate in mainstream food and income security mechanisms, programs, or mitigation strategies (see Box 5.4). Responding to vulnerability requires that a program understand such things as the likelihood of the situation reoccurring, the potential effects of the occurrence, the coping strategies used, and the mitigation tactics.[12]

Box 5.4 Understanding Vulnerability in the Livelihoods Context

Robert Chambers notes:

> Vulnerability . . . is not the same as poverty. It means not lack of want, but defencelessness, insecurity, and exposure to risk, shocks, and stress.
> . . .
>   Vulnerability . . . refers to exposure to contingencies and stress, and difficulty in coping with them. Vulnerability has thus two sides: an external side of risks, shocks, and stress to which an individual or household is subject; and an internal side which is defenselessness, meaning a lack of means to cope without damaging loss. Loss can take many forms—becoming or being physically weaker, economically impoverished, socially dependent, humiliated or psychologically harmed.

Sources: Quoted in *IDS Bulletin: Anthology* 37, no. 4 (September 2006): 33, from Robert Chambers, "Vulnerability, Coping and Policy (Editorial Introduction)," *IDS Bulletin* 20, no. 2 (1989). First published as "Vulnerability: How the Poor Cope."

The CSRL Experience

This strong commitment to addressing the special needs and concerns of the most vulnerable households was also a core commitment of the founding CSRL benefactors. Indeed, it was a commitment that the benefactors required the program to write into the original gift agreements and one on which they wanted the program to report.

To ensure that the most vulnerable households were targeted, the program adopted a series of PRA tools that helped identify these households (see Chapter 8). The first of these tools was an appraisal exercise that provided a mechanism for the participatory identification (with local leaders) of the poorest of the poor and what types of activities would be needed to reduce the vulnerability of this group. The second tool was a standard set of questions that many NGOs in Africa use in quantitative surveys as a basis for classifying the respondents in terms of their food security levels.

The baseline PRAs identified a number of households that were classified as extremely vulnerable. Many of these were households that had neither the labor nor the land to benefit from the regular CSRL-sponsored projects, and often were headed by older people without children or were households affected by human immunodeficiency virus/acquired immunodeficiency syndrome (HIV/AIDS). The goal of CSRL's activities was to build the assets of these vulnerable groups through a special needs fund that would help them reach a point where they could participate in the activity groups that the program was supporting. The program extension officers—program-funded agents who trained and supervised the community-based volunteers—were expected to target at least five extremely vulnerable households in each community they covered and report regularly on their progress. Since an officer was responsible for about six villages, this meant that each targeted about thirty extremely vulnerable cases per year. Over time, most of the extension officers converted from a system of helping individual households to working with groups of vulnerable households such as the eight HIV/AIDS support groups that have continued to receive different levels of extension officer crop and livestock support since 2005. Many of the HIV/AIDS-affected household members that belong to these groups received two start-up animals from the program's rotating herd safety net program.[13]

As the CSRL program expanded, it added a number of subprograms that targeted an even wider circle of extremely vulnerable households and individuals in the communities. One example of these new initiatives was the CSRL school lunch program. Although the principle focus of the program was agriculture and nutrition education and providing a more nutritious school lunch, the CSRL program supported a full-time extension officer to teach improved farming and livestock practices to the teachers and the students through a school gardens program (explained in greater detail in Chapter 7). It was anticipated that the children would provide the mechanism for transmitting this newfound information to their families when they returned home.

A second initiative was the development of community-based programs for the rehabilitation of chronically malnourished children, which was first pilot tested in 2005 (see Chapter 6). Again, the principal focus was vulnerable children and their families—not just the CSRL-targeted farmers. When the first group of children was released from the pilot Nutrition Education Center (NEC) in early 2013, each mother received a technology kit to help improve food production and was put in touch with one of the CSRL extension officers if the released child and mother were living in one of the CSRL villages.

Although it is clear that a high percentage of the children being targeted by the CSRL school lunch program and NEC projects are from vulnerable households, this is not currently being tracked. Thus, with the present system of tracking, it is not possible to see if and how the program is impacting the students' households or what other types of complementary activities might be needed.

Early Evidence of Impact

With a few notable exceptions, which were linked to unpredictable rainfall,[14] the number of households classified as extremely vulnerable has shown a consistent decline since the program's first baseline survey (Table 5.2). As the number of households classified as extremely food insecure has decreased, the program has increased its commitment to a more diversified set of activities for the households that are better off (i.e., those classified as having average vulnerability or being least vulnerable).

Although the CSRL system for tracking household vulnerability helped identify the growing diversity in the target population, the program has not yet developed a system for graduating the more successful target farmers or target villages, nor has it trained the local communities to collect and analyze this information on their own.

Also, the standard indicator that was used to track household vulnerability in the target farmers was never extended to the two most important new pilot initiatives: the school gardens program and the

Table 5.2 Household Food Security Status, 2005–2011 (in percentage)

Status	2005 ($n = 800$)	2006 ($n = 292$)	2007 ($n = 336$)	2008 ($n = 308$)	2009[a] Old ($n = 263$)	2009[a] New ($n = 55$)	2011[a] Old ($n = 263$)	2011[a] New ($n = 55$)
Food secure	9.2	48.6	82.1	63.7	43.7	43.6	67.3	56.4
Food insecure	48.3	17.8	10.4	18.8	24.0	25.5	23.2	36.3
Extremely food insecure	42.5	33.6	7.5	17.5	32.3	30.9	9.5	7.3

Source: Haroon Sseguya, Robert Mazur, and Dorothy Masinde, "Evidence of Impact and Transformation in Kamuli" (Ames: Center for Sustainable Rural Livelihoods, Iowa State University, 2012).

Notes: n = number of households. In 2005, the CSRL program used a program-generated food security rating participatory tool to measure household food security status. Since 2006, the program has used the Household Food Security Scale (HFIAS) indicator and guidance from the Food Aid and Nutrition Technical Assistance (FANTA) project sponsored by the United States Agency for International Development (USAID). This scale indicator has changed slightly over time in terms of the questions asked and mode of calculation (see Chapter 8).

a. Old households are households with which CSRL had worked for seven years. New households are households that were added later; the program had been working with them for only two years.

NECs. This was a missed opportunity since it could help the program staff determine other actions needed to sustain the positive impact of these activities.

Capacity Strengthening

Key Challenges

The concept of *local capacity* is central to most development programs. This is because many of the new technologies and management practices that development programs introduce require new knowledge and skills, or they require that existing skills be improved. New or improved skills must be learned and practiced. The concept of *local capacity strengthening* generally refers to a program's plan for improving the core capacities that it needs to sustain its activities once the program downsizes or exits. The particular program that is introduced will influence the type of capacities that are needed. Some of the key capacities required for a food security program are typically:

- Technical and human development capacity—knowing about new technology options and how to use them to strengthen people's livelihoods;
- Training capacity—having local-level trainers and training institutions that can ensure the sustainable training and retraining of community volunteers and experts;
- Technology and services access capacity—having community-level systems for updating and improving household access to the technology and services needed to build stronger livelihoods;
- Technology and knowledge transfer capacity—transferring the new knowledge needed to develop stronger livelihoods to others who need it and are receptive to receiving the information;
- Service delivery capacity—building the ability of people to deliver the essential services needed to improve livelihoods;
- Market access capacity—the hardware issue of having physical access to competitive markets and the software issue of having the knowledge needed to access the more profitable markets, including information on prices and quality standards for the more competitive markets;
- Capacity to demand social services and good governance—lobbying for the social services and good governance that communities need to strengthen livelihoods;

- Capacity to think strategically—analyzing a situation and developing a plan to address constraints and build on strengths and new opportunities;
- Capacity to organize—organizing individuals in groups so that they can take advantage of economies of scale, improve their bargaining power, and draw in the resources they need to strengthen their livelihood systems; and
- Entrepreneurial capacity—offering services for which there is a cash market demand.

The CSRL Experience

The shift toward a more people-centered, human development paradigm puts more emphasis on learning and training, creative problem solving, leadership development, social equity, empowerment processes, and so on, which are all dependent on the interconnectedness among different types of stakeholders and their ability to work together for the good of all. All of these competencies, and others, are integral to local human and institutional capacity development, the key to assuming active and sustained roles in taking over and adapting the CSRL programs that are making a difference in people's lives.

Various CSRL activities have contributed to capacity development at each of these levels. In almost every case, the CSRL educators were responsible for most local-level training and technical assistance activities that built this capacity.

Technical and Human Development Capacity. To date, CSRL—working in close collaboration with the Iowa State University (ISU), Volunteer Efforts for Development Concerns (VEDCO), and Makerere University (MAK) staff affiliated with the program—has developed field-level activities in 177 villages (a population of 98,000 people) to promote crop, livestock, value-chain, nutrition, or other related educational activities. As of February 2013, a total of ninety-four community-based trainers skilled in nutrition, agriculture, and livestock-related education were still living in the villages where they continued to provide outreach.

Training Capacity. The program has helped identify, develop, or adapt thirteen separate training modules. Especially important, all of the community-based trainers and some of the local partners have been trained in the use of the modules, which enhances the chance that the local communities can use them to renew their technical and human development capacity once the program exits. Many of the training modules have been reviewed and are in the process of being simplified to make them easier for the volunteers and partners to apply.

Technology and Services Access Capacity. This capacity has been built via a series of activities designed to increase local people's access to crop and livestock inputs, including (1) limited subsidies to reduce the cost of some inputs; (2) purchasing the materials used in demonstration trials from private sector vendors and private seed and seedling producers; (3) providing safety nets to facilitate vulnerable households' access to the technologies they need to strengthen their livelihoods; (4) providing community volunteers and educators with technology for on-farm demonstrations that link the farmers and the program with the major CSRL technology partners; and (5) targeting assistance for the most food secure households to help them develop their commercial activities.

Available qualitative and quantitative data confirm the rate of adoption of certain improved technologies, which the target farmers needed to improve their nutrition, has increased; and these farmers have become more resilient.

Technology and Knowledge Transfer Capacity. The best evidence of this increased capacity has been the accelerated rates of adoption of the new, more resilient crop varieties and livestock technologies promoted by the program.

Service Delivery Capacity. The program has helped communities build many of the essential services they will need to sustain stronger livelihoods, including water use committees to manage the new waterholes as well as building the capacity of various subcounty marketing associations.

Market Access Capacity. The program has also helped the farmer groups that it works with to organize new crop associations and livestock associations or join existing ones. These associations enable farmers to obtain better prices by helping them consolidate their products into larger bulk amounts that food processing plants and slaughterhouses want to buy. CSRL has reinforced these activities by providing prices in larger markets using both cell phone and paper formats to help farmers plan their marketing strategies.

Capacity to Demand Social Services and Good Governance. CSRL has helped train and retrain a network of community-based monitors in every parish where it works. The original role of these community monitors was to collect the basic M&E data that the community chose to use to evaluate its action plan. There is a growing body of anecdotal evidence from the biannual parish- and community-level meetings that this system has helped build the capacity of the local communities to demand more accountability from their local service providers—both governmental and nongovernmental.

Capacity to Think Strategically. CSRL has worked with each group and the parish leaders to develop a baseline action plan that is updated and revised annually. The records of the biannual meetings show that the community-based, CSRL-supported groups have tracked the execution of their action plans. The same records show a growing number of instances where villages have used their action plans to prepare proposals for other programs.

Capacity to Organize. Since 2004, the CSRL program has increased the number of farmer groups that it supports through training and technical support from 78 to 141, and has increased the number of marketing associations for crop and livestock producers from 1 to 7 in the villages where it works. Especially important, 140 of the 141 groups now belong to associations. Once groups decide to join one of the CSRL-sponsored associations, they are trained in farming as a business, negotiation skills, lobbying and advocacy, marketing, quality control, value addition, and postharvest handling.

Entrepreneurial Capacity Building. CSRL has assisted a number of extension groups and associations in developing income-generating activities. There is anecdotal evidence from the biannual meeting notes that an increasing number of individuals are breaking off to become private sector entrepreneurs. The program has sought to reinforce this capacity by buying the various inputs for its activities from these emerging entrepreneurs, including buying improved seed from farmers who have been trained to be certified seed producers; purchasing the high protein baby food or porridge from the nutrition and health workers who have been trained to grow and process the dry porridge ingredients; and buying other inputs from private sector vendors in the region, some of whom have received start-up loans from the program.

Early Evidence of Impact

There is a great deal of evidence that the CSRL program's capacity-building efforts have also strengthened capabilities in almost every one of the key capacity areas identified above.

Three of the major weaknesses in the program's start-up phase that probably had a detrimental impact on each of these core capacities are: (1) there was no viable mechanism for compensating the community-based trainers with a monthly salary for their services during the first five years;[15] (2) many of the original training modules and curricula were too complicated for community-level learning; and (3) the CSRL PM&E system overlooked the development of a capacity assessment tool to track the key capacities needed to execute and sustain the core program activities.

When the CSRL program was designed, it incorporated the concept of farmer-to-farmer extension that VEDCO, its principal NGO partner, had used successfully in Luwero District. But this earlier program did not support the wide range of intensive development activities instituted by CSRL and, by 2008, it was clear that changes were needed. The volunteer trainers, who were central to the program, needed regular compensation as well as greater support for farmer training. In 2009, the decision was made to create a new system of salaried trainers. The educational requirements of these trainers were higher, and they received a modest but regular salary. One of the most critical challenges facing programs of this type is to find a mechanism for sustaining the contributions of the community-based volunteers and trainers once the program ends. If this is not done, the program will lose the trainers as the principal link between the local farmers and the major national and international centers of excellence.

Most of the original training modules were borrowed from other organizations or developed by university personnel. Little of the training focused on learning styles and training methods. As a result, most of the training for volunteers and farmers used a classic lecture methodology.

Although there is a great deal of anecdotal data that the CSRL-sponsored training sessions increased the capacity of the community-based groups, the staff never developed any systematic way of tracking this information. This was a missed opportunity because it has been difficult to develop a system for assessing the link between specific types of training, training modules, and the different types of capacity that are needed.

Program Exit Strategy

Key Challenges

The ultimate goal of an aid organization is to help people apply and implement livelihood strategies in a sustainable way. This requires attention to capacity-building strategies that will enable local and national institutions to assume increasing levels of responsibility for successful program initiatives and models. Hence, a development partnership needs to model and plan a transition and exit strategy from day one. Some of the key questions that need to be addressed from the first appraisals should include:

- What systems will the program build so that, when it is gone, the successful initiatives will continue?
- What knowledge and skills do the local people need to continue to develop?
- What partnerships and capacities need to be modeled and shaped to look after the special needs of the most vulnerable?

The CSRL Experience

The concept of an exit strategy was implicit in the CSRL program's concept of empowering local people to continue improving their local livelihoods by (1) encouraging the local communities to develop and monitor action plans; (2) developing a network of local educators; (3) developing simple, user-friendly training modules on topics that communities need to build more sustainable livelihoods; and (4) building the capacity of producer groups and their transformation into more powerful cooperatives and federations that local communities need to ensure steady access to inputs and more competitive markets. An exit strategy was also explicit in the benefactors' visions for the program and in many of the CSRL Advisory Board's discussions.

Early Evidence of Impact

The partners never did, however, develop a formal written exit strategy that spells out the actions that the local communities and local governments should undertake to sustain the interventions once CSRL starts to phase down its support to certain communities and certain categories of activities or steps that will be needed to ensure that these activities are in place when the program funding diminishes or is redirected.

One reason for this was the fact that the exact duration of the program in Kamuli was never determined—it kept changing as more was learned. The same fluid time line meant that there was no formal plan about what criteria would be used to graduate local communities or households from the program, or what types of local government and private sector support the communities would need to sustain the CSRL activities.

During the next phase of the program, it will be important for the partners to engage the local staff and farmers' groups in discussions about needed links with public and private sector partners to sustain important CSRL activities should funding be decreased or redirected elsewhere. Another important focus will be on developing a written transition and exit plan, outlining criteria that can be used by the partners to determine the status of the target communities and households.

Lessons Learned and Recommendations

The CSRL start-up model for its crop and livestock activities was flexible. There was no preconceived program implementation plan, and the team worked hard to "start where the people are" and build on the institutional strengths of its principal partner, VEDCO. This same flexibility enabled the program to add new activities as the staff noted the need for them and new donors became interested in funding them. However, this also encouraged the start-up program to permit less emphasis on certain areas like livestock and natural resources. In retrospect, these areas should have been revved up much earlier.

One of the principal challenges in the next phase will be to reduce the focus of the program to a smaller number of core interrelated activities and identify the partnerships needed to sustain them. A second challenge will be to define a limited number of indicators with which to track the more focused set of activities. These indicators are needed to make sure that the CSRL PRA process and action plans (1) stay on track toward the achievement of a smaller number of critical objectives and important partnerships; (2) monitor the effectiveness of the program's past and present activities in achieving these objectives and nurturing the most critical partnerships needed to sustain them; and (3) identify what measures will be needed to ensure that the communities and their institutions have the capacity and partnerships that they need to sustain their activities once the program funding ends.

The team is in the process of developing an exit strategy that will address these issues for the beneficiaries with whom they have been working over the past ten years.

Program Start-Up

Local ownership is key to the continuity and advancement of program initiatives. It begins with participatory processes in early planning, and continues throughout implementation and routine monitoring. Soliciting input, in-kind contributions, and regular feedback from local leaders and community members will build loyalty and support for program efforts. This can also include the community's observations of conditions of vulnerability and indigenous knowledge of the local environment. All of these inputs will also help to ensure that program initiatives are appropriate to local conditions and cultures.

> **Lesson 1:**
> **Develop a well-conducted baseline participatory appraisal to ensure that local priorities are identified.**

Recommendations:
- Choose simple appraisal tools that the communities and staff can use to collect standard information, which can be updated annually.
- Keep the same appraisal tools throughout the program to adequately track the program's impact.
- Conduct the appraisal in the first year of the program so that the information represents a true baseline.
- Take a multidisciplinary approach that addresses all of the community's needs, not just the particular interests of the principal field partner or partners.
- Train staff and community leaders in the appraisal's methodology both prior to and during the baseline appraisals.

> **Lesson 2:**
> **Include a well-thought-out process for taking advantage of indigenous knowledge, technology, and available assets, which can be updated and strengthened as the program evolves.**

Recommendations:

- Ensure that the baseline appraisals engage local people in a two-way open dialogue about local knowledge and practice in relevant areas where the program is planning to intervene.
- Identify a form or format that will encourage staff and any community-based volunteers or experts associated with the program to conduct an extensive review of relevant indigenous knowledge prior to embarking on new activities.

Lesson 3:
Build strategies for developing local ownership into the initial program design and implementation.

Recommendations:

- Encourage cost sharing, but adjust it to the local context.
- Focus on a few core activities that link directly to the program's objectives, and scale up gradually.
- Adjust activities to the capacity of different beneficiary groups.

Participatory Monitoring and Evaluation

A PM&E system helps to build local ownership and understanding of the program. It can also provide program managers with good information in real time. For the program to be most effective, however, it needs to track a few key variables that can be monitored over time in order for the program management and major partners to grasp some of the bigger trends in program implementation. Any new activities need to adopt the same basic methodology. Care also must be taken to avoid responding to every new idea that the program beneficiaries, partners, or new donors propose.

Lesson 4:
A well-designed planning and participatory monitoring and evaluation system helps community members gain confidence in articulating their needs.

Recommendations:

- Encourage all program partners to agree on a flexible methodology for PM&E that includes a standard system for reporting.

- Identify a small number of variables that communities can track and report on annually for each of the main activity groups.
- Incorporate a summary table that tracks the evolution of the variables being tracked into the PM&E annual reports and the appraisal reports.
- Build capacity to use the PM&E system through staff and community-level PM&E training and include regular updates to the program's M&E manual.
- Minimize change in the appraisal data collection processes to avoid confusion and inconsistent data.

Targeting Household Vulnerability

Very vulnerable groups may always be present. However, with appropriate support, many vulnerable groups will take greater advantage of their own assets and gain much-needed social support, so that their livelihoods will improve. It therefore is important for any program seeking to emulate the CSRL model to develop a solid well-focused appraisal methodology that can be used to identify the principal target group and their assets.

Many of these groups will have neither the resources nor the labor to participate in the mainstream programs in their early stages. It thus is critical to build a special subset of activities that they can manage on their own with limited labor and resources.

If this targeting is successful, a certain percentage of the most vulnerable households are likely to be able to benefit from the mainstream program's activities. But a small percentage may never graduate.

Lesson 5:
Adopt a simple consistent methodology for identifying the first-generation target beneficiaries.

Recommendations:
- Develop a standard methodology for identifying and tracking the program's impact on vulnerable groups, individuals, and communities from the start.
- Train all staff, volunteers, and government partners in the methodology for identifying and tracking the program's impact on vulnerable groups so that they can use it whenever possible to classify any primary or secondary beneficiaries of the program.

- Train staff to prepare case studies that document the program's impact on vulnerable individuals to put a human face on the program's tracking data.

Lesson 6:
Develop special interventions that target the needs of the most vulnerable.

Recommendations:
- Have a budget line for each technical component of a program that can be used to support activities that benefit the most vulnerable.
- Ensure that all staff members who backstop these activities are trained in the program's standard vulnerability tracking tool.
- Encourage the program staff to use these techniques to track the impact of program targeting on the vulnerable groups that these programs are designed to benefit.

Capacity Strengthening

Education is the key to fostering a people-centered development program. It is therefore critical to create a system for tracking the impact of training on key local capacities. The goal of the process should be to produce training modules that are simple, relevant, and applicable both during and after the program's special funding stops.

Lesson 7:
Create a network of community-based development educators and the systems needed to sustain it.

Recommendations:
- Train community experts in the technical fields and participatory processes that the program supports.
- Involve local communities in the nomination and choice of the community workers so that they trust and believe the workers and are willing to work with them.
- Pay careful attention to recruitment criteria and processes to ensure community ownership and appropriate staffing.
- Build strong links between the community-based experts and the wider network of government, NGO, and private sector partners.

- Supervise the activities of the community-level experts in ways that strengthen their connection to the local communities, their technical expertise, and their leadership capacity.
- Reach agreement on how the community-based experts will be compensated and how this compensation will be linked to their performance and supervision.
- Track progress toward the execution of these key capacity-building functions through the community-based PM&E system.

> **Lesson 8:**
> **Develop a training module process that can be adapted as community-based educators increase their competencies, community members' needs are better understood, and capabilities improve.**

Recommendations:
- View curriculum development as a process that will evolve in response to new opportunities and constraints, not just a product.
- Ensure that the training modules are simple, straightforward, and geared to practical learning applications; pilot tested to ensure that the target audience can relate to the teaching methodology and the materials; timely and applicable to the target audience's day-to-day situations; and replicable so they can be reproduced at different scales.
- Track the impact of specific training sessions and modules as part of the PM&E system.
- Plan the program budget so that it will include the staff financial resources that this type of iterative curriculum process will require.

Program Exit Strategy

It is tempting for a program to focus on the immediate needs and the community's most pressing humanitarian problems. This is a big mistake because it can lead program planners to ignore some of the key government and public-private partnerships that the communities will need to sustain the program's interventions over time. Start with the end in mind, and work backward. A good plan is to draft a written exit strategy in conjunction with the baseline appraisals that influence the program design. This strategy should be reviewed, updated, and tracked as part of the routine operation of the PM&E system.

Lesson 9:
Build an exit strategy from the start that is monitored and updated as part of the participatory monitoring and evaluation system.

Recommendations:
- Involve all the partners in planning a formal written exit strategy that is updated and tracked as part of the PM&E system and discussed at the biannual and annual PM&E report meetings.
- Work with local communities to develop their own community-specific exit strategies that outline the process that the program will use to progressively disengage from these communities.
- Work with local communities and local governments to develop a list of critical government and private sector partnerships that the communities will need to sustain important activities once the program is ready to begin exiting.
- Track each community's progress toward the execution of the key measures in their exit strategy as part of their PM&E plan and summarize the progress being made.

Lesson 10:
Integrate sustainability mechanisms from the start to ensure adoption and continuity of the improvements that the program has stimulated.

Recommendations:
- Nurture relationships with local leaders, permanent institutions, and private businesses within the communities being served.
- Involve the beneficiaries in identifying the most important interventions that they would like to see retained and in recommending ways to sustain these activities.
- Anticipate the need for any essential community-level experts or support to be self-sustaining by the time that the program funding ends or is reduced.
- Provide occasional recognition for the program staff and local groups to recognize their commitment, innovation, and progress.

Appendix Table Initial Poverty and Food Insecurity Rankings from the 2005 Baseline Participatory Rural Appraisal

Criteria for Household Wealth Ranking in the Program Area

Wealthy	Ordinary	Poor
• Owns much land (minimum of ten acres) • Owns many livestock (minimum of ten cattle)	• Owns about four acres of land • Owns about two cattle and three goats	• Has less land (about one acre) • Owns no livestock (in some instances, they own hens)
Human capital • Attained good education and children are in good schools • Members rarely fall sick • Has fewer children (around five)	Human capital • Attained medium education (up to standard seven years) and children attend school • Has many wives and many children (more than one wife and over ten children)	Human capital • Children do not attend school • Members untidy most of the time • Appears sickly and pale
Social capital • Usually entertains visitors • Has hired laborers	Social capital • Relates well with other people • Does not use hired laborers • Occasional quarrels occur in the home	Social capital • Does not relate well with other people—is averse to interaction with others, is a laborer for others • Rarely entertains visitors • Regular misunderstandings common in the home
Financial capital • Has regular and diverse sources of income	Financial capital • Has minimal sources of income • Sometimes in debt	Financial capital
Built capital • Owns a car and a good house (may be made of burnt bricks and has a tin roof, plastered with a cement floor or carpet)	Built capital • Has a fair house (may be made of burnt bricks or mud, with a tin roof, no cement floor or carpet, no plaster) • May have a bicycle for means of transport	Built capital • Has a grass thatched mud house, sometimes with holes • Has no means of transport
Political capital • Has easy access to traditional and local government leaders	Political capital • Has easy access to traditional and local government leaders	Political capital • Rare or no relations with either local government or traditional leaders

(continues)

Appendix Table Continued

Criteria for Household Food Security Rating in the Program Area

Food Secure	Food Insecure	Extremely Food Insecure
• Has a full granary or store of food • Eats four times a day • Eats a variety of foods • Happy most of the time • Rarely falls sick • Possesses cultivated land with a variety of crops	• Has a half-full granary or store of food • Eats two times a day • Occasionally eats a variety of foods • Occasionally falls sick • Buys food at times	• Has no granary or store of food • Eats once a day • Does not change foods eaten at home • Works for food from other community members • Usually appears sickly • Children usually eat from the neighbors' homes • Has malnourished and stunted children • Husband and wife always absent from home

Criteria for Household Nutrition Status Ranking in the Program Area

Good Nutrition	Ordinary Nutrition	Poor Nutrition
• Rarely falls sick • Has bright children • Energetic • Happy most of the time	• Has a fairly healthy appearance • Rarely falls sick • Has pale-looking children	• Frequently falls sick • Sad most of the time • Has violent, malnourished, and low-weight children

Sources: Haroon Sseguya and Dorothy Masinde, *Towards Achievement of Sustainable Rural Livelihoods in Kamuli District, Uganda: A Baseline Assessment* (Ames: Center for Sustainable Rural Livelihoods, Iowa State University, 2005); Haroon Sseguya, Robert Mazur, and Dorothy Masinde, "Harnessing Community Capitals for Livelihood Enhancement: Experiences from a Livelihood Program in Rural Uganda," *Community Development* 40, no. 2 (2009): 123–138.

Note: Based on a PRA survey that was conducted over a four-week period in the middle of Year 1 of the program (early 2005) in thirty-two villages in the six parishes where the program planned to focus (see Chapter 8).

Notes

1. "Participatory rural appraisal (PRA) is a label given to a growing family of participatory approaches and methods that emphasize local knowledge and enable local people to make their own appraisal, analysis, and plans. PRA uses group animation and exercises to facilitate information sharing, analysis, and action among stakeholders." For more information, see World Bank, "Social

Analysis: Participatory Rural Appraisal," 2013, http://go.worldbank.org/H2OX FLV650.

2. Haroon Sseguya and Dorothy Masinde, *Towards Achievement of Sustainable Rural Livelihoods in Kamuli District, Uganda: A Baseline Assessment* (Ames: Center for Sustainable Rural Livelihoods, Iowa State University, 2005).

3. Ibid.

4. Examples of PRA tools are community or social mapping, cropping calendars or time lines, transect walks, wealth ranking, focus group discussions, and Venn diagrams. See, for example, Robert Chambers, *Whose Reality Counts? Putting the First Last* (London: Immediate Technology, 1997); and Robert Chambers, *Rural Development: Putting the Last First* (London: Longmans, 1983).

5. The CSRL program officers—focal persons for specific components like crop production livestock, value chain activities, or nutrition—train the program extension officers who then train the community volunteers (i.e., the rural development extensionists and community nutrition and health workers from 2005–2009, and the community-based trainers after 2010), and community-based volunteers train the farmers together with group subject matter leaders such as nutrition and health workers and lead farmers who are in charge of demonstrating technologies to group members.

6. Africare, "How to Measure the Months of Adequate Household Food Provisioning" (Washington, DC: Africare, 2005). See also Africare, "Guidance: How to Measure the Number of Months of Adequate Household Food Provisioning (MAHFP) Based on Participatory Rural Appraisals in Food Security Interventions," *Africare Food Security Review*. No. 1. September 2007.

7. Jennifer Coates, Anne Swindale, and Paula Bilinsky, "Household Food Insecurity Access Scale [HFIAS] for Measurement of Food Access: Indicator Guide," Version 3 (Washington, DC: FANTA, 2007).

8. Twelve paid community-based trainers were recruited in 2010 to provide education and training programs.

9. For more information on community-based volunteers, see Dorothy Masinde, Lorna M. Butler, and Mary Nyasimi, *Livelihood Improvement Through Training and Experience: An Analysis of Uganda Volunteer Trainers,* Unpublished Draft Report (Ames: Center for Sustainable Rural Livelihoods, Iowa State University, 2014), 36 pages.

10. For more information on livestock technologies, see Chapter 6 in this volume and Patrick Sangi, Jane Nakiranda, Nadiope Gideon, Charles Kategere, and Mark Westgate, "Strategic Objective One (SO1): Promote Resilient Climate-Smart Agricultural Technologies to Increase Food Availability," in Della E. McMillan, ed., *Sustainable Rural Livelihoods Program: Summative Monitoring and Evaluation (M&E) Report: 2005–2012,* Draft Report (Ames: Center for Sustainable Rural Livelihoods, Iowa State University, 2012).

11. For more information on marketing, see John Sembera, Ronnie Balibuzani, and Jane Sempa, "Strategic Objective Two (SO2): Build Diversified Livelihoods and More Resilient Markets to Improve Food Access," in Della E. McMillan, ed., *Sustainable Rural Livelihoods Program: Summative Monitoring*

and Evaluation (M&E) Report: 2005–2012, Draft Report (Ames: Center for Sustainable Rural Livelihoods, Iowa State University, 2012), pp. 38–65.

12. Vulnerability is a dynamic concept that is usually viewed on a continuum over time. For example, there may be three levels of vulnerability: "improving" poor (some social mobility); "coping" poor (little capacity for social mobility); and "declining" poor (little or no capacity for social mobility). Canadian Hunger Foundation (CHF) Partners in Rural Development, *Sustainable Livelihoods Approach Guidelines* (Ottawa, Ontario: CHF Partners in Progress, 2005), pp. 19–20.

13. For more information on the CSRL programs that targeted the HIV/AIDS-affected groups, see Esther Matama, Benon Musaasizi, and Laura Byaruhanga, "Strategic Objective Three (SO3): Reduce Malnutrition Levels Among Women of Reproductive Age and Children," in Della E. McMillan, ed., *Sustainable Rural Livelihoods Program: Summative Monitoring and Evaluation (M&E) Report: 2005–2012,* Draft Report (Ames: Center for Sustainable Rural Livelihoods, Iowa State University, 2012), pp. 66–118.

14. There are two rainy seasons in Kamuli, the main season from March through May and the short season from August through October, each of which is becoming less reliable; that is, rain may come down in torrents at some times, and at other times the area suffers from extreme drought. During the main season, the average annual rainfall is about 110 mm or about 4.3 inches. These conditions and others contribute to the vulnerability of Kamuli and other dryland communities in Uganda. See Kamuli District Planning Unit, Republic of Uganda, "District Development Plan for 2010/11–2013/15, Kamuli Town (May 2011)"; Yuko Kurauchi and Sarah Anyoti, "Enhanced Resilience of Drought Prone Communities Through Conservation Agriculture: The Case of Uganda," Forum for Agricultural Risk Management in Development (FARMD). Washington, DC: FARMD, 2013.

15. In the first five years, they were not compensated in cash, but given job-related tools and supplies. Since 2009, trainers have been compensated in cash.

6

Leaving the Door Open to Emerging Needs and Opportunities

Dorothy Masinde, Della E. McMillan,
Max Rothschild, and Gail Nonnecke

No program design is perfect; something will be missed.
Either a program will have overlooked some key constraint, or it will
need to respond to a new opportunity. This may require the tweaking of
the original design, which can be difficult—if not impossible—in a traditional agency-funded program with a preconceived program document
and fixed budget. In a flexible, privately supported model like the Center for Sustainable Rural Livelihoods (CSRL), change is an option.

This chapter shows some of the innovative ways that private sector
funding can be used to help programs adapt to new opportunities and
constraints. For the CSRL program, these innovative responses focused
on two key areas important to local people's livelihoods—nutrition and
livestock.

The challenges that CSRL faced in adjusting to these new opportunities and constraints were typical of most programs:

- Identifying new constraints and opportunities—creating a
  process to encourage a flow of new ideas from the program staff
  and beneficiaries;
- Pilot testing initiatives to address the new constraints and
  opportunities—developing and refining new methodologies for

The authors wish to acknowledge the helpful input and contributions of Gideon
Nadiope.

145

addressing the identified constraints and responding to new opportunities;

- Scaling up the new initiatives with additional funding—finding the funding sources to expand on pilot testing of the most promising activities; and
- Integrating the enhanced initiatives with other program components—integrating the new activities into the program's ongoing systems for accounting, monitoring, and communication.

Evolution of the CSRL Program's Nutrition Component

Identifying New Constraints and Opportunities

From the onset, the CSRL management team planned to integrate a human nutrition component into the program. However, nutrition had not been one of the original subprojects of the Volunteer Efforts for Development Concerns (VEDCO), so there was no specific plan for how this would be done and there was no field staff member who had this expertise—other than the field program manager. There was an international nutritionist on the early management team, and the budget included funds to consult with an in-country technical nutrition specialist to develop needed staff training sessions and training modules. A trained nutrition officer was hired in the middle of the first year (in January 2005) and replaced by a second trained officer after one year.[1] These officers were key to the proper training of the field staff and to the recruitment and support of thirty-six community-based health and nutrition workers.

The successful execution of these initial nutrition activities highlighted a number of new and emerging needs, one of which was to rehabilitate seriously malnourished children.[2] Prior to CSRL interventions, these children were simply regarded as sick children since few local people made the connection between children's food intake and their vulnerability to other illnesses (Box 6.1). Many of the sickest children had been hidden during the baseline survey. As the program progressed and built local people's capacity to identify malnourished children, more of these sick children were brought to the attention of the field staff. With only modest interventions in the original program to offer to the mothers, the only option was to refer them to the local health unit. Although the health unit might help children get better in the short run, the children often relapsed to another illness when they returned home and were reexposed to the same dietary conditions and unsanitary water supply. The existing CSRL budget was insufficient to cover the type of

---

Box 6.1 Emerging Needs Identified

"Most of the sick children we were introduced to had a small health records notebook with them. This health record notebook documented all of their shots and visits to the health unit. Almost every one of them included a prescription for 'better food.' The more we saw this, the more we realized that the root cause of the problem was that the mothers had no concept of what this meant or how to provide it. We could not simply stand by and do nothing."

Source: Dorothy Masinde in conversation with Della E. McMillan, April 25, 2013, Ames, Iowa.

---

direct intervention and education required by this newly recognized need in addition to the other program components.

Pilot Testing Initiatives to Address the New Constraints and Opportunities

Initial Pilot Activities to Develop Better Methodologies for Rehabilitating Malnourished Children. To address this issue, the CSRL nutrition and human immunodeficiency virus/acquired immunodeficiency syndrome (HIV/AIDS) adviser and field program manager started pilot testing a new protein-rich porridge made from local ingredients with ten malnourished children, and trained a small number of nutrition and health workers to use the methodology.

In conjunction with the intensive feedings, which were held in a group, the mothers of the ten malnourished children were trained in new crop production techniques and sanitation practices needed to sustain their children's progress when they returned home. This positive deviance model was highly successful in bringing about a sustainable weight gain for the children in the pilot test.[3]

The initial pilot program was self-funded by the CSRL nutrition and HIV/AIDS adviser and field program manager from their personal funds in 2006 because there was no line item for this activity.[4] Based on the results of this program, CSRL used some of its core funding to support a second pilot test involving ten additional children in 2007 and another ten in 2008, which helped the nutrition and HIV/AIDS adviser further refine the model and training modules. As word spread about the protein-rich porridge, some of the local community members started coming to the trainers who were leading the tests to buy the enriched porridge.

Creation of the Student-Led Establish and Grow Fund. The first Iowa State University (ISU) service-learning students arrived in the summer of 2006. One of the students, nutrition undergraduate Eric Nonnecke, accompanied the VEDCO nutrition and HIV/AIDS adviser as he worked with the first pilot rehabilitation efforts. Unbeknownst to the local CSRL staff, Nonnecke returned to the United States and started fund-raising—reaching out to other service-learning students and faculty. The result was the creation of the Establish and Grow Fund in 2007. Although tiny at the start with only $6,000 in donations, the Establish and Grow Fund sponsored a number of pilot initiatives to strengthen the program's capacity to rehabilitate chronically malnourished children (see Chapter 7). Even more important, the fund-raisers for the Establish and Grow Fund created a powerful lobby for the program to expand its community-based nutrition activities.

In 2008, Nonnecke returned to Kamuli and conducted a small research project on the nutritional status of the mothers and children that were affected by these first pilot rehabilitation activities. These results—combined with the quantitative data on the first pilot tests in 2005 and 2008—helped continue to build the interest in nutrition of both CSRL and VEDCO senior management and the CSRL program benefactors.

Initial Scale-Up of the Community-Based Initiative. Convinced of its utility, CSRL scaled up its support for community-based rehabilitation efforts to 110 additional malnourished infants in 2009 using core program funds. Although this initial scale-up was successful, it coincided with the program's decision to shift its focus from nutrition and health workers and rural development extensionists to community-based trainers in late 2009, so it was not repeated in 2010.[5]

Pilot Testing of a New Model of Nutrition Education Center. In 2010, the first disbursement of monies from the Establish and Grow Fund was deposited in a separate CSRL account. This coincided with the hiring of a third community nutritionist.[6] The CSRL field program manager seized this opportunity to expand the job description of the new nutritionist to include heading up the Nutrition Education Center (NEC) as well as the school lunch program (see Chapter 7).

The first pilot NEC started in one village in Naluwoli Parish in 2011. In contrast to the previous model, which was managed in the affected children's homes, the new NEC model provided intensive nutrition education through a former nutrition and health worker in a fixed location. The new program offered a more intensive opportunity to train mothers in the skills that they would need to rehabilitate their children and keep them healthy. As of December 2012, sixty-four children and twenty mothers had participated in the program, and thirteen mothers had graduated with their children.[7] Based on lessons learned from the first year and a half of execution, certain adjustments were made in the core model. The program is currently expanding the number of NECs, involving some of the mothers who have graduated in leadership roles in the satellite centers, and assisting some of the mothers to establish income-generating activities. As of August 2014, there were six centers reaching a total of 291 clients.[8]

Scaling Up the New Initiatives with Additional Funding

Since 2006, when CSRL started to report more regularly on its nutrition activities, a growing number of smaller CSRL donors—mostly ISU graduates and parents of CSRL service-learning students—increased their interest in nutrition. In 2010, this resulted in some small grants to support a school lunch program (see Chapter 7).

Pleased with the result of these small starter grants, one of the new private donors expressed an interest in supporting further nutrition interventions in October 2012. In response, the CSRL Advisory Board chair and the CSRL staff developed a short proposal to integrate the nutrition education subprogram with some smallholder livestock interventions. This was envisioned as a potential way to help young women start a small business, which also offered the possibility of providing animal source foods for their children. The donor showed interest in the idea, and started off by providing salary support for both a livestock and a nutrition officer. If the concept continues to attract support, this will contribute to one of CSRL's emerging objectives for the next program phase—to encourage the integration of program subcomponents (nutrition and livestock production) and to target the young women graduates of the nutrition education program to ensure that their skills are directed to a sustainable future.

Integrating the Enhanced Initiatives with Other Program Components

The chief challenges for integrating these activities into the larger program have been managing the special funds, hiring and retaining staff, and developing appropriate tracking systems.

Financial Systems. To ensure the autonomy of the special funds that were raised for the pilot projects in nutrition, these funds were—and still are—routed through a special account. Although cumbersome, this has enabled CSRL to report on all of the special funds to their individual donors. It has also made it easier to keep these funds from being used to make up some of the budget shortfalls in other areas.

Senior Staff Recruitment and Retention. Given the high demand for trained nutritionists in Uganda, it has been difficult to retain qualified staff for more than a few years. One of the principal activities of the CSRL field program manager was to ensure that future vacancies were advertised and filled with minimal delays.

Monitoring and Evaluation. Since nutrition was not part of the initial VEDCO program, neither the baseline appraisals nor the first quantitative evaluation measured the nutritional status of the children in the target households. There was also no consensus about how the program's nutritional impacts would be measured. At first, the program responded to only severe cases, and did not attempt to train the entire population. Gradually, the nutrition and health workers became a well-trained cadre of educators, and their contributions to household knowledge on nutrition were, and continue to be, widely recognized. Because the nutrition program was not integrated with the ongoing monitoring and evaluation (M&E) efforts, it has been difficult to track its efforts in the same way as the rest of the program. Standard measures of tracking nutrition were not used until 2011 (see Chapter 8). Before this time, much of the documentation was qualitative in nature (e.g., case studies), with only a modest amount of quantitative data. However, the data that were available for the early years suggested that the nutrition program had a substantial impact due to (1) increased dietary diversity and knowledge about the importance of having a balanced diet; (2) the promotion of flour made from the traditional grain amaranth plant; and (3) improved feeding and food preparation techniques, especially for infants.

The same lack of standard measures for tracking the program's nutritional impacts has also made it difficult to develop the types of partnership needed to sustain these activities should the program begin to decrease its input to Kamuli. The program is planning to develop a more standardized model for nutritional assessment in the next phase.

Evolution of the CSRL Program's Livestock Component

Identifying New Constraints and Opportunities

Livestock improvement was an integral part of the CSRL program from the start; however, it was funded at a modest level and limited to providing livestock to the community-based volunteers for demonstration units and breeding stock.[9] Like many livestock improvement and training programs in rural Africa, the community-based volunteers were expected to rotate breeding animals and to cost-share the construction of livestock housing. Since these volunteers represented only 10 percent of the original group of target households, this limited the program's outreach. The turnover of the animals to the second-tier beneficiaries was slow—taking at least two years.

The program lacked a full-time livestock specialist in the field with the necessary skills in animal science and veterinary medicine to train the farmers and provide technical backstopping to the extension staff. A full-time livestock faculty member at ISU or Makerere University (MAK) had not yet been identified to provide leadership to the livestock field activities and to fund-raise for potential program expansion, and the training module or curriculum was not adequate to teach farmers what they needed to know to manage the animals.

In this case, the chief catalyst for change was a chance encounter between senior ISU livestock specialist Max Rothschild and ISU deans Cathy Woteki and David Acker during a September 2004 bus ride in— of all places—South Korea. Intrigued by their discussion of the CSRL program, Rothschild, who had never worked in Africa before, combined some residual funds from one of his commercial grants with some internal seed grants from ISU to fund a visit to Kamuli in March 2005. During his ten-day stay, he participated in the livestock activities that were already under way and conducted some workshops in Kampala, Kamuli, and Luwero. After this visit, Rothschild joined forces with CSRL field program manager Dorothy Masinde to expand the focus of the program's livestock activities.

Pilot Testing Initiatives to Address the New Constraints and Opportunities

Use of Pilot Programs to Test New Methodologies. Since there was no money in the core budget for additional livestock activities, Rothschild started fund-raising. Most of the initial donations came from his family, friends, and business associates. The first private donations, approximately $4,500 in 2006, were transferred to a special account that was not part of the core budget. These funds were used to purchase additional animals for a wider range of households than the first animals, which had been given exclusively to community volunteers for demonstration purposes.

The second and third set of small donations—approximately $4,500 in 2007 and $5,000 in 2008—supported the purchase of additional animals and a 2008 pilot test of livestock units in two primary schools, a poultry unit at the Nakanyoni primary school and a piggery at the Kasambira school.

Rothschild visited about every nine months during this time period to provide technical support and training to the farmers and CSRL field program manager. The same visits and debriefings on the pilot program helped build a much greater understanding of livestock among the members of the program management committee and CSRL benefactors.

Use of Small-Scale Private Benefactor Support as a Means of Developing the CSRL Beneficiaries' Access to Markets. During a second visit to Uganda in February 2007, the CSRL field program manager and Rothschild co-organized a meeting of key stakeholders—leading representatives of the slaughterhouses, breeders, finishers,[10] breeding material suppliers, and so forth—in Uganda's pig industry to develop a more realistic strategy for expanding livestock ownership and production in Kamuli that would address some of the macroissues in the value chain as well as the more micro-level issues that had been the focus of the earlier livestock strategy. One output of the meeting was clear evidence that most pork buyers were coming from Kenya and paying low prices, partly due to infrequent production levels. In the absence of more effective marketing strategies to help Kamuli farmers obtain better prices, it was unlikely that any additional investment in the development of more intensive pork production would be sustainable.

Scaling Up the New Initiatives with Additional Funding

Monsanto Fund Three-Year Grant. A critical turning point occurred in the fall of 2007, when a grant proposal was submitted to the Monsanto Fund and accepted. CSRL received a $100,000 grant from the Monsanto Fund, which started disbursement in 2008. The activities under this grant helped the program to pilot test a more commercial model of production for the pig value chain in Kamuli's rural areas. Based on the results of the Monsanto-funded pilot test, CSRL rolled out a new set of livestock activities funded from the core budget in 2012–2013.[11]

Complementary Funding from Established CSRL Benefactors and New Private Sector Fund-Raising. As the Monsanto program advanced, it became increasingly apparent that it needed someone with higher-level technical experience to oversee the program and also be capable of providing veterinarian support.

Near the end of the fifth year of the program (in July 2009), VEDCO hired a senior livestock adviser.[12] Since neither the Monsanto Fund grant nor the core CSRL budget could cover his salary, additional private fund-raising from an established CSRL benefactor as well as other sources found by Rothschild was required.

New Potential Partnerships: Proposed Links to the International Livestock Research Institute. When the Monsanto Fund announced that it would not renew CSRL's livestock grant in mid-2011, it threatened the long-term sustainability of the three newly developed livestock cooperatives—comprised of 66 producer groups representing 347 farmers—that were critical to helping farmers sustain their new productivity increases by helping them develop better links with the most stable private sector feed and veterinary product supply outlets as well as wholesale markets.

Rothschild took the lead in trying to identify new potential donors. When he approached Heifer International—one of the few international nongovernmental organizations (NGOs) primarily focused on livestock—its officials informed him that they needed a start-up grant to expand into Kamuli. And several attempts to approach the United States Agency for International Development (USAID) mission about potential funding opportunities were unproductive due to the agency's limited interest in livestock.

Then, Rothschild learned that the International Livestock Research Institute (ILRI) was planning to launch a value-chain initiative in one Asian and one African country. He successfully lobbied for ILRI representatives to visit the CSRL program in July 2011. Subsequently, ILRI chose Uganda and recently completed a formal cooperative agreement with VEDCO to be its principle contact agency for the new value-chain activities. Although this collaborative agreement does not provide any cash for operating costs, it should strengthen the livestock program by providing critical technical support for developing new systems of livestock feed as well as staff- and farmer-level training in value-chain activities.

New Potential Partnerships: Future CSRL Funding for Human Nutrition. Due in large part to the growing evidence of the critical role of livestock in helping the poorest of the poor improve their living standards and food intake, there has been a strong lobby to make livestock a central focus of the new follow-up initiative that CSRL is developing with support from some of its existing and new ISU benefactors with interests in human nutrition. Based on the initial reaction of the donors in 2013, this is a promising area that potentially could lead to a separate endowment to provide private funding to underwrite the CSRL livestock activities as part of its broader commitment to nutrition.

Integrating the Enhanced Initiatives with Other Program Components

The chief challenges that CSRL has faced in integrating the expanded livestock activities into other elements of the program are similar to those faced by human nutrition.

Financial Systems. To ensure a sound accountability for the pilot funds, these funds—including the Monsanto grant—were kept in separate budget lines. While this made budgeting more challenging, it helped the CSRL program provide clear reports to benefactors about how their money was spent.

Senior Technical Staff Recruitment and Retention. The issue of identifying and retaining qualified senior staff was more daunting, chiefly because the original budget did not foresee the recruitment of a senior livestock adviser. Since having this type of senior specialist with training at the level of Doctor of Philosophy (PhD) or Doctor of Veterinary Medicine (DVM)—as opposed to training in animal science or general agriculture at the Bachelor of Science (BS) level—was an essential precondition to the effective execution of the Monsanto grant, the program made this a top priority for private fund-raising. During the first three years of his contract, the senior livestock adviser for CSRL was paid through these private funds. New program funding for nutrition made it possible to start paying for a more highly trained adviser through the core program budget for 2013.

Monitoring and Evaluation. The program has been able to track the use of the livestock activity's animals that it distributed to the target households. To date, however, there has been little analysis of the household-level impact of these activities in the CSRL program's quantitative surveys, mainly because the quantitative surveys collected almost no baseline data on livestock ownership or production techniques due to the early program's limited focus. There is, however, a great deal of qualitative evidence that these activities have had a positive impact on household-level nutrition and income. One of the major challenges of the next phase will be to better integrate the livestock activities into the program's routine quantitative surveys.

Responding to New Opportunities and Constraints

Although the goals and objectives of the CSRL program's human nutrition and livestock activities were very different, the staff used similar mechanisms in responding to these similar major challenges.

Identifying New Constraints and Opportunities

The Critical Role of the Program Management Team and Its Partners. The initial design of the CSRL nutrition program was strongly affected by the fact that neither of CSRL's two principal partners—MAK or VEDCO—had strong expertise in community or international nutrition. Having a senior ISU nutritionist on the US-based management team at the start of the CSRL program ensured that the job advertisement for the first CSRL field program manager listed nutritional experience as a critical requirement. The same effective lobby from the management team—combined with Masinde's background—made it easy to add nutrition. But until the nutrition extension officer was hired, the CSRL nutrition activities had a slow start and, even then, the first nutrition officer was in place for only about a year before another individual had to be recruited. This affected the progress of the educational program because time was needed to develop teaching materials, recruit the nutrition and health workers, and train all of the extension officers. Looking back, there may have been a different trajectory if the program had identified a local partner with strong nutrition expertise, or if the original international nutritionist on the early management team had not been recruited by another university.

The VEDCO staff were better trained in livestock, which made it easier to support this component from the start even though neither of the program's local partners had a strong interest in or support for livestock before the CSRL program began. Once Rothschild—who was not on the original ISU CSRL management team—got involved, he and the field program manager provided critical assistance in developing the short-term pilot scale-up initiatives as well as a larger grant that helped the program respond to these new needs.

The Critical Importance of Having Good Communication to and from the Field. Emerging program needs and issues must be identified by the local staff and community members, who will then inform management about them. It was the field staff who noted that the initial program model was not addressing the needs of the chronically malnourished children who were too sick to benefit from the program's routine education programs. It also was the staff who first communicated the farmers' desire to own more livestock. These ideas were shared with the field program manager during her frequent visits to the field. She then made follow-up investigations and spoke with the CSRL director as well as technical specialists about these needs. Open bottom-up communication was key to the program's development of a policy response.

The Critical Role of Networking. It was the CSRL director's networking through the ISU-based plant genome project that identified a source for grain amaranth seed in Uganda. It also was through the same network that the CSRL field program manager acquired the first recipes for the protein-rich formula used to rehabilitate the malnourished children in the pilot programs. The fact that grain amaranth could be grown in less than sixty days in even the most impoverished Kamuli soils made it accessible to the mothers of malnourished children.

Pilot Testing Initiatives to Address the New Constraints and Opportunities

The program's willingness to let the CSRL nutrition officer organize a pilot program to rehabilitate the malnourished children in 2006 set in motion a series of activities. It helped the officer perfect the community-based rehabilitation methodology and led to the founding of the Establish and Grow Fund, which created a student-led lobby to expand the CSRL program's nutrition activities. The same fund also supported the first Nutrition Education Center (NEC) in 2010. These successful pilot initiatives have attracted new ISU donors and inspired some of the existing CSRL benefactors to expand their financial support.

Rothschild's private fund-raising efforts in 2005–2009 were small but critical because they paid for the animals that were distributed to farmers who were not rural development extensionists (RDEs). Since the other costs of the pilot program (e.g., extension worker salaries and training) were covered by the core budget, this was all that the program needed to support the initial pilot test. These pilot initiatives showed an untapped demand for on-farm pig production and the types of marketing support that would be needed to help the farmers sell the pigs once production increased. When it became clear that the program needed a full-time senior livestock specialist to help manage the Monsanto grant, Rothschild's fund-raising shifted to raising the necessary funds to cover the specialist's salary.

Scaling Up the New Initiatives with Additional Funding

The pilot programs in livestock and human nutrition encouraged existing CSRL benefactors to expand their giving in these areas. Their increased exposure to the pilot programs' initial results occurred as a natural output of both groups' presentations during biannual meetings to which donors and potential donors were invited. This eventually led an existing CSRL contributor to support the salary of the nutritionist who oversaw the implementation of the NECs and improved school lunch program and another existing donor to fund the salary of the livestock veterinarian. It also led to the gradual development of a whole new set of privately funded activities focused on human nutrition and livestock that underwrote child nutrition, young mother's education, and livelihood improvement.

It is unlikely that any of these new initiatives would have occurred without the pilot projects. The pilot studies also provided the basis for grant applications by CSRL and VEDCO to outside agencies and foundations.

Integrating the Enhanced Initiatives with Other Program Components

The Critical Role of Identifying and Retaining Qualified Staff. Over time, the program has employed four different nutrition and HIV/AIDS officers and one senior livestock extension specialist. The continuity in their leadership has been critical since even a short gap would have resulted in a major setback. Strong oversight from the field program manager and the ISU-based livestock expert was necessary to ensure the recruitment and hiring of CSRL's first senior livestock specialist in 2009.

The Critical Role of Expanding the Program's Monitoring and Evaluation Plan. If CSRL had been inflexible, it might have missed the opportunity to address the new needs identified for human nutrition and livestock, both of which have dramatically increased the program's impact. This same analysis, however, shows some problems that often result when a program adds new activities but does not adjust other systems to accommodate them. To date, the majority of the CSRL program's nutrition and livestock activities have been managed as separate budget lines using their internal M&E systems. Although this information is useful, it makes it difficult to see the crossover between the old and new activities. Such tracking information is critical for gauging the community-level impact of the program and is an essential prerequisite to building strong partnerships between the volunteers, local health and veterinary services, and international partners.

Lessons Learned and Recommendations

One of the dangers of adopting the livelihoods concept is that, if it is not focused from the beginning, a program can go in many directions at once. Eventually, it became necessary to narrow the CSRL program's focus and integrate related interventions. In the course of doing so, important issues like livestock and nutrition were underfunded.

The CSRL program was willing and able to correct some of these initial oversights in the course of program execution. This flexibility was possible because the program had access to small pots of private benefactor funds. These discretionary funds helped the program pilot test new initiatives, providing the evidence to help the program expand in the two critical program areas of livestock and nutrition.

Certain aspects of the CSRL design—in particular, the financial and M&E systems—did not anticipate this high level of flexibility. This accounts for the fact that the program developed parallel systems for accounting and M&E, which made it difficult to determine how many local communities were affected by the new activities and which communities were successful enough to graduate. One of the principal challenges of the next phase of the program will be to develop a more integrated system of accounting and M&E for these new activities.

Although this chapter focuses on the CSRL program in Kamuli, the basic principles and lessons learned can be useful to any privately funded program that is attempting to develop the same type of flexible local programming. All of these programs will face the same key challenges in responding to new opportunities and constraints that emerge after the initial design:

- Identifying new constraints and opportunities;
- Pilot testing initiatives to address the new constraints and opportunities:
- Scaling up the new initiatives with additional funding; and
- Integrating the enhanced initiatives into the other program components.

Identifying New Constraints and Opportunities

No program design is ever perfect. Something will inevitably be understudied or underfunded during the start-up phase. Two of the most important factors that affect the initial design and execution of a program are the technical background and experience of the original management team and the principal NGO partners. As programs evolve, they should anticipate the need to adjust the background of the senior management team and local partners. Far from being a sign of instability, this is a sign of mature growth. All programs need experienced managers who facilitate an inflow of new ideas from the staff who implement the program as well as other organizations that work in the same field.

Lesson 1:
Consider ways that initial partner and management team choices can affect early program design.

Recommendations:
- Be conscious of the potential pitfalls of having only one or two partners with limited foci—they will affect what is seen and done.
- Be aware of how the composition of the management team may affect both partner choice and what is seen and done.
- Add new people to the core management team when a key technical area has been overlooked.
- Be aware that the physical location and cultural predisposition of the communities may affect the initial design.

Lesson 2:
Create open communication with staff to empower them to be aware of and communicate emerging needs.

Recommendations:
- Encourage the recruitment of an experienced program manager and give him or her the latitude to identify emerging needs.
- Facilitate continual communication between and among all team members of each partner organization to allow new ideas to percolate up and down.

Lesson 3:
Network with other organizations and programs to allow new ideas to circulate.

Recommendations:
- Encourage senior staff to network with regional centers of excellence in the program's technical interventions to identify and bring new technologies and best practices into the early program design.
- Continue staff networking and expand it to encourage the circulation of new ideas and potential synergies with other organizations.

Pilot Testing Initiatives to Address the New Constraints and Opportunities

Not all constraints are fatal flaws, and not all new opportunities pan out. This is why a program needs a filter. One of the best ways of filtering is to conduct a pilot study. Pilot studies are critical because they enable the program staff to better define the new intervention methodology and assess the likely impact of scaling up the new interventions to a wider audience.

To ensure that programs have the ability to pilot test promising initiatives, they may need to identify new, but small, sources of funding to achieve specific pilot tests. Many donors are attracted to the idea of supporting something new and innovative. A successful pilot test can turn a small donor into a major donor. It can also create the data to justify a larger grant application or endowment.

> **Lesson 4:**
> Develop innovative ways that small donations can be solicited and managed to sponsor pilot tests of new initiatives.

Recommendations:

- Ensure that all donors—however small or insignificant they may seem in the total budget of a program—receive regular updates on how their funds are being used.
- Court small private donations—through online techniques or at special events—to support promising new initiatives that can lead to larger grants to support further initiatives at a later date.
- Adjust the core budget if a pilot project shows the value of a new approach, even if this means downsizing another less critical program component.

Scaling Up the New Initiatives with Additional Funding

Armed with the results of the pilot studies, the program staff is better equipped to identify new funding sources—by convincing the existing donor base to support the new initiatives and by identifying new donors. Each option requires a program to present its results in a way that the potential donor understands.

> **Lesson 5:**
> Use pilot test results to sell the added initiatives to new and existing benefactors as well as private foundations and collaborative research programs.

Recommendations:

- Report regularly on results to the current donor base as well as any private foundations that are supporting elements of the program.
- Tailor all reports to the interests and reporting requirements of the contributors, and integrate the case study material with the program's more quantitative M&E data showing impact.
- Encourage the program manager to report on any new sectors that are relevant to emerging needs not covered by the current program.

- Help staff apply for private donor and foundation funding for emerging areas.

Integrating the Enhanced Initiatives with Other Program Components

Once the program funding is expanded, the next challenge is to build the technical capacity of the program to execute the new activities. The program will then need to (1) train the existing program management and staff members with the skills they will need to support the new activities and expanded program; (2) recruit and hire the types of technical experts that are needed to backstop the new activities; and (3) integrate the new activities into the existing program's ongoing management, financial, M&E, and communication systems.

Lesson 6:
Build the technical capacity of the program staff to support the new initiatives.

Recommendations:
- Before committing to a large-scale start-up to respond to new needs, anticipate the costs of a program from start to finish.
- Recruit and retain senior staff that have the requisite skills and experience in the new areas before committing to a larger-scale start-up.
- Train the field agents and community-based experts who deal directly with the beneficiaries in the new areas being supported.
- Ensure that qualified people are recruited and deployed for the key technical positions in new program areas.

Lesson 7:
Build flexibility into the design, culture, and communications of the program from the start so that new activities can be added and appropriately integrated into the program subsystems.

Recommendations:
- Consider ways that the concept of flexibility can be built into the program culture from the start so that new ideas from the pro-

gram's field office and management team are entertained and discussed.

- Adjust the M&E plan of a program to incorporate new initiatives, and update this process regularly based on lessons learned.
- Adjust the program's financial systems so that new line items can be added and fed into a central planning and accounting process.
- Develop a formal communication plan for the program to ensure that all partners, donors, and senior staff receive routine updates on the entire program.

Notes

1. The first nutrition officer, Henry Nsereko, was hired in January 2005. The second nutrition officer, Benon Musaasizi, joined the program in February 2006.

2. For a more detailed explanation of these new needs and how they evolved over the first eight years of the CSRL program, see Esther Matama, Benon Musaasizi, and Laura Byaruhanga, "Strategic Objective Three (SO3): Reduce Malnutrition Levels Among Women of Reproductive Age and Children," in Della E. McMillan, ed., *Sustainable Rural Livelihoods Program: Summative Monitoring and Evaluation (M&E) Report: 2005–2012,* Draft Report (Ames: Center for Sustainable Rural Livelihoods, Iowa State University, 2012), pp. 66–118.

3. In nutrition, the concept of positive deviance is a model of behavior change that uses a group approach to promote positive behavior change. This particular study was not a true research project since it had no control group for comparison.

4. They were later reimbursed for this from CSRL operating funds.

5. For more background on the rural development extensionists, community nutrition and health workers, and community-based trainers, see Chapter 5.

6. This third nutrition officer, Laura Byaruhanga, focused on the school lunch programs. A fourth nutrition officer, Esther Matama, who joined the program in August 2012, was responsible for providing technical support to staff, trainers, and the community in identifying and screening cases of malnourishment in the community for counseling and referrals.

7. For more information on the first NEC pilot program, see Matama, Musaasizi, and Byaruhanga, "Strategic Objective Three (SO3)," pp. 66–118.

8. Dorothy Masinde, Laura Byaruhanga and Gail Nonnecke, "Nutrition Education Programs," presentation to CSRL Executive Committee Meeting (Ames: ISU, September 24, 2014).

9. The original plan was that each extensionist and nutrition and health worker would receive two animals for demonstration purposes and breeding

stock. Each recipient received 1 male and 1 female pig or, for Muslims and other farmers not able to work with pigs, 100 birds per farmer.

10. Finishers are individuals who fatten livestock by providing appropriate feed and other conditions to prepare the animal for slaughter and eventual consumption.

11. In contrast to the earlier training sessions, which focused on basic restocking and on the new technologies, the focus of the commercial model activities program was on (1) training the more commercially oriented farmers on three key value chains; (2) facilitating the linkages that fulfilled the need for feed, buyers, and traders; (3) training the livestock marketing associations; and (4) facilitating farmers' access to collective marketing. This new commercial model for livestock production was developed through a series of four interlocking activities that included building public awareness of the model, providing value-chain training, fostering linkages, and helping organize marketing associations.

12. Nadiope Gideon is a veterinarian with extensive experience in animal science who grew up in Kamuli.

7

Leaving the Door Open to New Beneficiaries

Gail Nonnecke, Della E. McMillan,
Donald Kugonza, and Dorothy Masinde

In the course of executing a development program, new needs emerge as local leaders and communities become better known and relationships are developed. The partners' and benefactors' goals and priorities also are likely to change. Private benefactor funding gives programs greater options for responding to new opportunities as they emerge. Chapter 6 describes how the Center for Sustainable Rural Livelihoods (CSRL) program used private benefactor funding to scale up its nutrition and livestock activities. This chapter focuses on how the program used a similar model to pilot test and scale up a new prototype of service learning with university students. Service learning engages students in a three-part process: classroom preparation through explanation and analysis of theories and ideas; service activity that emerges from and informs classroom content; and structured reflection that ties the service experience back to specific learning goals.[1] These service-learning activities provide the vehicle for a new wing of CSRL activities that focus on increasing the agricultural knowledge of Kamuli's children, who will be its future farmers, and helping the local schools to develop more nutritious school lunches.

The challenges that CSRL faced in adjusting to these new opportunities and constraints were similar to those described in the previous chapter:

The authors wish to acknowledge the helpful input and contributions of David Acker and Lorna Michael Butler.

- Identifying new constraints and opportunities—creating a process that will encourage the identification of new beneficiary groups and the existing partners buying into the new initiatives;
- Pilot testing initiatives to address the new constraints and opportunities—developing and refining new methodologies for addressing the identified constraints and responding to new opportunities;
- Scaling up initiatives with additional funding—exploring ways to provide more sustained funding for the service-learning activities once the pilot tests show value; and
- Integrating the enhanced initiatives with other program components—integrating this set of activities into the program's ongoing systems for accounting, monitoring and evaluation (M&E), and communications in ways that increase the chances that they will be sustained both during and after the program.

Identifying New Constraints and Opportunities

Progressive Identification of New Institutional Partners in Kamuli

When the CSRL program was conceived, its principal focus was on developing a plan that would impact targeted Kamuli farmer participants and their families. In making this initial commitment, the founding benefactors were adamant that the program be hands-on and dedicated to results, not just an extension of the traditional international study abroad and faculty research programs of Iowa State University (ISU). For this reason, the initial program focused almost exclusively on a small, relatively restricted number of target farmers who were considered to be some of the poorest of the poor. Initially the goals did not include training or research opportunities for undergraduate or graduate students from either ISU or Makerere University (MAK).

With a few exceptions, this initial group of farmers was chosen to reflect a disproportionate number of the poorest of the poor who were left out of, or not able to participate in, the more conventional development activities supported by the Ugandan government or other organizations.

In the course of executing these activities, the program leaders and donors became aware of the broader cross-cutting needs of the surrounding communities that were likely to affect the sustainability of everything else that they were doing for the most vulnerable population groups. It was at this juncture that the CSRL team started thinking about what types of institution could enable it to affect the wider community. Since all of the communities had children enrolled in schools, the program began to look for ways that it could help strengthen the connection between the schools and the CSRL program. The local schools represented a new set of institutional partners beyond the existing partnership with Volunteer Efforts for Development Concerns (VEDCO) and MAK.

Progressive Identification of MAK and ISU Students as a New Beneficiary Group

During this period, ISU and MAK began to explore ways to strengthen the link between the program and their core mission of educating students.

In 2005, ISU was part of a national effort to internationalize university curricula. At that time, only 1 percent of all US undergraduate students studied abroad for academic credit. Of these, one-third chose locations outside of Western Europe, yet an estimated 95 percent of the world's population growth is expected to occur outside of that area in the next fifty years.[2] The ISU administration and faculty were aware that most of the university's study abroad programs reflected the trend at the time and initiated efforts to expand high-quality immersion programs in developing countries. Peer review and selection of a competitive grant application for funding validated the need to train students, many of whom would become future leaders in food and agriculture, about development activities in sub-Saharan Africa.

Another contextual issue was the growing national concern that the agricultural universities needed to reinvigorate the student experience through more hands-on partnerships with the general public.[3] This trend was being reinforced by a new elective classification of US universities that recognized community engagement through curricular engagement, outreach, and partnerships.[4]

Several ISU faculty members became interested in the concept of developing academic study abroad courses to create and enhance school gardens in the program communities to educate rural children about agriculture and provide a school-based gardening and lunch program. In 2005, they developed a United States Department of Agriculture (USDA) Higher Education Challenge Grant to support the development of two ISU study abroad, service-learning immersion programs that integrated multidisciplinary food and agriculture topics in Uganda and India.

About the same time, MAK began to require internships in some of their curricula, and a new partnership in support of experiential learning was seen as being valuable to the university. This new requirement was strongly influenced by MAK's experience with the Innovations at Makerere Committee (I@MAK), which began in 2001 as an initiative to enable the government, higher education, and community councils to work together to strengthen government capacity to support Uganda's antipoverty decentralization policy and service delivery by stimulating innovations in education and research. Educational programs were modified to improve students' capabilities for assisting with rural poverty. The pilot stage, which ended in 2006, was followed by another phase with partnerships between central government, higher education, the private sector, and local government councils with greater emphasis on innovations.[5]

The Role of Donor Interest in Getting the Program to Explore This New Opportunity

Finally, during a lunch in March 2004 following the biannual CSRL meeting of the management team with the founding benefactors, one of two lead donors who had helped found the program said, "Let's not talk about what you are doing now. Where are you going? What is the next big idea?" After a moment of silence, several faculty blurted out, "Students. Let's involve students in CSRL." The donors were clearly interested and encouraged the team to explore various ways that the CSRL program could strengthen its involvement of students.

Pilot Testing Initiatives to Address the New Constraints and Opportunities

The Initial Needs Assessment

In May 2005, grants from the ISU's Foreign Travel Grants Program, Henry A. Wallace Endowed Chair for Sustainable Agriculture, and office of the dean of the College of Agriculture were used to conduct an initial needs assessment mission.[6]

During his initial meeting with the assessment team, MAK dean of agriculture Mateete Bekunda reiterated his support for the program, which he felt would help MAK to develop and fund the types of student internship that were required for all undergraduate agricultural students. As an indication of his support, Bekunda assigned MAK lecturer

Bernard Obaa as the first MAK faculty adviser and granted permission for MAK students to participate in the program.

In November 2005, the service-learning needs assessment team presented the results of its participatory assessment to the founding benefactors. The assessment team indicated that a school garden program was feasible as a service-learning activity that could fulfill curricular requirements of both universities (see Box 7.1).

Box 7.1   Key Recommendations from the 2005 Reconnaissance Mission for the Service-Learning Program

---

Start-Up Resources Needed
- Inputs and technology (plants, seeds, tools, new technologies such as disease-free cultivars and planting stock)
- Water
- Technical information for site-specific plans

Organizational Considerations to Strengthen Program Impact
- Generating cuttings for distribution to children's homes or other schools
- Creating scholarships to pay school fees to students who participated in the school garden program
- Developing teaching materials and training
- Linking of the gardens to the school meals—typically, lunch
- Selling some garden crops or products to pay for school lunch costs
- Community support led by local officials, school administrators, and parents

Potential Constraints
- Access to land at school sites, garden tools, water, planting materials, other agricultural inputs (e.g., sprayers)
- Diversity and sequencing of crops for a balanced diet and continuous production
- Teachers or community might take food and children would not benefit

(continues)

Box 7.1 Continued

- Security during school breaks and holidays
- Fences to protect gardens from animals
- Labor availability during school breaks and for timely garden operations
- The students' negative attitude toward agriculture as a profession
- The students' negative attitude toward the school gardens because working in the garden had often been given as a form of punishment
- Management of a reasonable number of pupils in the garden to optimize hands-on learning
- Lack of animal projects due to acquisition, space, feed, and maintenance costs
- Preservice and in-service training of teachers
- Lack of any curriculum guides on school garden programs for teachers
- The teachers' insufficient knowledge of agriculture, food preparation, and nutrition
- Lack of school, community, and interministerial support or facilities for cooking and storing food
- Availability of fuel wood and a cook

Source: David Acker, Grace Marquis, Dorothy Masinde, and Gail Nonnecke, "Key Elements of a School Gardening and Feeding Program: Kamuli District School Gardens Plans Resulting from Participatory Visit," unpubl. report (Ames: Center for Sustainable Rural Livelihoods, Iowa State University, September 27, 2005).

During the presentation, which focused on the constraints analysis and resource requirements of the service-learning component, it became clear that water availability was a critical constraint at some of the schools. Specifically, the presentation highlighted (1) that primary schools needed agricultural tools, supplies, and a source of water for the gardens to thrive; (2) that children should not spend precious time or energy walking to and from a local borehole (water hole or well) or river to gather water for crops; and (3) that two children in Namasagali had drowned while gathering water from the Nile River for their families just before the team arrived.

Based on this analysis, CSRL's founding benefactors agreed to finance a one-year pilot service-learning program in the Namasagali primary school as well as fund a new borehole.[7] The borehole was deemed necessary to ensure that the school had a more secure water supply. This first borehole catalyzed a whole new initiative within CSRL—to solicit continuing donor support for borehole construction at schools and in communities where there is an insecure potable water supply.[8]

Design Appropriate Curriculum and Support Systems

The next step was recruiting the first group of students and designing an appropriate curriculum.

Faculty Advisers. Once the benefactors agreed to fund the first service-learning mission and a new borehole, the two colleges of agriculture selected the faculty advisers and faculty support staff. In each case, department and college administrators endorsed the faculty members' participation. Faculty worked with their department chairs to determine how teaching of the service-learning courses fit into their position responsibilities.

Student Grants. In contrast to traditional study abroad programs where students and their families pay the entire cost of their participation, ISU offered a competitive study abroad program fee.[9] Each student's total cost was offset by a scholarship from the private gift funds; thereby, students paid part of the study abroad costs and tuition fees. The conditions for the ISU service-learning study abroad program were advertised during the 2005 fall semester, with student applications and interviews completed by the end of the semester. A similar process was used to select the first group of MAK service-learning students. MAK students incurred no costs for their participation; all costs were paid by the CSRL service-learning endowment, including the lecturer's stipend.

Curriculum Requirements for ISU Students. The ISU study abroad structure was course based and met the ISU international requirements for students. The commitment was for one year that was divided into three course segments: (1) predeparture orientation (one semester at ISU, one credit hour); (2) study abroad service-learning program (one month, later extended to six weeks, in Kamuli, four credit hours); and (3) postprogram study and outreach (one semester at ISU, one credit hour).

Curriculum Requirements for MAK Students. The MAK students' enrollment in service learning satisfied the MAK College of Agricultural and Environmental Sciences (CAES) requirement that each student complete an internship. Currently, MAK students pay a fee each semester, which is then provided to the students as a $150 scholarship to offset the costs of completing an unpaid internship. MAK students participating in the service-learning program receive the scholarship but, because their living and transportation costs are paid by the ISU gift funds, they are able to use the $150 for scholastic materials in their degree program.

The first year of the service-learning program (2006) was a pilot year with participating students from MAK having completed most of their curricular requirements. After the pilot year, a change was instituted that allowed MAK students to remain in the Kamuli for ten weeks to fulfill the internship requirement of their curriculum. Over the next four years, the length of the program for ISU students was extended to approximately six weeks in the summer to allow for time in Uganda to enhance team building and program activities of the newly formed binational service-learning student team.

Housing. In the first three years of the program (the summers of 2006, 2007, and 2008), students and faculty lived in a house at the local high school, Namasagali College. Several ISU students cited the experience of living with their MAK colleagues in a dorm facing the Nile River with no electricity, running water, or Internet connections —and having to walk one mile to and from the school where they worked—as one of the most memorable bonding and transformative experiences of their lives.

In 2009, CSRL began to lodge the students in the CSRL guesthouse in Kamuli town, which provided access to electricity, running water, Internet connections, and supplies. Given the greater distances involved from the town to the rural schools, the students traveled to and remained at the schools for the entire day for program efficiency.

Orientation for ISU Students. Once the ISU students were accepted into the program, they were required to enroll in a one-semester orientation class that introduced them to the concept of sustainable livelihoods and rural economic development. They were also given a broad overview of the CSRL program and some of the technical and personal issues they were likely to confront when traveling and living internationally. The service-learning faculty members taught the orientation course with help from other ISU faculty, including those with direct involvement in the CSRL's field activities. By midsemester, ISU and MAK students communicated with each other electronically through e-mail and social media, and began discussions about the current status of the school garden program and its related projects.

Each spring, the ISU students staged a series of fund-raisers to collect cash and in-kind donations for the schools where they would be working. This enabled the students to arrive with much-needed school materials like pencils, erasers, pencil sharpeners, maps, notebooks, and soccer balls as well as funds for some of the tools and construction materials needed for their larger projects.

Orientation for MAK Students. The MAK faculty and CSRL field program manager completed the orientation for the MAK service-learning students. The students attended an orientation seminar every two weeks throughout the semester, including a four-day immersion experience in Kamuli, with visits to program schools and selected farms.

Binational Service-Learning Group Projects. The ISU and MAK students were organized into binational teams in the predeparture orientation classes. Each binational student team (1) completed a project that benefited the primary school, its children, and their families; (2) contributed labor and technical expertise to the school garden; (3) assisted in teaching primary school subjects of integrated science (agriculture, nutrition, sanitation); (4) worked with local farmers on the farmers' enterprise(s); (5) lived together in dormitory-style housing; and (6) visited the local community for cultural events and shopping for everyday needs.

To strengthen the partnership capacity of the school administrators, the program added a new activity in June 2012 that focused on mentoring the primary school teachers. Faculty from ISU and MAK offered a training course on agriculture that included head teachers and agriculture teachers from the five schools and district officials from the Ministry of Education. The workshop emphasized the theory and pedagogy of using experiential learning in agriculture instruction at primary schools.

Postservice Training and Outreach. At the end of the field season, each binational team presented a summary of its activities and projects at the local level to the VEDCO staff, Kamuli government personnel, and MAK faculty and administration just prior to the departure of the ISU students from Uganda.

Binational team reports by ISU students. Each ISU service-learning student prepared a binational team report, including personal reflections, and participated in a university-wide seminar highlighting their activities and accomplishments.

Each student was encouraged to speak to ISU undergraduate classes and share lessons learned with the university community. The twenty students who participated in the program during 2011–2013 and responded to the January 2014 service-learning survey reported that they (1) spoke to forty-four classes that were attended by approximately 1,300 students; (2) used knowledge gained in the service-learning program in Uganda to help interpret material in 105 other university classes; (3) presented thirty-three papers and posters at four different professional meetings, including the annual World Food Prize Norman E. Borlaug Lecture Poster Session on the ISU campus; (4) spoke at seven meetings in which program donors were present; and (5) organized four fund-raising activities to benefit CSRL activities in Kamuli.[10]

Binational team reports by MAK students. Each fall semester, the MAK service-learning students presented their internship activities and findings to MAK's college faculty and students. The college-wide students' seminar, comprised of current and sometimes former service learners, is among the most highly attended academic events of the college.

The MAK service-learning students also have implemented a number of outreach activities: (1) a three-day return visit during the fall semester during which the students visit school gardens and binational projects at the primary schools and local farmers' compounds, locations where the university students had completed work during their internship; (2) discussions with Kamuli school teachers about sustaining the accomplishments of the gardens and team projects; (3) organization of a one-day farmer's field day at the Nakanyonyi primary school; and (4) informal talks with other students in CAES.

In September and October of 2009, the program started a visiting scholars program that has hosted nine former MAK service-learning students for two months at ISU.[11] Since 2010, the program has drawn on some of the most successful MAK service-learning students who completed their baccalaureate degrees to mentor the other students in subsequent years.

Scaling Up the Initiatives with Additional Funding

The first three years of the program were funded through a separate appeal, which was made at the CSRL executive committee meeting each October, during which the service-learning coordinator provided a brief overview of the recent service-learning activities. In a separate poster session for donors and college administration, individual students presented their team projects. The enthusiasm of the early groups of ISU students was contagious. Their heartfelt debriefings to the benefactors and interviews in the ISU alumnae magazine fueled a steady expansion of the types of activities and the student numbers.

A critical turning point in the service-learning activities occurred in December 2008 when the two lead donors who funded the core development program continued their support through a separate endowment for the service-learning activities. Once this endowment was created, the faculty could make longer-term plans for the student projects and the schools. In May 2013, the same benefactors expanded the service-learning endowment. Because the service-learning funds were established outside of the main endowment that funds core CSRL activities, they have been managed through a separate budget line.

Even with this expansion, the total cost of the service-learning component of the program has remained low—about $4,500 per student for twenty-six students and five faculty members.[12] This amount includes expenses paid for all transportation to, from, and within Uganda; housing; food for all ISU and MAK students and faculty; the twelve-month salary, including benefits, of the VEDCO staff person who works in the school garden programs; the cost of the garden plots; supplies and maintenance; and all binational team projects.

Integrating the Enhanced Initiatives with Other Program Components

Monitoring and Evaluation

From the start, the service-learning component of the CSRL program has kept meticulous records on each student's activities and group projects. In addition, the service-learning faculty members complete annual focus group assessments and an analysis of students' reflective writings to determine student learning and program effectiveness. The design of these participatory assessment tools was facilitated by ISU's Center for Excellence in Learning and Teaching. Each October, a brief summary of these assessments, as well as of the students' activities, has been presented to the CSRL benefactors.

Although the service-learning program assessed learning outcomes, for several reasons these assessments were not integrated into the core M&E system of CSRL. The initial and continuous assessments were academic in nature and focused on improving the design and quality of the service-learning program and courses, not CSRL's rural development activities. Another reason was that the initial M&E system (see Chapter 8) was designed before the service-learning activities were started, and continued to use the same survey format and indicators to be comparative. Thus, many of the outcomes of the service-learning community outreach activities were not captured.

The CSRL program formulated a five-year—as opposed to annual—strategic plan in October 2013. This plan, codesigned by MAK service-learning faculty adviser Donald Kugonza and the ISU service-learning faculty advisers, includes five strategic goals for service learning[13] and a separate M&E plan to track the progress toward the execution of these goals and their anticipated outputs.

Sustaining MAK's Commitment to Service Learning

The CSRL service-learning model remains heavily dependent on CSRL donor funding. For MAK to scale the model up, it needs to find internships sites willing to take teams of students as well as ways to obtain faculty and staff support for visiting and evaluating the teams of students. In a country like Uganda, the issues come down to funding.

One of the principal challenges is for the partners to work together to help MAK fund teams of students to be placed into excellent internship opportunities, regardless of the Uganda location. If MAK is able to attract the generosity of private businesses or philanthropic organizations to support the undergraduate team-based internships, it should be possible to scale up the service-learning model, adapted to MAK's needs, beyond CSRL's current areas of intervention.

Sustaining the School Lunch Program

The conditions for sustaining the school gardens and the improved lunch program that it supports are not yet in place. This is still highly dependent on the full-time VEDCO employees for basic leadership. During the next five years, the CSRL program will try to help the schools and parent-teacher associations sustain the activities. Meanwhile, there is increasing evidence that the communities associated with the primary schools where the service-learning program has been involved are beginning to take greater responsibility for the provision of school lunches (see Box 7.2).

Box 7.2 Early Evidence of the Impacts of the CSRL Service-Learning Program on Children and Their Schools

In Kamuli, climatic conditions for rainfall are unreliable, soil quality is low, pest incidence is high, and availability of tolerant or resistant crop cultivars is low. The growing conditions are less than optimal, and consistent products from the school garden are insufficient for a year-long, daily school lunch program.

In a recent study, CSRL-VEDCO community nutritionist Laura Byaruhanga found that children in Kamuli consume about 1,070 kilocalories per day, compared to 2,000 to 3,000 kilocalories per day recommended for children in this age group. Of the kilocalories consumed on average each day by the children, 79 percent are from the school lunch alone. When the nutrient-dense lunch was introduced in 2010, it was supported 100 percent by the CSRL program. Today, through garden outputs and parents' contributions, the CSRL program's contribution is 34 percent, with outputs from the gardens at 32 percent and parents' contributions at 34 percent. As garden productivity increases through improved horticultural, agronomic, and pest management practices, the CSRL program's contribution toward the cost of the lunch will continue to decrease. Since part of the output from the garden is reinvested into the gardens, the overall cost of the school lunch program to CSRL is less.

The contributions of the school garden and parents have improved the quality and diversity of the children's diet. Two of the four service-learning primary schools are on the verge of having a self-sustaining, nutritionally balanced school lunch program. Over 350 children at one school used to have an occasional 50-calorie lunch comprised of a dilute maize porridge. Currently, they are eating a solid meal of maize, beans, and vegetables with iodized salt and vegetable oil added; eggs are served once per week. The nutritional lunch provides about 850 calories. In a second school, the same meal is consumed twice a week by over 600 children, with the goal of increasing it to every school day.

Source: E-mail communications between Laura Byaruhanga, Dorothy Masinde, and Gail Nonnecke, January 26, 2014.

CSRL is still leading the program, but the vast majority of the schools in the district are not involved in the school garden and lunch programs. CSRL currently works with five primary schools in Kamuli out of a total of approximately 365 primary schools.[14]

Early Evidence of Impact

Student-Level Impact

University Students. Fifty-six ISU and seventy-three MAK undergraduate students had directly participated in the service-learning program as of 2013. As of 2013, fourteen MAK students had come back as service-learning mentors and eleven MAK students had gone to ISU as interns since that new phase of activities started in 2009.

Program records indicate that service-learning students are choosing training at the Doctor of Philosophy (PhD) or Master of Science (MS) level in food and agriculture areas: (1) twenty-two (58 percent) ISU service-learning students have entered graduate or professional school soon after their graduation as of 2013; and (2) twenty (49 percent) MAK students who participated in the service-learning program have entered graduate or professional school after their graduation as of 2013.

School Students. Abundant anecdotal evidence and a few quantitative studies—completed mostly by graduate students—suggest the CSRL service-learning activities to date have (1) improved child nutrition by helping build students' and parents' awareness of nutrient-dense foods—fruits and vegetables; (2) strengthened the quality of the existing school lunch programs in two schools (Namasagali and Nakanyoni); (3) transferred agriculture, health, and sanitation knowledge and skills to children and their families; (4) helped improve primary school children's and leaders' attitudes about opportunities in agriculture, working in the school gardens, and working in the family fields; (5) provided information on nutrient-dense vegetable or grain crops and higher-yielding production techniques that helped several students to develop small gardens on their own, which have helped to pay secondary school fees; (6) generated food for school lunches, planting materials for the children, and teaching about agriculture—all contributing to more sustainable school lunches and knowledge transfer to children and their families; and (7) sold high-value garden products to assist in purchasing inputs for school lunches.

One of the most important impacts, which distinguishes the CSRL school garden activities from other school garden programs, is the model of raising high-value crops and animal products to be sold to purchase additional inputs for a nutritionally balanced school lunch throughout the school year. Another noteworthy outcome is the positive impact of the school lunch program on children's diets, and the increasing importance of the garden produce in helping to decrease its costs (see Box 7.2).

While these school lunch programs are highly dependent on CSRL support, the center hopes to make them more autonomous in the future. If they are successful, CSRL and others can adapt the model for Uganda and for school lunch programs in other low-income food insecure areas.

Program-Level Impacts

The development of the service-learning component has helped to transform the traditional model of school gardens into a more holistic food, agriculture, and health program within the schools and surrounding communities, and has highlighted the critical importance of clean drinking water and irrigation for the schools. It has also played a role in creating the student-led Establish and Grow Fund, which provides a mechanism for service-learning students and their families—as well as other students at ISU—to support the CSRL nutrition education center in Uganda,[15] and has provided a lobby for strengthening CSRL's emphasis on human nutrition (see Chapter 6).

Community-Level Impact

In Uganda and Kamuli. The involvement of ISU and MAK faculty and students in the school garden program has helped validate the program to the local education authorities, participating students, and their parents. An indirect consequence of having university students involved in the community is providing the children and their parents with positive role models for agriculture as a profession.

Recent research, discussed in Box 7.2, suggests that there may be potential for schools that actively participate in a school garden program to achieve a self-sustaining, nutritionally balanced school lunch program over time. While this possibility needs further study, it could be highly important to the schools and the community.

At ISU. From 2011 to 2014, the service-learning students conducted thirty-three presentations outside of a class setting, and a wide variety of university and alumnae publications carried articles about individual students and the program at large. All of this community outreach and publicity has helped build internal university and external alumnae donor support for the CSRL program in general and international studies in particular (see Chapter 9).

Lessons Learned and Recommendations

This chapter has highlighted the fact that the CSRL service-learning program faced many of the same challenges that confronted the livestock and human nutrition programs in Chapter 6:

- Identifying new constraints and opportunities;
- Pilot testing initiatives to address the new constraints and opportunities;
- Scaling up the initiatives with additional funding; and
- Integrating enhanced initiatives with other program components.

There was, however, an important difference since both livestock and human nutrition were part of the original program. This meant that the chief challenge was pilot testing new initiatives to scale up what was already under way. In contrast, the service-learning program involved the addition a completely new set of activities involving university and primary students and some new institutional partners such as the primary schools.

The fact that CSRL's service-learning program supported two existing school district initiatives—school lunches and school gardens—was critical to building the local school district's interest in the program. Having the program associated with an ongoing community-based program was also an advantage. Had the CSRL program not existed, the ISU and MAK service-learning team would have had to identify local partners to help develop the program. Without the connection to existing benefactors, fund-raising to get the program started would probably have taken much longer. Having VEDCO's continuity in the communities also helps to maintain the people's interest in the program throughout the year.

Strengths of the CSRL service-learning curriculum include: (1) its organization into three distinct phases: orientation, service learning, and after service learning; (2) the strong involvement of both MAK and ISU as team leaders and student mentors; (3) its binational nature; (4) its partnership approach, which relied heavily on partnering with a Ugandan nongovernmental organization (NGO); (5) its heavy emphasis on using local experts and cultural guides to orient students and faculty members and create bridges to the community; (6) its strong central administrative support; and (7) its trust in—and relative autonomy of— staff from partner institutions that lead the program.

This structuring of the curriculum and scholarships helped CSRL minimize the typical problems of study abroad programs such as student culture shock or drop out. To date, no student has been asked to go home or been forced to return home because of an accident or inappropriate behavior. The same organization has helped minimize some of the in-country and postservice adjustment problems that characterize many global immersion experiences on return to the United States. Having a clear curricular model for the ISU students made it easier for ISU to engage MAK in adapting its preexisting model for student internships to the service-learning model.

The chief weakness of the CSRL system was that it focused on the collection and analysis of the data that the program leadership needs to ensure compliance with the three educational partners' rules and regulations for courses, curriculum, and risk management. This decision had two important consequences: (1) it meant that it has made it difficult to track the substantial impact that some of these activities have had on some of the larger program objectives, and (2) it did not establish a system for tracking the broader long-term impact of service learning on the lives of the participating students.

To address these two issues, CSRL recently adopted its first strategic plan for service learning in January 2014. That plan identifies a simple list of indicators to track the program's progress toward the achievement of five major objectives over the next five years.

Identifying New Constraints and Opportunities

When the CSRL program was conceived, its principal focus was on developing a program that would benefit a small group of vulnerable households that were experiencing extreme food and income insecurity. In the course of executing these activities, the program leaders and benefactors became aware of the broader cross-cutting needs of the surrounding communities and their institutions. They were also thinking about more permanent institutions to which they could connect to help sustain certain community-based interventions. During this same time period, ISU and MAK started looking for ways to strengthen the connections between the program and their core mission of educating students. The program was also under pressure from the lead benefactors to come up with "the next big idea."

> **Lesson 1:**
> Develop a flexible program structure that can accommodate the addition of new program beneficiaries if and when they can strengthen the core impact of the program.

Recommendations:
- Encourage staff and beneficiaries to identify new groups of beneficiaries for program activities.
- Consider adding service-learning and university students to established community-based programs.
- Involve all of the existing partners in the initial discussions about whether or not to add new beneficiary groups.
- Allow enough time to determine if and how all of the partners will be affected by the addition of new beneficiaries.
- Decide up front what mechanisms will be put in place to manage the new activities without detracting from the core mission of the partnership.

Pilot Testing Initiatives to Address the New Constraints and Opportunities

CSRL's willingness to support the pilot tests for service learning helped the program explore different educational partners, which enabled the program to choose the most appropriate initial pilot test sites carefully and to link the program to an established initiative in the same area.

The same pilot tests helped the program develop a well-balanced curriculum before scaling up and made sure that it was compatible with ISU and MAK requirements.

> **Lesson 2:**
> Screen potential partners carefully to ensure that each partner has a solid vested interest in the service-learning activity's success.

Recommendations:

- Design service-learning programs that provide service and added value to the ongoing activities of the educational institution as well as the overarching development program.
- Support service-learning activities that complement and are not competitive with the mainstream activities of the educational institutions and development programs they support.
- Ensure that the service-learning activities are supervised by the staff of any and all educational institutions and the development programs they are designed to support.
- Anticipate the need to have a small number of program staff dedicated to service learning.

Lesson 3:
Execute the student program so that it complies with the partner institutions' curriculum, mission, and risk management strategies.

Recommendations:

- Link international students with students from the country or area where the program is being executed.
- Link service-learning programs to existing academic curricula, including the rules and regulations for academic courses and internships.
- Make sure that the students have safe places to live.
- Make sure that the service-learning program complies with all of the risk management rules and regulations of the participating institutions.
- Screen all applicants carefully to ensure their suitability for the program.
- Insist that all students participate in a rigorous predeparture orientation course that provides background information on the issues they are likely to experience and projects they are to complete.
- Help students process any stress or cultural adjustment issues by having regular group discussions in the field.
- Require all students to participate in a postservice course that helps them process and write up their experience.
- Encourage student outreach to promote appropriate processing of their experience and pride in their accomplishments.

Lesson 4:
Facilitate the students' after service-learning efforts to keep them engaged in the program.

Recommendations:
- Anticipate student-led initiatives in the initial design, including how these student-led initiatives may need to be mentored.
- Encourage students to form student-led alumnae groups.
- Encourage the program to manage the student-generated funds, even if the dollar amount is small.

Lesson 5:
Consider ways to reduce student costs to ensure wider participation.

Recommendations:
- Encourage benefactors and businesses to sponsor individual students.
- Require students to report back to donors on lessons learned from their experience and the impacts on their education and career choices.
- Develop stable methods of funding service learning through the creation of a funded endowment or private business sponsorships once the core curriculum has been defined and pilot tested.

Lesson 6:
When partnering with government bodies or agencies (e.g., school, medical, or health facilities), strengthen the capacity of the local organization to manage and sustain associated service-learning activities.

Recommendations:
- Conduct baseline training and retraining of the administrators and staff in the key areas where the service-learning program is operating.
- Build the capacity of any committees that oversee the institutions with which the service-learning program is collaborating—such as parent-teacher associations for schools or community health

and sanitation committees for local health facilities—so that they participate in the design, execution, and monitoring of the activities, including systems that can help these oversight groups to self-assess their capacity in key areas.
- Provide detailed briefings before and after service-learning activities to make sure that the government officials who oversee the local institutions supported by the service-learning program understand the activities and their compliance with the institution's mission and rules for risk management.

Scaling Up the Initiatives with Additional Funding

The CSRL experience shows how adding a service-learning component to an established program can encourage deeper connections with existing benefactors and energize an existing program with new ideas. The original benefactors were attracted to the idea that the program was trying out new ideas. It was these same private benefactors who provided the seed money to test the model before scaling it up to an ongoing five-year program. The founding benefactors' seed funding helped attract other benefactors. Some of the new benefactors were willing to fund ISU and MAK students or support complementary projects like the boreholes.[16] Once the CSRL students returned to ISU and MAK, they became an important lobby for the program and new initiatives and funding.

Lesson 7:
Develop creative ways that private benefactor support can be used to design, pilot test, and scale up service learning.

Recommendations:
- Ask benefactors about their interest in adding some activities that target university students or local students in the area being affected once a program is semiestablished and focused.
- If benefactors are interested, consider soliciting a small privately supported needs assessment and design mission before embarking on the activities.
- Solicit donor interest in funding a one- to two-year pilot program that can help refine the program and key partnerships before incorporating the service-learning program into the core endowment.

- Mainstream the support for service learning into the core endowment once the program has been refined and the core curriculum, leadership, and partnerships defined.

Integrating the Enhanced Initiatives with Other Program Components

Since the service-learning activities were added later, they had their own tracking system. The CSRL experiences highlight the critical importance of tracking the execution and impact of the service-learning activities during and after the pilot programs were completed as part of the program's overall M&E plan. This system should track the execution of the service-learning activities as well as their impact on the program and the students' lives and career choices.

> **Lesson 8:**
> **Document the direct and indirect impacts of service learning over time.**

Recommendations:
- Develop an initial list of indicators that can be used to track the students' activities, their outputs, and their impacts on the current program, which can be updated and revised as the program is conceived, continued, and expanded.
- Identify an initial list of indicators that can be used to track the service-learning program's wider impacts on the participants and the involved communities.
- Develop a service-learning M&E subplan that describes the methodologies that will be used to collect and analyze this data.
- Consider ways that graduate student and faculty research studies can collect and analyze some of the data that the program needs to track these indicators and the broader impact of the program.
- Produce reports, papers, and case studies on this data, and share the findings with the partners and beneficiaries.

Notes

1. Julie S. Johnson-Pynn, "Success and Challenges in East African Conservation Education," *Journal of Environmental Education* 36, no. 2 (2005): 25–39; Janet Eyler and Dwight E. Giles, *Where's the Learning in Service Learning?* (San Francisco: Jossey-Bass, 1999), 1–22, 64, 165–185, 194, 195.

2. National Association of State Universities and Land-Grant Colleges (NASULGC) Task Force on International Education, *A Call to Leadership: The Presidential Role in Internationalizing the University* (Washington, DC: NASULGC, 2004).

3. Ibid.

4. Carnegie Foundation for the Advancement of Teaching, "IU Research Center to House Carnegie Classification of Institutions of Higher Education," News Release (Carnegie Foundation for the Advancement of Teaching, Washington, DC, October 8, 2014).

5. The Rockefeller Foundation initially funded I@MAK, followed by a loan from the World Bank's International Development Association (IDA) and grants from the Rockefeller Foundation and the Carnegie Corporation. Some of the outcomes increased education and training for government employees; enhanced research performance of faculty members; supported undergraduate student internships to central and local governments, NGOs, the private sector, and other agencies; and established several decentralized learning centers equipped with information and communication technologies (ICT). For information on this program, see Karen Theroux, "Makerere at the Crossroads," *Carnegie Reporter* 4, no. 1 (2006); Makerere University, *Makerere University Annual Report (2007)* (Kampala: Makerere University, 2007), pp. 1–29; Department of Open and Distance Learning, School of Distance and Lifelong Learning, Makerere University, "Distance Education," (Kampala: Makerere University website, 2014); Samwiri Katunguka, "The Learning Innovations Loan Funding Towards Capacity Building for Decentralization in Uganda," paper presented at a World Bank workshop on the organization and management of innovation funds, Maputo, Mozambique, October 11–13, 2005.

6. The team then (1) met with the dean of agriculture and faculty members at MAK as well as officials at the Ministries of Agriculture, Education, and Health in Entebbe and Kampala; (2) met with VEDCO's executive director and staff; (3) visited schools with and without school garden programs in Luwero and Kamuli; (4) gathered ideas on the elements of successful school garden programs, along with beneficial outcomes and constraints; and (5) conducted a participatory workshop with twenty-two current stakeholders, including Kamuli officials, representatives from the Ministry of Education, other elected officials, local primary school administrators, and teachers, parents, and VEDCO staff working in Kamuli.

7. In contrast to traditional open wells, which are only about 12 meters (40 feet) in depth, a borehole well uses a slender shaft to go much deeper, for example, between 60 and 73 meters (200–240 feet) in the Kamuli area. Since borehole construction requires special equipment, borehole wells are more expensive to build than traditional wells. This initial support for $75,000 was for one year. The agreement anticipated that, at the end of that period, the team would review the impact of the program as a basis for determining whether this was an appropriate model for service learning.

8. The district water officer and local communities or school officials determine borehole locations. A water users committee is trained to manage and maintain the new water source. Because of their depth, they provide a protected

water supply, which is less likely to harbor microorganisms. Communities contribute about $300 toward the borehole cost, some of which goes to the district water account and the remainder to the community borehole account. The current cost of establishing one borehole in Kamuli is about $15,000. The first borehole was installed in 2006, and a total of fourteen boreholes had been installed as of 2012. At least eight are situated near primary schools. A borehole supplies between 10,000 and 40,000 liters of safe drinking water per day.

9. During the first year of the service-learning program, each ISU College of Agriculture and Life Sciences (CALS) student participant paid a program fee of $500; the student cost has increased since this time. Participating students from other ISU colleges pay a higher fee, but often their colleges or departments help to cover the costs.

10. These numbers are based on an e-mail survey conducted by the faculty leaders in January 2014, to which twenty of the twenty-three participants in 2011–2013 responded.

11. During their visit, each scholar is attached to an ISU faculty member who facilitates the student's learning experiences in their discipline.

12. Based on the total cost of the program divided by all of the ISU and MAK students, using 2013 data.

13. The strategic goals for the next five-year phase of service learning are (1) build a service-learning facility; (2) increase the impact on more students; (3) increase MAK and ISU faculty engagement; (4) increase community engagement; and (5) develop a plan for succession.

14. Republic of Uganda, "Kamuli District Local Government Five Year Strategic Plan, Orphans and Other Vulnerable Children Programme, Fiscal Year 2008/09–2012/13," Kamuli, Uganda (April 2008). The early years of CSRL's service-learning initiative focused on two Kamuli primary schools— Namasagali and Nakanyonyi primary schools. Activities at these schools included classroom education, school gardens, school lunch programs, and other types of support, including the construction of wells (boreholes), which serve both the schools and surrounding communities, and construction and improvement of some school buildings and facilities. For example, a girls' boarding dormitory, latrines, and a school kitchen were built at Namasagali Primary School, and a teachers' house and latrine were constructed at Nakanyonyi Primary School in 2014. Work with these two schools continues. Beginning in 2011 the CSRL program started at additional schools: Namasagali College Staff's Children's Primary School (2011), Naluwoli Primary School (2012), and Namasagali College (2013). A school lunch program was introduced at Naluwoli primary school in 2014. In 2013, a youth entrepreneurship initiative, involving poultry care and production and vegetable production and marketing, was introduced at the secondary school, Namasagali College.

15. CSRL and CSRL-VEDCO employees founded the CSRL program's first Nutrition Education Center in 2011 (see Chapter 6). A former community nutrition and health volunteer houses the program in the compound of her home. The program began with about twenty-five young mothers who needed assistance with, and knowledge about, feeding and caring for their malnourished infants. By 2014, it has evolved to six additional satellite women's sup-

port groups that are mentored by graduates of the program who train and assist more young mothers.

16. Having the CSRL community-based program already in place made it easy to add separate budget lines so that these funds could be tracked and reported on to the other donors by the ISU Foundation. Many of these new donors—who often were businesspeople—were attracted by the low cost of the activities and the fact that individual donors could see a visible return to the students, the community, and the wider university within a short period of time. The donors also were impressed that MAK and ISU students had to compete for program acceptance and scholarships, and by CSRL's efforts to ensure that at the end of the term they were properly thanked and debriefed by each student they had supported. A significant number of the service-learning donors went on to fund larger CSRL initiatives based on their positive experience with the service-learning students and activities.

8

Tracking Progress and Planning for the Future

Haroon Sseguya and Della E. McMillan

Everyone wants a successful program. One of the best ways to learn if a program's efforts are making a difference is to track what is being done. Which elements are working? Which elements are not working? Which elements should be strengthened and expanded and which should not? Tracking a program's progress should help lead to good decisions.

This chapter provides a brief overview of some of the creative ways that the Center for Sustainable Rural Livelihoods (CSRL) program responded to the special challenges of designing—and redesigning—its tracking system:

- Developing a flexible start-up monitoring and evaluation plan and related training programs—creating a flexible monitoring and evaluation (M&E) plan and training needed to carry it out will ensure that programs can be scaled up and down as new activities, partners, and interventions are added or deleted;
- Defining baseline measurements and planning—determining what types of information the program will need as a basis for measuring future impact;
- Monitoring program execution and outputs—determining the type of program information that is needed to monitor the execution of specific activities in ways that inform decisionmaking;

The authors wish to acknowledge the helpful input and contributions of Jane Sempa, Muhammad Senkumba, and Kato Steven.

- Periodic objective measuring and assessing of program outcomes and impacts—assessing as systematically and objectively as possible the five main aspects of an intervention—its relevance, effectiveness, efficiency, impact, and sustainability—to improve the program;
- Reporting to different audiences—disseminating results of the program's M&E activities to the program administrators, donors, and beneficiaries who need them to inform strategic planning and action; and
- Setting up and maintaining program documents—organizing annotated bibliographies and filing systems to document the summative impact of the program and the lessons learned for different audiences.

Monitoring and Evaluation System: 2004–2008

The Baseline Participatory Rural Appraisal

The CSRL program began implementing its activities in Kamuli in September 2004. Since CSRL did not have preconceived ideas for the types of activity that it would support, the management team decided that the program needed a full review of the local livelihood systems as a basis for strategic planning.[1]

To assist with this process, the leadership team decided to execute a baseline participatory rural appraisal (PRA),[2] which is a methodology that enables local people to assess their own situations and identify solutions that may improve them (see Chapter 5). The CSRL appraisal was designed and executed by a Makerere University (MAK) junior lecturer and an Iowa State University (ISU) senior sociology professor,[3] with extensive input from all partners. It used standard PRA methodologies,[4] resulting in an action plan for the first year of the program.

Two critical pre-PRA steps involved the preparation of a data collection guide and a training workshop for field staff. The actual appraisal was conducted over a four-week period in early 2005 in thirty-two villages in the six parishes where the program planned to focus.[5] The research team collected two types of data from the group meetings: (1) information about the local communities' access to different types of agriculture, nutrition and health services, local institutions, and gender roles and relations;[6] and (2) community-generated profiles describing the percentage of households that fit into different categories of wealth, nutrition, health status, and food security, and what types of intervention would be needed to reduce the percentage of households in the lowest ranking of each of these four categories.

After data collection, a joint analysis of the community-level data was conducted, followed by the development of a parish-level action plan for the coming year. Based on the results of the baseline PRA, the senior managers associated with the three principal program partners proposed three priority objectives for the program's first multiyear strategic plan: (1) enhancing food production; (2) enhancing community nutrition and health; and (3) building the capacity of the local farmers' groups to design and execute appropriate interventions. A second tier of priority needs—such as enhancing access to water, credit, income-generating opportunities, and markets—were tabled for a later date.

The Program's First Monitoring and Evaluation Plan

Once the CSRL program started to execute its first multiyear strategic plan in early 2005, it also put in place the program's first M&E system, consisting of three broad categories of M&E activities with different audiences for reporting. This original plan was presented as a table in the final report of the baseline PRA (Table 8.1).

Field Activity Monitoring. An M&E assistant was tasked with the development of the standard templates needed to track the rollout of the program's activities and the compilation of a monthly progress report based on the analysis of this data for the Volunteer Efforts for Development Concerns (VEDCO) regional team leader in Kamuli and the CSRL program (Activity 1, Table 8.1).

Participatory Monitoring and Evaluation System. The M&E assistant was also responsible for the CSRL participatory monitoring and evaluation (PM&E) system, which focused on the organization of a series of stakeholders' meetings. Several levels of participatory review and planning sessions were organized at different levels of the program intervention area, including (Activities 2–5, Table 8.1):

- Quarterly zonal meetings (covering two to three contiguous villages) to monitor the work of the community-based volunteers (i.e., the rural development extensionists and community nutrition and health workers);
- Quarterly parish-level meetings to deliberate issues coming up from groups, extensionists, and nutrition and health workers;

Table 8.1 Monitoring and Evaluation Plan for the CSRL Program, 2004–2008

Activity	Level	Frequency	Participants	Responsibility for Data Collection	Documentation
Field activity monitoring					
1. Field activity monitoring	Household/group	Weekly or monthly	Household and group members	VEDCO technical staff with help from the CSRL M&E assistant	Monthly reports submitted to CSRL and VEDCO
Participatory monitoring and evaluation system					
2. Community-based volunteer monitoring meetings	Zone	Quarterly	Rural development extensionists and community nutrition and health workers	VEDCO technical staff with help from the CSRL M&E assistant	Quarterly reports submitted to CSRL and VEDCO
3. Parish community-monitoring meetings	Parish	Quarterly	Representatives of groups on a rotating basis; local leaders		Quarterly reports submitted to CSRL and VEDCO
4. Subcounty community-monitoring meetings	Subcounty	Biannually (August and December)	Discuss issues raised in the parish and lower-level interactions	Community members, with assistance from the VEDCO technical staff and the CSRL M&E assistant	Biannual reports submitted to CSRL and VEDCO
5. District stakeholders' meeting	District	Annually (April)	Group leaders, local leaders from district, subcounty, other district partners		Annual report extract presented to CSRL administration and donors

External evaluations and quantitative surveys

6. Annual household survey and evaluation	District	Annually	Households and groups	ISU graduate research assistant	Annual evaluation report presented to the CSRL administration and donors at ISU
7. External/internal evaluation	District	Every three to five years	CSRL partners, local leaders, government department heads, farmers, and NGO representatives	External consultant	External/internal evaluation/assessment to be presented to partners

Source: Table was the product of discussions between Haroon Sseguya, Dorothy Masinde, and Della McMillan, Evanston, IL, July 25, 2012. It was further validated during a meeting between Haroon Sseguya, Jane Sempa, and Della McMillan, Kampala, Uganda, August 27, 2012.

- Biannual subcounty community-monitoring meetings to deliberate issues coming up from the parishes and develop solutions for any new emerging problems; and
- An annual district stakeholders' meeting to share the results of the parish and subcounty meetings and program activities, and to make decisions on issues affecting the program's execution and strategic planning.

External Evaluations and Quantitative Surveys. The original M&E plan anticipated that the program would organize two types of external evaluations:

- An annual household survey and evaluation conducted on a fixed sample of households over the life cycle of the program. The goal of this survey was to provide a mechanism for assessing the program's impact on its initial target households to inform program planning (Activity 6, Table 8.1); and
- An external/internal evaluation, with an external assessment of the program conducted by an outside evaluator every three to five years, which is the standard for most development programs (Activity 7, Table 8.1).

During 2004–2008, the program carried out a simultaneous M&E process that evaluated the program based on the existing plan; analyzed the program's progress in achieving its objectives with the resources and activities at its disposal, making needed modifications; and reviewed the adequacy of the existing tracking systems in relation to the needs of the program.

Activity Monitoring Activities

For each major component of the program, a list of indicators was developed and used to track the execution of activities. When new activities were added—like the expanded livestock and nutrition program and the service-learning school garden program—additional indicators were developed. The data for these indicators were collected by the field-based program staff members who then transmitted the data to the program's M&E assistant.

Participatory Monitoring and Evaluation Activities

The CSRL program's M&E system was committed to converting the baseline appraisal into a PM&E system. To accomplish this, the CSRL M&E assistant or his or her designated representative from among the program staff conducted a full review of each group's action plan and each parish's action plan—based on the group plans—every three months, with a subcounty review conducted twice a year. Based on this analysis, each parish and subcounty prepared a new annual plan that was presented at the annual district stakeholders' workshop that brought together leaders from all of the groups and parishes.

It is a testament to the high-quality baseline training workshop that the VEDCO staff were able to replicate this model in every parish where the program worked in 2005–2008 (Table 8.2). The same exercise helped identify a large number of issues that the program was able to address (see Box 8.1).

However, this exercise generated a huge paper trail. Specifically, the quarterly review of each group generated a short handwritten report; each parish generated a short report; each of the biannual subcounty reviews generated its own stand-alone report; and each stakeholder meeting its own stand-alone report. Care was taken to ensure that the community leaders at all levels of the program (group, subcounty) received hard copies. In addition, a soft copy was filed with the CSRL program office in Kamuli and the VEDCO M&E office in Kampala. This was done to ensure local ownership of the results and to help the local communities and three main stakeholders build their capacity for data-based strategic planning.

Annual Quantitative Surveys and Evaluations

Baseline Quantitative Survey. Although the baseline PRA provided useful qualitative information, it did not provide any sort of meaningful quantitative baseline (see Box 8.1). For this reason, it was important to collect this data during the first annual quantitative survey and evaluation.

Unfortunately, this survey was organized in June 2006. One of the unintended consequences of this delay was that it meant that the baseline quantitative survey was not really a "baseline" since it occurred eighteen months after the baseline appraisal survey and twenty-four months after the first CSRL activities had begun. About a third (320) of

Table 8.2 Time Line for Key CSRL Program Monitoring and Evaluation Activities, 2004–2013

	2004[a]	2005	2006	2007	2008	2009	2010	2011	2012	2013
Field activity monitoring	X	X	X	X	X	X	X	X	X	X
PM&E system										
Baseline PRA		X								
Community-based extensionist/ educator monitoring meetings		X	X	X	X	X	X	X	X	X
Parish community-monitoring meetings		X	X	X	X	X	X	X	X	X
Subcounty community-monitoring meetings		X	X	X	X	X	X	X	X	X
Annual district stakeholders' meeting		X	X	X	X	X	X	X	X	X
External evaluations and quantitative surveys										
Annual household survey and evaluation under CSRL leadership			X	X[b]	X					
Annual household survey under VEDCO leadership						X		X		
First nutritional assessment survey								X		
Midterm external evaluation					X[c]					
M&E plan		X								
M&E training workshop	X									
M&E summative report/review									X	

Source: CSRL program documents.

Notes: Implementation years run from July 1 of one calendar year to June 30 of the next.

a. Program started last quarter of the year in Kamuli.

b. Abbreviated survey.

c. Report completed in January 2009.

Box 8.1 Issues Raised by the PM&E and Annual Survey Activities that Informed Program Management

Job Description and Compensation of the Community-Based Volunteers

The original plan outlined two categories of volunteer farmer trainers: (1) rural development extensionists, who were responsible for providing support to community members on food security issues; and (2) community nutrition and health workers, who were responsible for nutrition and health education. The 2006 annual household-level evaluations, as well as feedback received during the subcounty community-monitoring meetings, indicated that some of the volunteers were not doing a good job and that the beneficiaries who they were supposed to serve feared negative consequences if they reported them. Based on this information, the CSRL implementation team created a series of parish-level local monitoring committees. The committees allowed for a more culturally appropriate mechanism of critiquing the staff's performance—both positive and negative. This new system helped improve the performance of the volunteer trainers until the end of the first phase when CSRL introduced a new system of salaried community-based trainers.

Technical Support for Livestock

The original focus of VEDCO's activities in Kamuli was primarily crop production. In 2005, the program strengthened livestock. The livestock program had been operational for less than a year when the PM&E parish and group meetings reported that external veterinarian service providers were expensive and unreliable. Since VEDCO had no livestock expert on its staff, the information fell on deaf ears and, within one year, almost all of the poultry provided by the program was wiped out by diseases. In 2006, CSRL hired both an animal health and a veterinary extension officer to provide technical backup.

Format of the Annual Stakeholders' Meeting

The principal objective of the annual district stakeholders' meeting was to share program achievements, challenges, and lessons. One observation made during the first PM&E stakeholders' meeting in 2006 was that there were no field visits or other opportunities for the area partners to see what the program was doing on the ground.

(continues)

Box 8.1 Continued

Based on this observation, the program added a field day where all of the area stakeholders and partners were invited to see what was being done in the program.

Agricultural Support

In the first phase, the CSRL program promoted a wide range of enterprises: maize, beans, bananas, cassava, sweet potatoes, grain amaranth, a variety of leafy vegetables, poultry, and pigs. By 2008, it was clear that the program could not accurately track all of these activities through its routine monitoring or annual surveys. It was therefore recommended in 2009 that the program focus on a narrower group of crops (maize, beans, cassava, and sweet potatoes) and livestock enterprises (goats and pigs) that the program thought would have the greatest potential impact on infant malnutrition and food security.

Seed Multiplication Gardens

The seed multiplication gardens were to be managed by group members, with the host (the owner of the land where the garden was located) taking a larger proportion of the seeds after harvest. During the 2006 and 2007 annual evaluations, it was determined that only the host and a few members actually managed the gardens, but that all of the members claimed a portion of the seeds. This feedback caused the CSRL program to shift from group-managed multiplication gardens to gardens that were managed by a single individual in the group who would get all of the proceeds, but would give a share (50 percent) back to the program. This seed would be given to the next farmer or group of farmers. To put this arrangement into effect, a Memorandum of Understanding was signed between the individual farmer and the program.

Source: Prossy Isubikalu, "Evaluation of the Sustainable Rural Livelihoods Program in Kamuli District, Uganda" (Kampala and Ames: Makerere University and Center for Sustainable Rural Livelihoods, Iowa State University, 2009).

the 800 target households that were the initial focus of the program were randomly selected for inclusion. The survey was timed to coincide with summer vacation at ISU to permit the same M&E leadership team that designed the baseline PRA to design the quantitative survey.

One innovative feature of the survey was that it included the questions needed to calculate two standard impact indicators that the Food Aid and Nutrition Technical Assistance (FANTA) Project funded by the United State Agency for International Development (USAID) had endorsed for measuring household access to food and the nutritional quality of household members' diets, the Household Food Security Scale (HFSS) and the Household Dietary Diversity Score (HDDS).[7] At the time, these were considered to be two of the best indicators that US government-funded programs could use to measure their impact on household food security. The use of these indicators provided a standard indicator of programmatic impact that could be compared with other US government programs in Africa, Asia, and Latin America.

Follow-Up Annual Surveys and Evaluations. As anticipated, the program supported two follow-up annual surveys in June 2007 and 2008. To ensure comparability, these surveys used the same basic questionnaires and sample households for all three years. If a household dropped out of the program—either because of death, illness, migration, or lack of interest—they were not replaced. Thus, the same households were studied by all three quantitative surveys.

The output of the exercise was a series of annual evaluation reports. Each report synthesized the results of the quantitative survey, folded in other evidence of quantitative and qualitative impact from group discussions, and developed a list of recommendations for better implementation and strengthening of the program's impact.

These annual quantitative surveys—combined with the PM&E—provided program managers with information that helped inform various decisions, including (1) reconfiguring the job description and compensation of the community-based volunteers; (2) providing greater technical support for livestock; (3) strengthening the annual stakeholders' meeting by adding a community-based field day; (4) focusing the program's agricultural support on a smaller number of crop enterprises; and (5) shifting from group to individual-managed seed multiplication gardens (see Box 8.1).

Each quantitative survey produced a detailed report summarizing the quantitative and qualitative data from the survey (see Box 8.2) and the major policy recommendations stemming from it.[8] The report was reviewed by all ISU faculty members working on the survey as well as the CSRL field program manager. A revised version of the report was always discussed at the biannual executive committee meetings. There was, however, no systematic distribution of the quantitative survey

Box 8.2   Quantitative Versus Qualitative Assessment
   Methodologies

"There are two major scientific ways of gathering information: quantitative methods and qualitative methods. Quantitative methods are those that express their results in numbers. They tend to answer questions like 'How many?' or 'How much?' or 'How often?' When they're used to compare things—the results of community programs, the effects of an economic development effort, or attitudes about a community issue—they do it by subjecting all of the things or people they're comparing to exactly the same tests or to the same questions whose answers can be translated into numbers. That way, they can compare apples to apples—everything or everyone is measured by the same standard. Quantitative measures are often demanded by policymakers; they are considered trustworthy because their results can be measured against one another, and because they leave less room for bias.

"Qualitative methods don't yield numerical results in themselves. They may involve asking people for 'essay' answers about often-complex issues, or observing interactions in complex situations. When you ask a lot of people for their reactions to or explanations of a community issue, you're likely to get a lot of different answers. When you observe a complex situation, you may see a number of different aspects of it, and a number of ways in which it could be interpreted. You're not only not comparing apples to apples; you may be comparing apples to bulldozers or waterfalls. As a result, researchers and policymakers sometimes see qualitative methods as less accurate and less legitimate than quantitative ones. That can be true, but, as we'll see, if qualitative methods are used with care, they can also yield reliable information.

"Qualitative and quantitative methods are, in fact, complementary. Each has strengths and weaknesses that the other doesn't, and together, they can present a clearer picture of the situation than either would alone. Often, the most accurate information is obtained when several varieties of each method are used. That's not always possible, but when it is, it can yield the best results."

Source: Work Group for Community Health and Development at the University of Kansas, "Qualitative Methods to Assess Community Issues," chap. 3, sec. 15, in Community Tool Box (Manhattan: Kansas State University, 2013).

results like there was for the PM&E reports. This may have resulted from the fact that the main analysis and write-up of the quantitative survey data was done in Ames, not Kampala. It may also have been overlooked because of the perception that the internal monitoring data was being collected to meet VEDCO's own internal objectives.

Reporting

The information from these three M&E tracking systems—activity monitoring, PM&E, and annual quantitative surveys—provided the basis for the annual report for the CSRL fiscal year, which runs from July 1 to June 30. Most annual reports provided a year-by-year explanation of the program with multiple personal case studies. CSRL encouraged its staff as well as several external individuals—MAK and ISU faculty, staff, and students—to submit annual case studies of specific households or individuals with which they had worked. Most of the early donors liked this format since it allowed them to see the human impact of the program. Although this system of reporting satisfied the original group of benefactors and helped the program maintain and grow its funding, there were some underlying problems that it failed to reveal.

Insufficient Baseline Data on New Activities. The first was the dearth of quantitative analysis of the new activities added by the program after the first year such as water sources, service learning, expanded nutrition education, and the livestock, credit, and food processing activities. This gap in the baseline data set was especially serious for nutrition, as lowering the area's high malnutrition rates was one of the principal objectives of the program. Since many of these new activities were not included in the annual survey, they developed their own tracking and reporting systems. Because there was almost no integration of these new internal tracking systems with the tracking systems that had been outlined in the original M&E plan (see Table 8.1), there was no way of assessing if and how these activities were contributing to the program's major objectives.

Insufficient Data on Training Program Efficacy and Impact. The program was unable to track the impact of its substantial investment in community-level training. While it was easy enough to say how many people had been trained in what subject matter during a single year, it was far more difficult to say where this training occurred, what it had accomplished, and where more was needed. In short, the program never developed an appropriate system for tracking how many people in different communities were being trained and on what themes, providing real-time feedback on training quality, assessing the local-level impact of the training on community capacity, or identifying what capacities remained unaddressed. This lack of feedback made it difficult to develop a realistic training plan.

An Insufficient System for Organizing Program Documents. The proliferation of reports from the program—activity monitoring, PM&E, and surveys and evaluations—was overwhelming. By the fifth year, it was impossible to find all of these reports in one single location either in Uganda or Iowa. The operational impact of this situation was that it discouraged the program administration from looking at more long-term trends for specific communities or the broader program area.

All three problems were masked by the program's tendency to focus on single-year results and human interest case studies in its annual reports and strategic planning sessions. The same focus on single-year reporting made it difficult to determine which communities were doing better than others, according to which parameters, and which communities might be ready to graduate from the program.

External Evaluations and Surveys

Under normal circumstances, the three lurking issues described above would have been identified during the program's first external evaluation. However, this did not occur because the mid-term evaluation— conducted over a three-month period in the middle of the sixth year (2009)—did not base its analysis on the existing data sets that the program was using to track its programmatic and financial reporting as is standard practice for a development program of this size and complexity. When it came time to pull the data together in some type of organized format, it became clear that this was a problem not easily solved. It was decided to adopt a more participatory methodology based on *sondeo* principles.

In the classic farming systems methodology, a *sondeo* consists of a small interdisciplinary group that circulates within a project intervention area talking to the project beneficiaries in the hope of getting a better understanding of the local situation.[9] At least twenty farmers or beneficiaries were selected from each parish for intensive interviewing by

the small interdisciplinary *sondeo* teams. A total of twenty-three partic-
ipants represented all of the stakeholders: community representatives;
MAK; CSRL; local government technical staff; Self-Help International,
VEDCO's partner nongovernmental organization (NGO) in Kamuli; and
VEDCO.

Based on these data sources, the external consultant who was hired
to oversee the midterm evaluation generated a report highlighting the
main program achievements and challenges, along with some recommendations for the next phase of the program (Table 8.3).[10]

Monitoring and Evaluation System, 2009–2014

Unfortunately, there was no structured monitoring of the partners' decisions on program modifications in response to recommendations of
either the annual evaluation studies[11] or the midterm evaluation,[12]

Table 8.3 Summary of Midterm Evaluation *Sondeo* Findings, 2009

Program achievements	Enhanced agriculture production
	Expanded or strengthened social networks
	Improved health
	Increased food security
	Improved awareness of activities leading to improved nutrition and health
Program challenges	Community-level volunteers wish to be paid for their work
	Community-level volunteers require refresher training
	Program is supporting too many different enterprises
	Farmers' excessive dependency on VEDCO with little knowledge of local alternatives
	VEDCO extension staff use less effective training and facilitation methods
	Partners need greater clarity concerning their role in program, e.g., MAK
	Proliferation of data from different sources
Next phase recommendations	Create new system of salaried community-based trainers
	Build facilitation capabilities of VEDCO extension staff
	Build capacities of local organizations in marketing and networking
	Focus agricultural activities on fewer enterprises
	Move annual planning meeting to Kamuli
	Develop an improved tracking system

Source: Prossy Isubikalu, *Evaluation Report: Sustainable Rural Livelihood Improvement Program in Kamuli District, Uganda* (Kampala and Ames: Makerere University and Center for Sustainable Rural Livelihoods, Iowa State University, 2009).

including the recommendation that the program develop an improved tracking system. This oversight occurred at a time when there were major administrative and accounting changes in CSRL. As a result, the program continued to use the same basic M&E system in Phase Two (2009–2013, postmidterm) that it used in Phase One (2004–2008, premidterm).

Activity Monitoring

Staff continued to use the new data entry templates that were developed to facilitate data analysis during the CSRL midterm evaluation. Each quarter, VEDCO summarized this data and reported it to CSRL. Although many of the indicators were the ones that the program was using for strategic planning, there was no complete summative analysis of this data until December 2012 (see Table 8.2).

Participatory Monitoring and Evaluation

The CSRL system of quarterly, biannual, and annual meetings worked well and continued to operate with the same frequency as it had in the early implementation years, producing the same types of reports. When the original VEDCO M&E assistant was promoted to a higher-level position in Kampala in 2010, there was little to no impact of this change on the organization of the community, parish, and subcounty-level PRA updates and action plans thanks to VEDCO's strong ownership of the PM&E model and its commitment to ensuring the model's continuity through regular steady staffing of the M&E assistant position.

Annual Household Surveys and Evaluations

The 2009 and 2011 Annual Household Surveys and Evaluations. As outlined in the original M&E plan, two additional quantitative household surveys were conducted in 2009[13] and 2011. To ensure comparability between years, the questionnaires used the same survey form and questions that were used in the 2006–2008 quantitative surveys. The principal shift was in the number and location of the households in the survey. Since the intervention area was expanded during the second phase, the sample frame was adjusted to include 263 of the 308 households studied in the June 2009 survey that had been in the CSRL program since the first year of the program and fifty-five of the new target households added to the program after the midterm (January 2009).[14]

These surveys included an important shift in leadership and oversight. Each of the earlier quantitative surveys was designed and executed by an external ISU-MAK leadership team. VEDCO staff members executed the 2009 and 2011 surveys with some oversight by the MAK professor who had supervised the earlier surveys (he did not control survey execution, data entry, or analysis). This shift in responsibility to a new group of VEDCO M&E assistants—without a written M&E manual to guide them—had some unintended consequences: (1) the new M&E assistants did not understand the critical importance of entering the data into a standard format so that the results of the 2009 and 2011 quantitative household surveys could be compared with the earlier years; (2) they had little understanding of the field programs and therefore had less capacity to clarify the data than the previous leadership team; and (3) since the original M&E plan did not outline any process for revising the survey questionnaires as new activities were added to the program, there was little information on any of the new areas that had been added after 2005 such as livestock, credit, and food processing.

These three factors contributed to VEDCO's failure to complete a full analysis of either the Implementation Year 2009 or 2011 data. Because of this, the CSRL program did not produce a report on the quantitative survey for 2009 and produced only a summary overview of the 2011 results.[15]

The First Nutrition and Health Survey. A second important shift was the addition of a separate nutrition and health practices survey in 2011, which was designed and executed by the VEDCO health and nutrition technical officer. In an attempt to link the nutrition and health practices survey to the 2011 annual household survey, the health team weighed all of the children in the 318 households included in the annual quantitative household survey for that year using the standard international protocols for nutrition surveys.[16]

Based on this data, the team produced the program's first comprehensive health and nutrition survey. A major strength of this survey was its commitment to collecting the data using the standard data collection techniques of the Ugandan government and major international donors. The chief weaknesses were that this type of nutritional data was not collected during either the baseline PRA or the baseline quantitative survey in the first and second year, which meant that even though there was clear evidence that the program had a measurable impact on the health and nutritional status of the target households, it was impossible to assess the global impact of the program on malnutrition.

Reporting

This incomplete analysis had several major consequences for reporting:

- Activity monitoring reporting—the VEDCO M&E assistant continued to produce the quarterly activity reports from the data turned in by the technical assistants. The speed and efficacy of this activity actually increased after the midterm due to the creation of standard reporting sheets that sped up data entry and analysis. Although a summative analysis of this data was done in preparation for the midterm, this type of analysis was not replicated until the 2012 summative report workshop, which meant that the CSRL Phase Two reports continued to focus their reporting on the activities in the current year as they had during Phase One.

- Participatory monitoring and evaluation—the program continued to help the local communities produce handwritten parish and subcounty stakeholders' meeting reports for both the old and new beneficiary areas of the program. These were then typed, proofread, and stored with the local communities as well as with the program. Most reports tended to focus on the current program year, making it difficult to grasp how much progress had been made. There also was almost no comparative analysis of one community with another. This lack of comparative analysis was a big problem since the program was starting to consider graduating some of the farmers with whom CSRL had been working for a long time. Since the program had never agreed on a few standard indicators that all of the communities would track— such as the percentage of households classified as extremely food insecure or infant malnutrition levels—there was no agreed-on basis for determining which communities had the greatest need and which ones were ready to graduate.

- Quantitative surveys and evaluations—since VEDCO was unable to complete the analysis of the annual household surveys and evaluations for 2009 and 2011, no additional household surveys and evaluations were conducted in 2012 and 2013. This meant that the program had no real-time quantitative impact data for the final five years of Phase Two.

- Annual reports—to offset the lack of quantitative impact data, the program leadership relied primarily on case studies to document local-level impacts in the 2009–2012 annual reports.

External Evaluations

Additional External Evaluations. No additional external evaluations were conducted on the program after the midterm. Had there been more external evaluations, the problems with data entry and analysis—which had not improved since the midterm—would have been exposed.

The First Internal Evaluation Based on the Program's Existing Monitoring and Evaluation Data. Another type of external evaluation brought these M&E issues to the fore—the first meeting of authors and stakeholders for this book. During the course of that meeting in July 2012, the MAK faculty member who oversaw all of the external evaluations explained why the quantitative analysis of the 2009 and the 2011 household surveys had not been completed. A plan was put in place to complete a longitudinal analysis of the data. At the same meeting, the authors noted that the CSRL had never established a central documentation system.

During the same meeting it became clear that, although CSRL invested heavily in local training and service learning, it was difficult to show the level of activities or their outputs because the program had not developed a system for tracking the types of training that had been conducted in different communities or with specific groups.

Various efforts to find this missing information were thwarted because the program had never developed a single integrated management information system or a system for archiving the hundreds of M&E and technical reports that had been produced. This lack of an integrated filing system made it impossible to document the program's impact on individual subcounties, even though the most recent PM&E reports made it clear that this impact had occurred.

In contrast to earlier analyses that had circumvented the lack of integration between the different tracking systems, this one received the high-level attention that the M&E issues required. Most critically, CSRL needed to (1) complete the analysis of the 2009 and 2011 quantitative surveys; (2) determine what types of longitudinal data existed with which they could track the evolution of the program's activities in different areas; and (3) start grouping the electronic version of all of the program documents into one database.

The First Field Staff Monitoring and Evaluation Workshop. The first workshop in September 2012 subdivided all of the technical staff into four teams by area of concentration: crop and livestock production, value-chain activities, health and nutrition, and local capacity building. During the workshop, each team developed an indicator performance tracking table (IPTT)[17] for its specific component of the program that summarized the existing activity-monitoring data for that particular activity set and any information from the annual household surveys or the 2011 health and nutrition survey that could be used to track the global impact of these activities on the local beneficiaries.

The Second Field Staff Monitoring and Evaluation Workshop. During the second workshop two months later, each of the four teams prepared a draft report that explained the evolution of the program's activities and any quantitative or qualitative evidence of impact for that component.

The output of this second workshop was the CSRL program's first summative M&E report. In contrast to earlier reports that analyzed each type of M&E data—the program's activity monitoring data, the PM&E data, and the quantitative surveys—separately, this report presented an integrated analysis of all three types of M&E data over the program's life cycle (2004–2012).[18] It also tracked the evolution of the CSRL program activities for each sector and any qualitative or quantitative evidence of impact. Although the staff discussed what type of documentation system would be useful, there was no time to begin putting it together.

The workshop also provided an opportunity for each of the CSRL technical teams to identify some key elements that they felt would need to be incorporated into the tracking system for the next phase: (1) a core set of indicators to track program execution and impact for specific areas and the methodologies to collect and analyze the data; (2) a clear IPTT summarizing the key indicators and targets for sector indicators; (3) a system for regular review of the IPTT as well as the individual indicators and data collection methodologies to determine whether or not they are functioning appropriately; (4) a line budget for basic training to ensure that all the key stakeholders—such as community leaders, community-based trainers, CSRL staff, and other partners—can use the new system to strengthen the program's efficiency and impact; (5) a plan for accelerating data processing; and (6) a written M&E plan that outlines the different systems, a management information system to integrate the different systems, and a plan for periodic review and updating.

Lessons Learned and Recommendations

The strengths of the CSRL program's M&E system included:

- Activity monitoring—the standard templates the program used to help the CSRL staff track its activities helped facilitate real time data entry and analysis;
- Participatory monitoring and evaluation—this system was linked to consistent community-based strategic planning that had buy-in, support, and participation from all of the partners;
- Annual surveys and evaluations—the annual surveys proved a regular objective assessment of the program's impact on about one-third of the program's target households; and
- All three subsystems provided useful information to the principal stakeholders that affected the program's execution and design.

There is also a great deal of evidence on how this information helped highlight new areas of concern and areas that were not being adequately addressed by the program.

The chief weakness of the M&E system was linked to the program's failure to build the capacity of its partners' staff to understand the need for a more integrated analysis of the three sources of program information. Instead, the three M&E subsystems operated more or less independently with the PRA-based PM&E data collected by the CSRL M&E officers, the quantitative monitoring data collected by the community-based trainers and technical officers, and the external survey data collected by a team under the leadership of a MAK professor.

The same parallel subsystems created a huge set of data and document management issues that made it difficult to document the program's longitudinal impacts. It also led to inconsistent baseline measurements for new activities that were started after the first year such as the program's expanded nutrition activities. Moreover, there was no system for tracking the efficacy and impact of the program's training programs, which the local people needed to operate the activities both with and without the program's support.

In retrospect, it is unlikely that, from the onset, the three partners could have sat down and drawn up one inclusive M&E system that would have been acceptable to everyone. However, it might have been possible to draft one by 2005 or 2006 when the program was fully up and running.

In the next phase, CSRL and its partners will be challenged to develop a simple and flexible M&E plan that will build on the program's extensive investment in different types of program tracking during its first eight years.

Developing a Flexible Start-Up Monitoring and Evaluation Plan and Related Training Programs

Although it is highly unlikely that all of the partners or staff will be willing or able to develop a real M&E plan at the start of this type of program, it nevertheless is well worth it to develop a simple draft M&E plan and then arrange for its periodic review.

The plan should provide clear guidance on who will be responsible for the collection and analysis of the different types of data; how staff will be trained to collect and analyze the data; and when the data will be reported to different stakeholder groups, including program beneficiaries, government and execution partners, and external donors.

Lesson 1:
Familiarize staff with basic monitoring and evaluation concepts and develop a written plan.

Recommendations:
- Develop a draft M&E plan in conjunction with the baseline appraisal and quantitative survey.
- Build into the draft M&E plan a process for regular review and revision to adjust the plan to new activities and partners.
- Conduct basic M&E training to familiarize the program staff with the global logic of the M&E plan and its intended role in program execution.
- Maintain a full-time M&E specialist on the program staff and a budget line to support the program's M&E activities.

Defining Baseline Measurements and Planning

Although a baseline appraisal is a useful start-up tool, it does not replace the need for accurate baseline measurements of the key indicators being used to track the program's impact. For this reason, it is useful to complement the appraisal with a baseline quantitative survey at the start of the program before activities begin. This allows any baseline measurements to be truly baseline and helps promote more consistent long-term tracking. There are no second acts on program baselines. Do it right the first time or spend the rest of the program playing an expensive game of trying to reconstruct it.

Lesson 2:
Link baseline appraisals to baseline surveys.

Recommendations:
- Train all staff, partners, and community leaders to ensure informed participation in the appraisal.
- Develop a written document that clearly defines the different tools and a standard methodology for recording and interpreting the information.
- Link strategic planning to the debriefing of the appraisals, and include a section in the guidance that describes this strategic planning process and how it needs to be written up.
- Whenever possible, conduct subsequent quantitative surveys during the same time of the year as the baseline survey.
- Harmonize appraisal questions and measures with surveys being used to collect the baseline quantitative data on a new project.
- Pilot test the appraisal and quantitative baseline methodology in one or more nonprogram communities to adjust the methodology.
- Hire a qualified outside trainer and coordinator to ensure that all topics and issues are being addressed.

Monitoring Program Execution and Outputs

An IPTT organizes a program's indicators like a road map. Without it, it is difficult for even the most seasoned manager to see how all the indicators being tracked relate to the program and whether or not specific project components are on target to achieve the goals that they are designed to address.

A well-designed IPTT lists all of the indicators that will be used to monitor the execution of the activities that the program is planning to support in its achievement of specific objectives, including indicators used for monitoring the execution of the activities that the program is planning to support, tracking the program outputs like training and technical assistance, and tracking whether or not these activities and outputs are achieving the desired impacts.

Using standard indicators will increase the chances that they will be meaningful to both the program and the wider community. When the indicator measurement standards are comparable with national and international standards, it inspires government confidence in a program.

Many programs underdocument their training programs, even though they often are one of the largest line items in the budget. A retroactive tracking system that tries to dig up this information looking backward is expensive and time consuming. To avoid this problem, care must be taken that the tracking table tracks all of the activities designed to build (1) the capacity of the program leadership, or partnership, to execute key activities such as community-level and staff training; (2) the outputs of this training in terms of staff assessments of training quality; and (3) the core capacity of the stakeholder or partner being targeted.

Even the best feedback on performance is useless if it comes too late. It therefore is critical that rapid reporting and sharing of results among stakeholders is ensured.

Lesson 3:
Develop an indicator tracking table to facilitate the tracking of program activities and outputs.

Recommendations:
- Identify a list of monitoring, output, and impact indicators based on the initial appraisal and adjusted program design.
- Review the list of standard indicators that each of the partners in particular sectors are using.
- Develop an initial table that summarizes what methodologies will be used to measure each indicator, the data collection frequency, and the individual responsible for collecting and maintaining the data.
- Ensure that the program uses appropriate data collection methodologies and trains staff to collect the data in a standard manner.
- Identify targets for each indicator.
- Propose a process for periodic review of all indicators as well as the targets and data collection methodologies for each indicator in the IPTT.

Lesson 4:
Encourage speedy and efficient data entry, analysis,
and reporting.

Recommendations:

- Use standard tools for data collection on a focused set of variables for each program objective. Too many variables can slow data entry and reporting; too few variables can make the data meaningless.
- Stay abreast of new trends—such as cell phone and PDA (personal digital assistant such as a mobile electronic device) technology—that can accelerate data entry and analysis.
- Maintain a consistent data dissemination strategy that provides a forum for reporting on results.
- Realize stakeholder needs for reporting may change over the life cycle of a program.

Periodic Objective Measuring and Assessing of Program Outcomes and Impacts

Any midterm or final phase evaluation should include the objective measurement of each major impact indicator and a complete review of the M&E system. Some of the key questions that need to be asked include:

- Is the program on line to achieve its targeted results?
- Are the indicators measuring program results?
- If not, how should the indicators be adjusted?

For a five-year programming cycle, this means measuring the indicators during the first year (i.e., at baseline), in the middle of the third year, and at the end of the fifth year. The midterm figures should tell the program leadership, partners, and donors whether the program is on track and allow them to make the necessary adjustments in program activities and anticipated outputs.

Case studies can be used to explain program impacts and major challenges. It is wise to encourage staff to collect and write up case studies as part of the M&E plan. Where possible, case studies should include related quantitative data as a backup to data being tracked in the IPTT.

Many institutions require all of their programs to have an external team leader for this exercise to increase objectivity. A program should anticipate a preevaluation planning process that will prepare all of the partners and implementation staff for the review. Most standard planning modules identify seven basic steps that are designed to ensure that all of the staff understand the goals, objectives, and intent of the evaluation. A typical preevaluation planning model includes:[19] (1) identifying and empowering the evaluation leader, who is the person on the evaluation team that will work most closely with the external evaluator on the subsequent steps of preevaluation planning as well as the actual evaluation; (2) clarifying donor and organizational guidance and expectations; (3) drafting the evaluation scope of work and work plan; (4) identifying the evaluation team and finalizing the scope of work; (5) organizing the project documentation; (6) organizing the project information; and (7) planning the evaluation logistics. Evaluation is like cleaning house. It is not fun, but in the long run it makes everything run better if it is well organized and well planned, and staff are trained to be receptive to the results.

Lesson 5:
Conduct objective impact assessments that measure program impacts using standard quantitative indicators.

Recommendations:
- Develop systems for the timing, objectives, and format of mid-phase and end-of-phase program evaluations.
- Establish a preevaluation planning process to organize the project documentation and M&E data for the exercise.
- Develop a formal debriefing exercise during which the principal results of the evaluation are explained and discussed.
- Include training modules on evaluation in the training program, including general principles of evaluation, preevaluation planning, and evaluation follow-up.

Lesson 6:
Combine qualitative and quantitative assessment methodologies to assess impact.

Recommendations:

- Develop a list of instructions for case studies in the program's M&E manual.
- Train staff to collect case studies that include quantitative data on some of the program's main activity monitoring and impact indicators.
- File all of the case studies that follow this standard format in a case study archive.
- Encourage staff to follow up on old case studies to see how the individual or household may have changed over time and update the indicator tracking data on that particular individual or group.

Reporting to Different Audiences

It is important to provide information in a way that the different stakeholders and donors in a program can understand, and to anticipate that a stakeholder's or donor's interest in different types of information is likely to change over the life cycle of the program.

Some private donors—especially family foundations or foundations run by businesses—have strict outlines for the types of information that they need. Other donors may want only individual case studies that document the program's impact on specific individuals or groups of individuals and a broad overview of the current program budget. A wise donor-funded program plans for any scenario.

It is never just a question of whether or not donors will require an M&E plan—create one either way. The first donor-funded endowment or grant should be thought of as start-up capital. A successful program will draw in other donors that may report to different constituencies. Having a broad M&E system in place helps a program respond to new opportunities and new donor requirements.

Lesson 7:
Tailor program reports to the needs of different audiences.

Recommendations:

- Build a draft reporting and communication strategy into the M&E plan.

- Review this communication strategy in conjunction with any M&E strategy review.

Setting Up and Maintaining Program Documents

A successful multidonor program generates hundreds of documents each year. Different stakeholders need different sets of documents. This is especially true when programs involve multiple partners and different stakeholders. An annotated bibliography provides the key to opening specific documents on specific topics from different time periods.

Even in a modest development program, the leadership should see that there is a widely accessible central filing system, and that it is regularly updated and reported on in program reports.

Lesson 8:
Develop a central filing system for program documents that is easy for everyone to access.

Recommendations:
- Develop a central system for filing all program documents in the first year of the program.
- Develop annotated bibliographies that cross-reference to an electronic filing system for all program documents.
- Require staff to submit an updated version of the annotated bibliographies that cross-reference to an electronic filing system for all program documents in conjunction with their annual reports.
- Keep electronic documentation in at least two completely separate sites.

Notes

1. For a description of livelihoods systems, see Box 3.2 in Chapter 3.

2. Baseline appraisal or assessment: "A set of data that measures specific conditions (almost always the indicators we have chosen through the design process) before a project starts or shortly after implementation begins. You will use this baseline as a starting point to compare project performance over the lifetime of the project. Example: If you are on a diet, your baseline is your weight on the day you begin." Mercy Corps, *Design, Monitoring and Evaluation Guidebook* (Portland, OR: Mercy Corps, 2005), p. 54.

3. MAK junior lecturer Haroon Sseguya was also an ISU Doctor of Philosophy (PhD) student in sociology and sustainable agriculture; ISU sociology

professor Robert Mazur is an African development specialist whose scholarship focuses on African food security, livelihoods, and health.

4. For more on standard PRA methodologies, see Chapter 5.

5. In Uganda the major geographical divisions are districts, counties, sub-counties, parishes, and villages. For CRSL's purposes, the subcounty is the main level of focus for interventions within the district. Program planning and review is more frequent at the subcounty level. The political leaders of these units are well educated and contribute productively to local activities. A subcounty usually has 30,000–40,000 people and comprises between six to eight parishes.

6. In addition to basic descriptive information, the researchers worked with local community representatives to execute three types of standard PRA interviews: (1) social mapping to identify all resources in their communities that might impact their development as a map—usually made on the ground—which was then reproduced onto paper for further use in research or development work; (2) gender analysis to illuminate the links between the existing gender relations in a community and the attendant development issues that need to be addressed to ensure meaningful development for all community members; and (3) institutional linkage diagramming to identify different government and local institutional activities and capacities.

7. The basic guidance for the creation of these indicators was downloaded from the USAID-funded FANTA Project website. See Jennifer Coates, Anne Swindale, and Paula Bilinsky, *Household Food Insecurity Access Scale (HFIAS) for Measurement of Food Access: Indicator Guide,* Version 3 (Washington, DC: Food and Agriculture Technical Assistance Project [FANTA], 2007); and Anne Swindale and Paula Bilinsky, *Household Dietary Diversity Score (HDDS) for Measurement of Household Food Access: Indicator Guide,* Version 2 (Washington, DC: Food and Agriculture Technical Assistance Project, 2006).

8. Haroon Sseguya, *Annual Evaluation of the Livelihoods Improvement Program* (Ames: Center for Sustainable Rural Livelihoods, Iowa State University, 2006); Haroon Sseguya, *Annual Evaluation of the Livelihoods Improvement Program* (Ames: Center for Sustainable Rural Livelihoods, Iowa State University, 2007). In 2008, the program executed an abbreviated two-page household survey that focused on household food security, nutrition, and health changes. The survey was conducted with 308 of the households that had been included in the 2006 and 2007 household surveys. Although the data was entered, analyzed, and presented, the survey leaders did not prepare a separate report because (1) original supervisor Haroon Sseguya was in the field collecting the information needed for his ISU PhD dissertation; and (2) it was anticipated that the data would be included in the report generated by the midterm evaluation.

9. Lorna Michael Butler, *The "Sondeo": A Rapid Reconnaissance Approach for Situational Assessment,* Western Regional Extension Publications, WREP0127 (Pullman: Washington State University, 1995), http://cru.cahe.wsu.edu/CE Publications/wrep0127/wrep0127.html.

10. Prossy Isubikalu, *Evaluation Report: Sustainable Rural Livelihood Improvement Program in Kamuli District, Uganda* (Kampala and Ames: Makerere University and Center for Sustainable Rural Livelihoods, Iowa State University, 2009). A summary of the report was prepared by the M&E adviser Haroon Sseguya since VEDCO's analysis of the data had not been completed until October 2012, when Sseguya oversaw a process that completed data cleanup and analysis for the 2009 and 2011 quantitative surveys. The final product of this analysis was presented in the 2012 M&E summative report, not in this initial report on the 2011 survey that was presented at the stakeholders' workshop in April 2011: Haroon Sseguya, *Evaluation of the Sustainable Rural Livelihoods Program in Kamuli District, Uganda: Summary Report* (Ames: Center for Sustainable Rural Livelihoods, Iowa State University, 2011).

11. Sseguya, *Annual Evaluation*, 2007, p. 25.

12. Isubikalu, *Evaluation Report*.

13. Even though the 2009 survey was conducted during Phase One (i.e., before the midterm), it was not analyzed until after the midterm, so it is counted as part of the Phase Two M&E activities.

14. Haroon Sseguya, Robert Mazur, and Dorothy Masinde, *Evidence of Impact and Transformation in Kamuli* (Ames: Center for Sustainable Rural Livelihoods, Iowa State University, 2012), pp. 18–19.

15. Sseguya, *Evaluation of the Sustainable Rural Livelihoods Program in Kamuli District, Uganda*.

16. Robert Magezi Winx, *VEDCO/CSRL Nutrition and Health Survey Report 2011–2012* (Kampala: VEDCO, 2012), p. 14.

17. Indicator performance tracking table (IPTT): the IPTT distills all of the information that staff, partners, and local people need to know in order to know where a project's activities are in relation to the achievement of its key objectives. The IPTT lists all of the indicators that a program is using to monitor its execution (monitoring indicators) and impact (impact indicators). Each objective is listed on a line. Under the objective, the table lists the baseline measurement for each impact indicator and what the program hopes to achieve after a certain number of years as well as the annual targets for each of the monitoring indicators. The IPTT table is a living document that is regularly updated; most of the monitoring indicators are updated annually and the impact indicators updated every two to three years. When the project's information is portrayed in this sort of table, it is easy for the staff and community leaders to see where the program is in relation to where it wants to be. Since the indicators are succinct short sentences, they are easy to read and translate into local languages, which increases transparency and communication. Della E. McMillan, Alice Willard, and Guy Sharrock, *IPTT Guidance: Guidelines and Tools for the Preparation and Use of Indicator Performance Tracking Tables.* M&E Module Series (Washington, DC: American Red Cross; Baltimore: Catholic Relief Services, 2008).

18. Patrick Sangi, Jane Nakiranda, Nadiope Gideon, Charles Kategere, and Mark Westgate, "Strategic Objective One (SO1): Promote Resilient Climate-Smart Agricultural Technologies to Increase Food Availability," in Della E. McMillan, ed., *Sustainable Rural Livelihoods Program: Summative Monitoring*

and Evaluation (M&E) Report: 2005–2012, Draft Report (Ames: Center for Sustainable Rural Livelihoods, Iowa State University, 2012); John Sembera, Ronnie Balibuzani, and Jane Sempa, "Strategic Objective Two (SO2): Build Diversified Livelihoods and More Resilient Markets to Improve Food Access," in Della E. McMillan, ed., *Sustainable Rural Livelihoods Program: Summative Monitoring and Evaluation (M&E) Report: 2005–2012,* Draft Report (Ames: Center for Sustainable Rural Livelihoods, Iowa State University,, 2012); Esther Matama, Benon Musaasizi, and Laura Byaruhanga, "Strategic Objective Three (SO3): Reduce Malnutrition Levels Among Women of Reproductive Age and Children," in Della E. McMillan, ed., *Sustainable Rural Livelihoods Program: Summative Monitoring and Evaluation (M&E) Report: 2005–2012,* Draft Report (Ames: Center for Sustainable Rural Livelihoods, Iowa State University, 2012); Nancy Rapando, Stephen Kato, Ronnie Balibuzani, and Henry Kizito Musoke, "Strategic Objective Four (SO4): Strengthen the Organizational Capacity of Farmer Organizations and Their Linkages to the Private- and Public-Sector Institutions that They Need to Build and Maintain Sustainable Livelihoods," in Della E. McMillan, ed., *Sustainable Rural Livelihoods Program: Summative Monitoring and Evaluation (M&E) Report: 2005–2012,* Draft Report (Ames: Center for Sustainable Rural Livelihoods, Iowa State University, 2012).

19. Della E. McMillan and Alice Willard, *Preparing for an Evaluation* (Washington, DC, and Baltimore: American Red Cross/Catholic Relief Services M&E Module Series, 2008).

9

Capitalizing on Impacts and CSRL's Multiplier Effects

David G. Acker, Henry Kizito Musoke, and Haroon Sseguya

Institutions become partners because they see potential benefits from the relationship. If the partnership is successful, each partner institution should achieve some of its goals and over time see the potential for greater returns. While some of the benefits are predictable, the multiplier effects of the partnership may generate unanticipated opportunities and outcomes. When staff members participate in a partnership, they are exposed to new networks, knowledge, and resources. The results can help leapfrog an institution into a new leadership role and open the door to new funding sources.

Four transformational challenges that institutions are likely to confront include:

- Conducting a baseline analysis of institutional strengths and weaknesses—performing a frank analysis of which strengths each partner already has and which it will need to develop;
- Developing a flexible plan to build institutional capacity— creating a solid plan to build the capacities that the institution will need to execute the program as it evolves;

The authors wish to acknowledge the helpful input and contributions of Joseph Bbemba, Mateete Bekunda, Lorna Michael Butler, Samuel Kyamanyawa, Dorothy Masinde, Robert Mazur, Linda Naeve, Henry Nasereko, Gail Nonnecke, Nancy Rapando, Max Rothschild, Annette Nakyejwe Sebulime, Shelley Taylor, Phinehas Tukamuhabwa, and Mark Westgate.

- Sustaining institutional achievements—deciding what types of institutional investment may be needed to maintain the new resource and organizational capacities once the partnership's initial program funding ends; and
- Rethinking the partnership to capitalize on multiplier effects—reassessing each partner's role in the partnership as its capacity grows and its objectives for the partnership change.

The Institutional Context

In the course of executing the Center for Sustainable Rural Livelihoods (CSRL) program, each partner committed to a preliminary set of activities that evolved over time in response to the changing needs of the program and the implementation team. Each partner institution was affected in four key areas:

- Human resources development—developing the technical capacity and quality of the staff;
- Institutional services—building the capacity of the individual partners to offer better services in the areas where they intervene;
- Management and financial systems—strengthening the core management and financial systems of the institution; and
- Financial resources—increasing the institution's total funding and networks for getting funds.

Some of these organizational impacts were directly related to the execution of activities while others were simply set in motion by some of the contacts that the different partners developed in the course of executing the program. In each case, the organizational impacts were major.

Volunteer Efforts for Development Concerns

Prior to partnering with CSRL, Volunteer Efforts for Development Concerns (VEDCO) worked for eighteen years in the Luwero District in Uganda's Central Region, where it helped transition a group of war-affected communities to diversified livelihood systems. VEDCO's original goal in partnering with CSRL was to help roll out its activities from the Central Region to other areas of Uganda.

The original signed protocol between VEDCO and Iowa State University (ISU) focused on expanding and strengthening its core livelihood activities in three subcounties of Kamuli from 2004 to 2009, which was later expanded to include four subcounties.

In the course of executing the partnership, VEDCO strengthened its core human resources, financial, and management systems in ways that attracted other donors, therefore propelling it to higher levels. It moved from intervening in two districts in 2004, to twenty districts in 2012, and from an annual budget of $400,000 in 2004, to an annual budget of about $2,000,000 in 2011 through programs that were funded by over eighteen different donors. VEDCO's next challenge is to continue to strengthen its personnel, finance, and global management systems so that it can manage its spectacular growth.

Conducting a Baseline Analysis of Institutional Strengths and Weaknesses

Human Resources Development. Because of the close proximity of ISU's field program manager and the VEDCO staff, it was relatively easy to get to know the staff and their responsibilities. The continual communication between VEDCO's executive director, the field program manager, and the CSRL director helped to identify some of the early staff competencies needed. Diagnoses were made in an informal way, by accompanying field staff to farmers' fields, sitting in on staff meetings, and listening to community members. ISU and Makerere University (MAK) faculty with different technical backgrounds also visited Kamuli frequently in the early years, interacting with staff and local farmers. The working relationships that evolved between these faculty members and VEDCO personnel also helped to informally identify existing competencies and skills.

When CSRL began working with VEDCO in 2004, the nongovernmental organization (NGO) had no systematic model for training the community-based rural development extensionists that were the foundation of all of its food security programs. There was also a tradition of unpaid volunteers who worked alongside the field staff.

Institutional Services. When the CSRL-VEDCO partnership began, VEDCO's extension programs were largely focused on improving agricultural practices to prevent food insecurity. This included working with existing farmer groups to develop small kitchen gardens, producing food under drought conditions, and introducing improved crop varieties based on national research. VEDCO had never intervened in community-based nutrition, nor had it worked with existing local institutions such as schools. Although VEDCO had always supported livestock as part of its core food security programs, these activities were basic and focused on helping vulnerable households build small herds through rotating stock (see Chapter 6).

Management and Financial Systems. The addition of a new partnership with ISU meant that VEDCO had to develop a new trust relationship as well as a new system of accountability. VEDCO did not have rigorous accounting and accountability systems in 2004. This became evident as the field program manager worked with the VEDCO office to ensure that ISU's accounting requirements were met. At first, neither field staff nor local beneficiaries took part in the development of program budgets. These early observations provided clues to future needs.

Financial Resources. One of the reasons that VEDCO was selected as a partner for CSRL was its financial openness. At the time the partnership began in 2004, VEDCO had three other partners with whom it held contracts and a budget of about $400,000. The partnership with two different universities brought a totally new source of resources, and the fact that the funds originated with private benefactors opened up a new way of looking at funding sources. From the beginning, VEDCO expressed interest in gaining a better understanding of how it could establish its own private endowment.

Developing a Flexible Plan to Build Institutional Capacity

Human Resources. Through its partnership with CSRL, VEDCO improved its human resources policies for field staff recruitment and training (see Chapter 4). In 2010–2011, CSRL also served as an incubator for VEDCO to pilot test a new system of paid community-based trainers to replace the unpaid community-based volunteers (see Chapter 5).

The same collaboration helped VEDCO improve the technical quality of its staff. In 2004, a high percentage of the VEDCO field agents were unpaid volunteers, none of the VEDCO senior management team had mainstream qualifications in agriculture,[1] and few field staff had training at the level of Bachelor of Science (BS) in these areas. The CSRL director developed tight job descriptions for the key technical positions in the program and worked with VEDCO to ensure a competitive review and hiring process. This process drew a new generation of trained staff at the BS and Master of Science (MS) levels—many of them MAK graduates—to the CSRL program. Almost all of these highly qualified first-generation CSRL hires went on to more senior VEDCO positions.

Imbued by the CSRL hiring model, VEDCO replicated this hiring process in other districts. A brief overview of VEDCO staff reveals that out of eighty staff members,[2] thirty-eight have a BS degree or are pursuing one; eighteen have a MS degree or are pursuing one; and two are pursuing a Doctor of Philosophy (PhD) degree. Many new VEDCO hires are identified through the ISU and MAK service-learning program, the MAK internship program, or the VEDCO internship program. Since 2004, VEDCO has hired over thirty former interns from MAK and Kyambogo University.

Institutional Services. Important institutional impacts of the CSRL-VEDCO partnership have included VEDCO's improvement of its training modules, a stronger integration of both nutrition and livestock into the food security programs, and a greater assimilation of research into the core programs.

Improving training resources. Although VEDCO had training modules, they were usually developed on a case-by-case basis, often by borrowing from other programs. By 2006, VEDCO had developed an integrated series of thirteen modules to train the community-based volunteers who backstopped technical components of the program (see Chapter 5). The extension specialists developed most of the modules with input from the CSRL director and MAK and ISU faculty members. Based on feedback from the field, the modules have gone through a series of reviews, revisions, and consolidations. With a few notable exceptions, this core set of modules is used by VEDCO's programs throughout Uganda, and several other organizations have borrowed them for their own use.

Strengthening integration of nutrition into food security programming. One of the major institutional impacts of the CSRL partnership on VEDCO was the program's addition of nutrition as a core intervention area. This knowledge was quickly scaled up to all of VEDCO's programs in Uganda. Since then, VEDCO has played a key role in the design of Uganda's first national Action Plan on Nutrition (in 2011). Important innovations like the establishment of feeding and educational centers for malnourished children and their caretakers are emerging and will provide viable benchmarks for scale-up—not only for VEDCO, but also for other institutions and government programs.

Strengthening integration of livestock into food security programming. Another wide-reaching impact of the CSRL partnership has been the strengthening of VEDCO's livestock programs. CSRL provided VEDCO with the internal Ugandan and regional East African networks necessary for improving livestock marketing and was instrumental in developing the funding—first from private benefactors, then the Monsanto Fund—that VEDCO needed to expand these activities and allow it to hire its first full-time professional animal scientist and veterinarian. Today, the CSRL program in Kamuli is widely regarded as an example of best practice that VEDCO is hoping to extend through all of its programs using a new collaborative research support program sponsored by the International Livestock Research Institute (ILRI), which began in late 2013.

Assimilating research into the core program. The CSRL partnership involved VEDCO in a number of strategic research partnerships for crop production, nutrition, postharvest processing, and marketing. CSRL underscored the need for a strong tripartite arrangement involving research, academic teaching, and extension that made the end users of the research findings (i.e., the farmers) active research participants. As a result, VEDCO is now regarded as a key player in applied research activities in the region—and throughout the country—involving crops such as sweet potatoes, bananas, upland rice, beans, grain amaranth, and cassava. This type of applied research has helped reintroduce soybean production into Kamuli (see Box 9.1). By 2012, VEDCO had signed partnerships with six collaborative research programs—most of which were facilitated either directly by CSRL or by individual MAK or ISU faculty affiliated with the program.[3]

Management and Financial Systems. The CSRL program assisted VEDCO in strengthening its weak first-generation accounting systems through on-the-job training of the VEDCO accountants (see Chapter 4). This training helped VEDCO introduce a strong monthly reporting schedule across the organization in 2008 that has allowed partners to institute periodic checks on operations and compliance following standard accounting procedures. The system has been strained by the addition of many new grants and projects within such a short period of time as well as by high rates of turnover in the accounting staff. Improved accounting software is being rolled out to nearly all field offices, and VEDCO plans to institute a wide area network (WAN) for accounts and monitoring and evaluation (M&E) in the next five years as resources become available.

Financial Resources. By the end of 2011, VEDCO's annual budget had grown to $2 million, and it held relatively steady in 2012 despite the

Box 9.1 The CSRL Impact on the Promotion of Soybeans in Uganda

Soybean, which is known for its high protein (40 percent) and oil (20 percent) content, was introduced in to Uganda in 1913 from the United States and South Africa. Following the Ugandan civil war in the 1970s, most of the soybean varieties, breeding lines, and seeds were lost. In 1996, an outbreak of soybean rust wiped out all soybean varieties. The release of several rust-resistant varieties between 2004 and 2010 and farmers' improved management practices accelerated Uganda's annual soybean production to 181,000 tons in 2009, or an annual growth rate of 2.4 percent.

The high adoption rate of the Maksoy variety, and eventually other varieties—augmented by private investment in the soybean value chain, government support for soybean research, high market demand, and more farmer income—has led to soybean's popularity among farmers, processing companies, and local factories for oil, livestock feed, and household consumption.

Between 2011 and 2013, the ISU-Uganda farmer-to-farmer initiative, funded by the United States Agency for International Development (USAID) and led by ISU Extension and Outreach, cooperated with VEDCO and 180 Kamuli women farmers to advance soybean (and maize) management and production, including soil fertility improvement. Few farmers had previously grown soybeans; however, the program generated interest and showed that there was the potential for soybeans becoming an important cash crop in the subcounties where it was introduced. It also proved to be a valuable addition to the family diet.

VEDCO is currently pilot testing a commercial model of soybean production in two subcounties (Butansi and Namasagali), through working with 16 farmer groups and a total of 295 women farmers and 15 indirect farmers. Labor-saving technologies have been developed with support from ISU, especially the seed-cleaning machines, which save 80 percent of the time spent by women cleaning and sorting produce. VEDCO continues to look for ways to bridge the gap on value addition of soybeans.

Sources: Bernard Bashaasha, *Soybean Research in Uganda USAID Manpower for Agriculture Development* (MFAD) (Washington, DC: USAID, 1992) pp. 1–14; Margaret Smith and Linda Naeve, *Strengthening Value Chains for Maize and Soybeans for Ugandan Women Farmers*, Final Report, Feed the Future (FTF) Niche Project No. 1071-20-505-1 (Ames: Iowa State University Extension and Outreach, 2012); Phinehas Tukamuhabwa, R. Kawuki, D. Nanfumba, T. Obus, and B. Bashaasha, "Overview of Impact Indicators of Soybean Rust Resistant Varieties on Uganda's Economy," research application summary presented at the biennial meeting of the Regional Universities Forum for Capacity Building in Agriculture (RUFORUM), Entebbe, Uganda, September 2012, pp. 2155–2160,

global economic slowdown in the eurozone and elsewhere. Between 2004 and 2012, the donor base has increased from three to twenty (Figure 9.1), representing both mainstream foundations such as the McKnight and Ford Foundations and nongovernmental organizations (NGOs) such as Agricultural Cooperative Development International/ Volunteers in Overseas Cooperative Assistance (ACDI/VOCA), Harvest Plus, and Oxfam International.

VEDCO has expanded from working in only the Central Region to working in all of the geographical regions of Uganda. Since 2004, VEDCO's outreach has grown from approximately 5,000 households to almost 35,000 households (Figure 9.2).

Although it is impossible to say that CSRL caused this transformation, there is a strong connection since (1) most of the programs are based on the scale-up interventions that were first pilot tested in Kamuli; (2) a high percentage of the senior staff who helped lead this development were trained entirely or partially under CSRL; and (3) many basic accounting systems that inspired this new round of program scale-up were developed by the VEDCO accountants working with CSRL (see Box 9.2).

Sustaining Institutional Achievements

VEDCO is currently facing several major challenges to sustaining the institutional gains that it made through the CSRL partnership.

Reduce Employee Turnover by Developing a More Competitive Plan for Employee Compensation. Currently, the VEDCO Board of Directors requires it to follow a salary scale that is considered by some to not be competitive with other NGOs in Uganda. This has resulted in many skilled staff leaving the program for better jobs within other VEDCO programs as well as outside of VEDCO as soon as they are available. If something is not done to stabilize staff turnover, VEDCO will not be able to sustain either the CSRL program or any of its newer programs without a constant infusion of new training and retraining. Recently, the VEDCO Board of Directors sanctioned the need to bolster its ranks by adding three new members with advanced qualifications in extension, agronomy, and agribusiness. This is expected to enhance the competencies of the board, thereby enabling it to better guide policy and program implementation, in addition to strengthening the advocacy role that VEDCO plays in Uganda.

Figure 9.1 Evolution of the Number of Donors and External Funding for VEDCO, 2004–2012

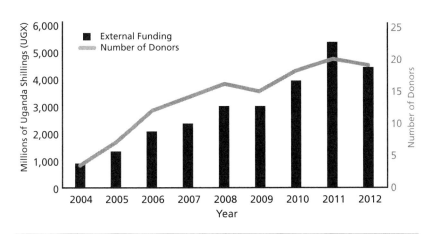

Source: VEDCO annual audited accounts. Data provided by VEDCO finance manager, June 2014.

Figure 9.2 Evolution of VEDCO's Program Outreach, 2004–2012

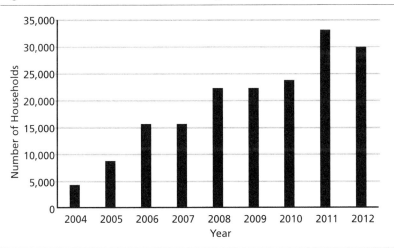

Source: VEDCO annual progressive reports for 2004–2013. Data provided by VEDCO agricultural program director, June 2014.

Box 9.2 Impact of the CSRL Partnership on VEDCO's Institutional Services and Strategic Planning and the Other Partners

---

"Many civil society organizations in Uganda, including VEDCO, were established to react to human need, in this case, post-conflict livelihoods. However, after twenty-five years, many NGOs continue to rely on a short-term-project model. For these organizations to have an impact in achieving more sustainable development, they will need to articulate strategic objectives, as well as the type of growth curve needed to accomplish these goals. The partnership with ISU's CSRL and MAK gave VEDCO an unprecedented opportunity to consider these two challenges, and to expand both technical and management expertise.

"ISU's decision to make VEDCO the primary partner, rather than the more conventional 'sister' university MAK, put its academicians in day-to-day contact with the field realities of Uganda. The addition of MAK as a third partner added more technical input and a one-on-one partnership between the students and faculty of both institutions. This was highly beneficial to all of the partners involved. Specifically, it forced the academics to translate their academic knowledge into practical field applications that helped deepen the training and knowledge of VEDCO's field technicians. All of the partners benefitted from one another's networks and contacts, and all three of the partners achieved their original objectives for the partnership and more."

Source: Former VEDCO executive director Henry Kizito Musoke, in telephone conversation with Della E. McMillan, October 19, 2013.

Develop Better Budget Review Processes to Ensure Adequate Overhead. The issue of developing a more realistic and competitive salary structure is complicated by the fact that many of VEDCO's new grants developed in the wake of its successful implementation of the CSRL program included little or no overhead.[4] While VEDCO's low overhead has made it popular for its low cost base per beneficiary ratio, it has also made the organization relatively noncompetitive on the job market, leading to an exodus of some well-trained staff to better paying positions elsewhere. The challenge for VEDCO is to develop a better system for budgeting and negotiating program budgets.

Develop More Robust Accounting Systems. A more robust system of accounting that can handle the current CSRL contracts as well as all of the new contracts that have been added is critical to VEDCO's growth. Since staff turnover in the accounting positions is a problem, the resolution of this third constraint is interrelated to the first and second.

Strengthen Core Institutional Capacity. Once the major challenges are confronted, there are areas where VEDCO would like to further increase its institutional impact.

Develop an endowment to help stabilize operations. To date, VEDCO has been completely dependent on donor assistance for almost all of its programs. This has affected its ability to attract and retain talented staff. VEDCO is committed to the idea of developing an independent funding base to support the core operations of the institution. This type of endowment is critical to VEDCO's development of a more stable base of senior technical staff.

Mainstream M&E throughout every level of the organization. During the first four years of the program, most VEDCO staff members saw M&E as a policing activity rather than a management tool. After the first comprehensive M&E training in 2007, they no longer saw it that way. Since 2012, VEDCO has been working to mainstream M&E at all levels of the organization, from the VEDCO board to the field extension workers and community organization leaders. Many of the key activities needed to build VEDCO's long-term capacity in M&E can be pilot tested as part of the CSRL partnership, and potentially scaled up at a later date.

Encourage private sector support to promote value chains. Since 2004, the Uganda government has progressively privatized agricultural research and extension. Creating more agribusiness interest in value-chain activities in Kamuli would increase the likelihood that agribusinesses might help support the modest cost of the National Agricultural Advisory Services (NAADS) needed to sustain households' access to extension services for some of the key value chains. VEDCO hopes that the same private sector partners—such as agribusinesses—might be willing to fund a specific service center that supports a value chain where they intervene.

Rethinking the Partnership to Capitalize on Multiplier Effects

In the next phase of the partnership, VEDCO will continue to be a CSRL partner in Kamuli. However, VEDCO has a much wider zone of intervention and more partners than it did ten years ago. Since the field program is also more mature than it was a decade ago, activities will likely become more targeted and integrated, and there may be additional partners to move toward greater local sustainability. VEDCO's continuing role in providing support for the community-based trainers will be important so that they too are able to achieve greater empowerment and independence. With its new NGO status, CSRL will be in a position to hire and manage its own staff; therefore, CSRL and VEDCO will have to determine which Kamuli activities they will carry out together (see Chapter 4).

Makerere University

In 2004, MAK was near the end of a long reconstruction period, during which the university had reasserted its role as the leading educational institution in East Africa, focusing its energy and resources on teaching and research. While there was an institutional commitment to extension, the university had almost no money to permit either the faculty or students to take this knowledge out of the university and bring it to rural communities.

MAK's original goal in partnering with CSRL was to improve the quality of the internships that all of MAK's College of Agricultural and Environmental Sciences (CAES) undergraduates were required to have. They were also interested in helping some of the CAES junior faculty complete their PhDs.

Although MAK helped CSRL identify VEDCO as a field partner, ISU never signed a formal contract with MAK. This meant that MAK was not an institutional partner with its own line budget like VEDCO. For this reason, MAK's institutional transformation was more subtle and less easy to trace because it was not part of any type of strategic planning exercise that was being tracked.

Conducting a Baseline of Essential Institutional Strengths and Weaknesses

Human Resources Development. While there was an implicit understanding that ISU would help MAK's junior faculty complete their PhD education in the United States, ISU and MAK did not jointly conduct a systematic diagnosis or strategic plan to determine which departments would be targeted. Probably because CSRL's focus was on rural community development and sustainable livelihoods, this objective fit well with the interdisciplinary interests of faculty members in MAK's Department of Agricultural Extension and Innovations. Early workshops and planning meetings did, however, include members of other academic departments as well as a number of nonagricultural colleges.

Institutional Services. The stated mission of MAK's CAES is: "To advance training, knowledge generation and service delivery to enhance agricultural development, sustainable natural resource utilization and environmental management."

Despite this commitment to rural development, many of the faculty had difficulty putting themselves and their students into the field. This may be attributed in part to the associated costs of extension outreach, the demands that are often involved in teaching large classes, and the pressure to spend time on grant writing to bring in external funds for research.

As CSRL and VEDCO began to consider how to strengthen community nutrition outreach to Kamuli families, they first looked to MAK's CAES and the Department of Food Technology and Human Nutrition. But in 2004, community nutrition was not an area of major expertise for the college; therefore, CSRL sought this support in other places. This highlighted the need for CAES to strengthen its own internal ability to backstop the need for nutrition education in rural areas. CAES has now introduced a human nutrition BS degree, which includes training in community nutrition.

Management and Financial Systems. Unlike VEDCO, CSRL did not have a major impact on MAK's management and financial system. This was largely because MAK was a different type of partner than VEDCO, and few activities were funded directly through MAK. When technical expertise was needed, MAK faculty could be identified to provide technical assistance through service contracts.

Financial Resources. Until the original CSRL management team sought out the CAES dean, there had been little (if any) contact between ISU and MAK. MAK did have previous associations with US universities (Virginia Polytechnic Institute and State University, Ohio State University), and private foundations also had a long history with MAK's reconstruction, and later, with the development of the undergraduate internship program. The internship was spearheaded in 2000 by the Rockefeller Foundation, in partnership with the World Bank, when they provided $5 million for university-wide undergraduate internships at MAK to promote innovation in local government. This became known as the Innovations@MAK initiative (also see Chapter 7).[5]

Developing a Flexible Plan to Build Institutional Capacity

Human Resources. For a wide variety of reasons,[6] CSRL's heaviest institutional impact was in the Department of Agricultural Extension and Innovations at MAK, similar to ISU's Department of Agricultural Education and Studies or Department of Sociology. When the CSRL program started in 2004, only two of the sixteen faculty members in this department had PhDs, and few had completed field-based research. In 2005, several junior faculty members took responsibility for the initial baseline participatory rural assessment and strategic planning process in Kamuli. Another junior faculty member from the department was tasked with helping ISU start up the service-learning program. Three MAK professors from this department obtained, or supplemented, their PhDs from ISU. All of them have continued to have strong communication with professors who backstopped the CSRL program, which helped promote publication, consulting, grant getting, and networking.

Thanks in part to this strengthened capacity, the department began the first multicountry PhD program in agricultural and rural innovation in the fall of 2012 through a grant from the European Union. The PhD program admitted twenty-seven students during its first year (2012–2013) and was scheduled to have seventeen in its second year, the highest number of PhD students in any MAK doctoral program.

Although it is impossible to say that the CSRL program caused this dramatic expansion of the department, it was an important contributing factor since (1) the CSRL program facilitated the training of three of the key faculty who are leading the expansion of the department; (2) seven of the current faculty in the department have worked on research projects that were completely or partially funded by the CSRL; (3) the heavy involvement of the undergraduate students in the CSRL program and the relatively high percentage of these students that have gone on to MS and PhD programs with assistance from the CSRL program and other donors have helped raise the profile of the department as one that attracts some of the brightest, most ambitious students in the university; (4) many of the programs are based on the scale-up interventions that were first pilot tested in Kamuli; and (5) a high percentage of senior staff members who helped lead this development were trained entirely or partially under CSRL.

Institutional Services. CSRL's partnership with MAK facilitated more faculty members spending time in the field. Not only did the partnership bring MAK closer to an NGO that was serving Uganda's rural communities, but the relationship opened up a unique opportunity to transform the student internship program and expose students to global issues and ideas.

Strengthening the faculty's ability to conduct applied learning and research. To date, CSRL records show that thirty-one MAK faculty members in nine departments have worked with CSRL either as mentors, consultants, or other resource persons. Several junior faculty members who conducted research with various ISU departments received scholarships from outside the CSRL core endowment, but CSRL helped them conduct their fieldwork in Uganda in conjunction with CSRL activities. Some of these faculty have continued working with CSRL or some of the CSRL-related research programs after returning home, which helped smooth the transition back to Uganda-based teaching positions. In addition, the partnership has contributed to these faculty members' external grant success, private consultations, and publication records.

Strengthening the inclusion of nutrition in MAK's core research and training programs. The CSRL partnership catalyzed stronger links between MAK's research and teaching on nutrition and the core agricultural disciplines. When the CSRL program began, there were few (if any) connections between the faculty associated with nutrition and faculty associated with the core agricultural disciplines involved in crop and livestock production. This was in large part because the nutrition expertise at MAK was dispersed between two different units of the university—the School of Public Health (SPH) and the Department of Food Technology and Nutrition (formerly the Department of Food Science and Technology) in CAES. Although the college had a Department of Food Technology and Nutrition, the principal focus of the program was on food processing and preservation techniques.

Since CAES did not have a department with this expertise, the CSRL program utilized several faculty members from the SPH as consultants. This link was strengthened when a member of the school agreed to serve on the CSRL Advisory Board. Another source of technical advice and support was the new Human Nutrition and Home Economics Department at Kyambogo University.

CSRL's active collaboration with human nutrition programs outside of the college may have encouraged CAES to strengthen its own internal nutrition capability to backstop community nutrition. This commitment was further strengthened by the involvement of several members of the Department of Food Technology and Nutrition faculty in the USAID-supported Pulse Collaborative Research Support Program (CRSP), now the Legume Innovation Lab,[7] which started in 2007.

Transforming the CAES model for undergraduate internships. CAES switched the focus for its mandatory ten-week internship program to a service-learning model. Since 2006, seventy-three MAK students have completed service-learning activities in Kamuli through the scholarship program set up under CSRL. In addition, approximately 150 students from both ISU and MAK have been affiliated with CSRL programs in Kamuli unrelated to service learning since 2004. Another seven MAK students received various types of financial assistance in the form of computers, stipends, and tuition from individual faculty, student, or family donations and CSRL scholarships (see Chapter 7).

Most MAK service-learning students reported a great deal of satisfaction from their experiences of facilitating technology transfer to farmers via the knowledge and planting materials that the primary school children took home. Their supervising professors reported (1) a substantial increase in students' self-confidence from exposure and adaptation to new cultures, views, and challenges; (2) a development of leadership and research skills among students due to the demands of coming up with appropriate projects for addressing some of the challenges facing farm families; and (3) a shift in the participating students' attitudes about agriculture as a profession and the utility of pursuing graduate study in an agricultural field versus the more traditional areas of postgraduate education for talented science students in Uganda such as medicine.

There is also emerging trend data that suggests a higher percentage of MAK service-learning students have gone on to graduate school—both in Uganda and abroad—than the agricultural student population at large.[8] These factors, combined with the cost effectiveness of the program versus other internship programs, have resulted in an increasingly competitive selection process. Based on successful feedback from CSRL, CAES decided to adopt a service-learning model for all of its internship programs.

Management and Financial Systems. As previously noted, few activities were funded directly through MAK. Most faculty and students received their stipends or scholarships directly from CSRL's Uganda office or through a direct contract for service. And ISU and MAK already had somewhat compatible financial systems. Although the policies were different, the accounting systems were similar; thus, the partnership required few adjustments in management or financial services.

Financial Resources. The program brought many direct financial benefits to MAK during its ten-year partnership. These benefits included supporting seventy-three MAK students' participation in the joint ISU-MAK service-learning activities in Kamuli and another 150 students for other types of training and research related to the program.

During the same time period, over thirty-one MAK faculty members have participated in the program's activities with different levels of CSRL-funded support. Other faculty benefited from further training and professional development from funds that the CSRL team obtained through research grants from other sources (see Box 9.3).

Box 9.3 CSRL Financial Support for MAK Faculty, Undergraduate, and Graduate Training, 2004–2013

- Provided full scholarships for seventy-three MAK students who participated in the joint ISU-MAK service-learning activities in Kamuli;
- Sponsored the participation of 150 MAK undergraduate and graduate students in other types of training and research activities related to the program;
- Facilitated scholarships to fund the PhD-level training of four junior faculty members from its own private gift funding sources, various departments, or USAID;
- Helped fund two MAK students' undergraduate and graduate studies at MAK; fifteen MAK students who were not junior faculty to attend ISU for graduate or undergraduate studies; eleven MAK student interns for two months at ISU; and
- Facilitated individual ISU faculty and alumnae and financial support to another seven MAK students through Friends of CSRL.

Source: CSRL program records with updates from Gail Nonnecke, Dorothy Masinde, and Haroon Sseguya, October 2013.

In addition to this core financial support, a number of ISU faculty and departments have provided support to some of the MAK faculty and their former students in developing larger grants and collaborative research support programs.

Sustaining Institutional Achievements

The heavy involvement of CSRL with MAK's Department of Agricultural Extension and Innovations helped transform the department into one of the strongest in CAES. In the course of MAK's collaboration with the CSRL service-learning program, the university has codeveloped a new model for the internship program that is a core requirement for all undergraduate programs. The same program has exposed MAK to the possibility of developing its own foundation and privately supported endowments like the ones ISU used to launch CSRL. MAK's next challenge is to develop a solid plan for consolidating and scaling up some of the newfound capacities and ideas that it acquired under the partnership.

Identify Ways that CSRL Partners Can Help Support a Scale-Up of MAK's Service Learning. MAK is moving forward with its current plans to reform its entire internship program by modeling it after the ISU-MAK service-learning and school garden program, and by creating regional learning centers. To achieve this, the college will partner with Ministry of Agriculture, Animal Industry, and Fisheries to ensure that internship students are integrated into, and supported by, the ministry's programs. It is expected that MAK will institutionalize ISU-MAK service learning so that it is recognized as a unique academic activity with a separate budget line and a coordinating office with a full-time service-learning and internship coordinator. In addition to the logistical challenges such as paying for the centers, this presents a host of new opportunities for MAK and its partnership with ISU and VEDCO. These new opportunities include considering (1) ways that the CSRL partnership can strengthen the service-learning curricula's local- and national-level impacts; (2) ways that the CSRL partnership can be used to develop more cost-effective methods of supporting MAK's service-learning activities and any physical infrastructure needed to scale up the CSRL program's unique model for building livelihood assets; (3) ways that the CSRL model can help strengthen the research impacts of the service-learning model in key areas needed for building household assets and resiliency in Uganda; and (4) ways that the CSRL model can help support collaborative development research between ISU and MAK faculty.

Attract a New Generation of MAK Faculty from More Diverse Departments to the CSRL Program. Many of the young faculty members who were the pillars of the CSRL program during its first eight years are no longer able to support the program because they have moved on to higher levels of responsibility in the university, where their top priority is to teach and bring in large grants to help fund their students and applied research programs. The overwhelming majority of the MAK professors who CSRL worked with during its initial phase came from two departments in CAES—the Department of Agricultural Extension and Innovations and the Department of Animal Sciences. As CSRL prepares to move into a new phase of engagement with MAK, the university must elaborate a strategy for bringing in a new generation of professors. The same challenge offers an opportunity to work with a wider range of departments within the college, and to work with other colleges like the SPH; the College of Veterinary Medicine, Animal Resources, and Bio-Security; and the School of Distance and Lifelong Learning.

Increase Second-Generation Grants that Complement CSRL's Kamuli Activities. When the CSRL program first started, there were a large number of lecturers who had not yet completed their PhDs. Today, this is far less of a problem since most new MAK professors already have their degrees. MAK is also no longer awash with external rehabilitation grants, which means the university is eager to develop externally funded grants, which carry high percentages of overhead to support some of its operating costs. To address this issue, CSRL must either find departments where the lure of funding young lecturers for external study abroad still holds; help these new professors and their students engage in externally funded applied research in connection with the program; or partner with MAK in applying for large grants that will benefit ISU, CSRL, and MAK.

Rethinking the Partnership to Capitalize on Multiplier Effects

The CSRL program's partnership with MAK was always very different from the one that it had with VEDCO. This is because MAK was never charged with executing a wing of CSRL activities and it was a mature international university whose financial, research, and teaching systems had been carefully reconstructed and expanded through a wide range of international support following the Ugandan civil war. ISU was only one of its many US and European partners.

The chief weakness of the collaboration during this initial phase was that it was informal in every area except service learning (Chapter 7) and the program's participatory monitoring and evaluation system (Chapter 8).

Once the service-learning program started, the collaboration was more formal and focused on the design, execution, and assessment of this student program as part of the core curriculum of both universities (Chapter 7). The same service-learning program provided a means for three junior MAK faculty to become actively involved. Since 2005, a MAK faculty member has led all of the program's external quantitative evaluations (Chapter 8). The chief problem with this arrangement was that, although the professor was tasked with the global design and execution of the survey, VEDCO was responsible for the analysis of the survey. This divided responsibility made it difficult to analyze programmatic impacts over time (see Chapter 8).

Three challenges for the next phase of MAK's participation in the CSRL partnership will be (1) identifying the best ways that ISU can collaborate with MAK as it seeks to scale up the concept of service learning to the other partners that host MAK interns; (2) clarifying the role of MAK in the design and analysis of the CSRL M&E system; and (3) developing a strategic plan for the next phase of the partnership.

Iowa State University

In 2004, ISU was at a critical crossroads in its international agriculture programs. Steep declines in US government and donor funding for international agricultural research were making it harder and harder to support the active research programs that had made ISU one of the leading international agriculture research institutions in the United States.[9] At the same time, the university was under internal and external pressure to internationalize its curriculum and student training.

When ISU began the CSRL program, it was interested in pilot testing the use of private benefactor support to back more sustainable development partnerships (i.e., partnerships that were less vulnerable to the volatile ups and downs of federal or other grant funding).

Although institutional capacity building was never a formal objective of the CSRL program, its activities set in motion a series of changes that have completely transformed the international programs of the College of Agriculture and Life Sciences (CALS). These changes are the result of (1) giving the ISU faculty and students an opportunity to work on real-world problems in a real-world institutional context; (2) creating a new interdisciplinary undergraduate major in global resource systems; and (3) helping to connect ISU students, faculty, and administrators with a large number of undergraduate and graduate students and faculty from Uganda.

Conducting a Baseline Analysis of Essential Institutional Strengths and Weaknesses

Human Resources Development. During the planning years before CSRL was formally established, there was recognition within CALS that only a few faculty and students had hands-on experience on the African continent, and there had been relatively few long-term relationships with an African institution—none with an NGO. The number of African students on the ISU campus was negligible. When the possibility of private gift funding emerged, it did not take long for a critical mass of the ISU community to recognize that the CSRL idea might be the perfect opportunity to create long-term learning experiences for faculty, staff, and students in a developing country.

Institutional Services. Within CALS, there was a clear recognition that, by selecting an African NGO as the primary partner to lead the field program, ISU would have to learn a whole new culture. This was one of the factors that made selection of an NGO partner an attractive option—everyone could learn together. By selecting VEDCO as the primary partner to lead the field program, ISU gained access to the workings of a tested farmer education model, vast rural Ugandan knowledge, and valuable networks with other NGOs and local governments. By partnering with MAK, ISU benefited from departmental knowledge of Uganda, a vast array of technical knowledge and expertise that was tested in Uganda, and important research and private sector networks.

Management and Financial Systems. While ISU had ample experience with US government and private foundation contracts, it had less of a track record with the financial realities of developing country NGOs and universities. This lack of experience is reflected in the fact that the partnership began without any sort of planning for joint accounting or accountability training to ensure that ISU's accounting standards could be met (see Chapter 4).

Financial Resources. When the CSRL program started, ISU had almost no private benefactor support or endowments for international work in developing countries—and no endowments to support any activities in Africa. It was hoping to pilot test this type of collaboration in conjunction with the program (see Chapters 1 and 2).

Developing a Flexible Plan to Build Institutional Capacity

Human Resources. One of the greatest impacts has been to increase the number of senior ISU faculty and staff with experience in Africa. A total of forty-three faculty and staff representing two-thirds of the academic units in the college and 50 percent of the administrative units in the university have collaborated with the CSRL program in Uganda.[10] This direct investment of the program in this type of human resources development has had a host of downstream consequences for the university's core institutional services.

Institutional Services. By law, US land grant universities have three core functions: teaching, research, and extension.

Teaching. One of the most important indirect impacts of this increased faculty capacity has been to strengthen ISU's teaching program at five levels:

- Creation of a new model for study abroad at ISU—based on lessons learned from the CSRL service-learning pilot test, ISU has added additional undergraduate study abroad programs on all seven continents, and the CSRL school garden program has inspired a second service-learning program in 2009 at Gifft Hill School in the US Virgin Islands;
- Revision of core courses and addition of new courses—to date, over eight courses in CALS have been revised by ISU faculty members based on their field experience in Kamuli;
- Creation of a new undergraduate major—the 2009 creation of a new CALS undergraduate major in global resource systems had over 100 students enrolled in 2013 and is one of the fastest-growing undergraduate majors in the college. This new major is a direct outgrowth of the CSRL service-learning program in the sense that it was created to respond to students' demand for more interdisciplinary courses dealing with development;
- New opportunities to expose students to international issues— the CSRL program has helped create a series of activities intro-

ducing a new model for internationalizing the student experience at ISU. By 2013, fifty-six ISU and seventy-three MAK students and nine faculty and staff have participated in the service-learning activities in Uganda, and a high percentage of the undergraduate CALS student body has been affected by the program's outreach activities; and

- Creation of a nucleus of students from Uganda—the same CSRL core and spin-off programs have helped attract a large number of Ugandan students—eleven undergraduates and twenty graduate students (from 2005 to 2013)—as well as international visitors from Uganda to the campus, ranging from five to ten per year.[11]

Some of the best indicators of the longer-term impacts of the CSRL on ISU's teaching mission are the early evidence of impact on service-learning students' lives: (1) it is estimated that, as of 2013, 63 percent of ISU service-learning graduates are in MS and PhD programs that will likely lead to careers in international agriculture and in global development–related fields; (2) of the four global resource systems interns who graduated and completed their global internship with CSRL programs in Kamuli, three are planning careers in international work; and (3) three global resource systems student interns were selected for the US Peace Corps, all of whom were in the service-learning and school garden program in Kamuli. Their Peace Corps assignments are in countries in West Africa.

Research. To date, the impact on funded faculty and student research and grants development has been most pronounced in the departments of agronomy, animal science, and sociology.

- Agronomy—since 2005, various faculty and students in the department of agronomy have strengthened ISU research ties with Uganda through a wide range of new collaborative USAID research programs focusing on cowpeas, beans, maize, and integrated pest management. To date, over thirty students have conducted or are planning MS- or PhD-level research related or connected to the CSRL support in Kamuli, and several faculty have developed and or are planning new research programs;
- Animal science—the early involvement of one senior livestock specialist helped strengthen VEDCO's livestock programs through a combination of support from CSRL, Monsanto Fund, and International Agricultural Research Center donors. Many of these same grants have supported ISU MS and PhD student pro-

grams and are encouraging more junior faculty to become interested in international research; and

- Sociology and rural sociology—to date, two faculty and five MS and PhD students have developed or are developing applied research programs, or have published on various aspects of the CSRL's activities in Uganda.

Extension. A USAID-funded extension initiative in 2012–2013 involved two ISU extension staff and three Iowa farmer-to-farmer volunteers working with 180 women farmers in Kamuli to help them improve maize and soybean crop management, postharvest handling, collective marketing, and recordkeeping skills.[12]

A wholly unexpected impact of the program was the creation of a series of student-led public outreach programs, public awareness presentations, and CSRL-related articles in university and college magazines, the ISU Foundation magazine, and the student newspaper. Also the recently remodeled Harl Commons in Curtiss Hall, which houses CALS, now features Ugandan coffee in its global café. Fifty percent of the college's commission from the global café goes back into the CSRL field budget.[13]

Financial and Management Systems. The CSRL program helped strengthen ISU's understanding of the financial realities of developing country NGOs and universities as well as what types of training and capacity building are needed to make them compatible with ISU's accounting standards (see Chapter 4).

The program has also highlighted some of the most important management strategies that may need to be devised in order to administer this type of partnership, including (1) the addition of earmarked flexible funding to facilitate a process for building interdisciplinary management teams like the one CSRL pioneered, and (2) making organizational development for team management a prominent goal from the beginning.

One of the best indicators of the university's ownership of the CSRL concept was its willingness to assist in every aspect of ISU's registration as an official NGO in Uganda in November 2013 (see Chapter 4). This registration facilitates the program's independent management of this and any other ISU program in Uganda.

Financial resources. CSRL pilot tested a new model for using private donor funding to support international programs. The successful implementation of this model has provided a model for two other CALS endowments. The same program has strengthened some of ISU's existing linkages to the International Agricultural Research Centers, National Agricultural Research Centers, foundations, and international donor agencies that ISU faculty can use to develop future donor-funded international programs.

The founding benefactors' original pledge in 2004 of $8 million to endow the CSRL program, plus the other $2 million provided to get the program started, has helped leverage approximately $2 million of additional internal support from CALS between 2004 and 2014—largely for salaries, graduate student support, and travel. Other leveraging has come in the form of research awards. Between 2005 and 2013, ISU faculty generated seventeen different competitive research grant awards— all of which have been focused on Uganda's development problems—of over $4.6 million. This does not account for the many additional forms of support that CSRL receives from ISU departments and colleges across the total university. There is also a certain amount of qualitative evidence that the ISU faculty's exposure to African opportunities and networks through the CSRL program has led to an increase in grant success in Africa and other developing country areas (Table 9.1).

Sustaining Institutional Achievements

ISU is justifiably proud that the CSRL program has had a host of positive spin-offs for each of its partners as well as itself. Since almost all of the partners' original objectives for the partnership have been achieved, it is time to rethink the next phase of objectives for each partner and the partnership as a whole. To facilitate this process, ISU received approval in 2013 to operate as an independent NGO in Uganda. This new status, which took over two years to accomplish, will give ISU more autonomy in managing its existing and any new partnerships. A critical next step will involve the development of a strategic plan with the existing partners to clarify their objectives for the future and to determine if any new partners should be added.

Execute and Monitor the First Strategic Plan for Service Learning.
The service-learning program has completed its first five-year strategic plan (see Chapter 7). This includes a provisional M&E plan that will allow it to more easily track the program's graduates as well as the impacts of some of the school activities that they support. This tracking system should make it easier for the CSRL program to determine how to sustain certain aspects of these activities as other parts of the program undergo change.

Table 9.1 External Grants for African-Related Research in the ISU College of Agriculture and Life Sciences, 2013–2014

Grant Name	Region Country,	Link Between CSRL and the Grant	Grant Source	Grant Amount
Enabling applied seed technologies	Africa-wide	Faculty and department; no direct link to CSRL	Gates	$3.2 million
Review of seed programs at African universities	Africa-wide	Faculty; CALS recommended MAK be included	Gates	$200,000
African plant breeding masters program	Africa-wide	Faculty; CALS recommended MAK be included	Gates	$1.6 million
Seed cleaning	Uganda	Faculty; CSRL directly involved in the implementation	Gates	$100,000
Agricultural technology transfer	Ghana	CSRL experience was attractive to prime and funding agency, made CALS more attractive as a partner	USAID, International Fertilizer Development Center	$1.6 million
Agricultural policy	Ghana	CSRL experience was attractive to prime and funding agency, made CALS more attractive as a partner	USAID, Chemonics	$1.1 million
Heat stress	Egypt	Associate director involved in livestock took the lead on this grant and used his experience in Uganda	Illumina	$45,000
Poultry disease resistance	Africa-wide	CSRL created high level of interest among animal science faculty when three visited Uganda; indirect link	USAID	$921,000
Food security model development	Global	No direct link	USDA, Economic Research Service	$35,000

Source: Compiled by David Acker, CALS associate dean, based on data from CALS Global Programs records. Table attached to e-mail from David Acker to Lorna Michael Butler, January 28, 2014.
Note: Totals have been rounded.

Encourage Participation of More Diverse Group of Faculty, Staff, and Departments. Within five years, almost all of the original faculty members who created the CSRL program will be retiring or moving toward retirement. This opens the door to creating new connections with different departments. This expansion should be much easier than the original start-up since the CSRL program is well established within the university.

Consider Ways that Students Can Conduct Applied Research to Strengthen the CSRL Program. One option for increasing the involvement of young faculty—many of whom still have to do research to secure their positions at the university—will be to identify various ways that ISU and MAK faculty and students can conduct applied research that will complement the program. This type of applied research is an attractive option to some of the small grant funds for East Africa since it offers an opportunity for immediate scale-up of research findings for the greater good.

Lessons Learned and Recommendations

The CSRL experience highlights how this type of creative partnership between very different institutions can build organizational capacity in new areas. When staff members participate in a partnership, they are exposed to new networks, knowledge, and resources. The results can help leapfrog an institution or a department within an institution into new leadership roles. For these results to be sustainable, home institutions need to build their internal capacity to support these new leadership roles. CSRL partner institutions were willing to capitalize on these achievements by (1) adding senior staff and support staff positions, and developing new systems for managing grants in some of the oversight offices (in the case of VEDCO and ISU); (2) reforming certain elements of the undergraduate curriculum (in the case of ISU and MAK); (3) designating core staff to manage new functions such as the service-learning program at MAK and ISU; and (4) seeking complementary funds from other sources within and outside of the university to help partners respond to some of their priority needs that could not be met by the gift.

These complementary investments helped to sustain the initial CSRL activities and to introduce a host of new activities that strengthened the achievement of the program's core objectives.

Today—ten years after the CSRL partnership began—each partner is at a different level from where it was when the program started. Many of the farmers and groups that the program has helped have increased their assets to the point that they can sustain their higher living standards with only minor program input. The next phase of the program presents a host of special challenges, which include determining how the partners will agree on (1) the best criteria to use to determine when villages and households are ready to graduate from the program; (2) what actions will be needed to sustain the graduated villages and households once they no longer are CSRL target households and villages; and (3) what types of M&E systems will be needed to track the program in the future.

During the same time period, the partners need to reassess their priorities for partnership in the future—both within Kamuli and in other areas of Uganda and globally.

Conducting a Baseline Analysis of Essential Institutional Strengths and Weaknesses

Once the partners agree on a core program, they must agree on what capacities they will need to execute the program, who will provide them, and how they will be provided. No one partner has all of the skills that the partners need, and certain skills—such as accounting, monitoring and evaluation, and reporting—are needed by everyone. Many of these may not have been apparent during the initial courtship. Each partner will have strengths and weaknesses that the other partners can help it to better understand, analyze, and utilize.

> **Lesson 1:**
> **Facilitate each institution conducting a self-assessment survey that will help it to understand some of the internal limitations and strengths that may be needed to carry out partnership obligations.**

Recommendations:
- Encourage a frank and open discussion of each partner's institutional objectives for the partnership from the start, and determine which objectives overlap with the objectives of the program.
- Review the core institutional capacities that each partner has and will need to execute the program.
- Identify which types of training and training programs will be needed to build each partner's capacities, and determine what

types of program-funded and institution-specific training will be needed to achieve these objectives.
- Agree to a system for assessing the effectiveness of training programs in building institutional capacity in the areas targeted by each institution's capacity-building plan.

Developing a Flexible Plan to Build Institutional Capacity

If a partnership is successful in building the core capacity of its partners during the initial phase, it creates a group of partners with greater capacity and more far-reaching objectives for a second phase. For this reason, any new program needs to create a means to continually review the core capacities of all partners.

Lesson 2:
Develop a flexible plan within each partner institution to take advantage of capacity-building opportunities and needs.

Recommendations:
- Agree to a preliminary plan for tracking each partner's progress toward the achievement of its own institutional objectives and projected growth curve for the partnership, and track this information as part of the program's M&E plan.
- Review the institutional capacity-building subplan each year.
- Consider interpartner Memorandums of Understanding (MoUs) to identify the need for institutional capacity self-assessment and tracking as part of the core partnership agreement.

Sustaining the Institutional Achievements of the Partnership

If the partners want to sustain the program-generated spread effects of a private benefactor–funded program, they will need to jointly decide how to adjust policies, resources, and programs to accommodate the innovations. This is equally true in a finite-length project as well as long-term partnership since no program or NGO is likely to remain the same indefinitely. Each member of the partnership may need to grapple with issues such as how to adjust human resources policies and salary structure to retrain new staff, how to continue to offer certain essential training to be competitive, and how to strengthen existing successful programs to take advantage of models that the program has piloted.

Lesson 3:
Build in mechanisms to help each institution maintain and absorb the capacities that it is likely to develop in the course of executing the partnership.

Recommendations:
- Conduct an annual review among all partners of the institutional capacities being developed under the partnership.
- Monitor the effectiveness of all institution-specific or partnership-wide training programs used in achieving the goals outlined in each partner's capacity building plan.
- Consider the value of each partner conducting an early baseline review of its human resources policies to determine which policies encourage or discourage staff participation and retention.
- Facilitate annual or biannual updates of the human resources review as part of the annual partnership planning process.

Rethinking the Partnership to Capitalize on Multiplier Effects

If a partnership is successful in its initial phase, it creates a group of partners with more ambitious objectives and greater capacity in a second phase. If these new, even more ambitious objectives mesh with those of the partnership, they can lift the partnership to even greater heights of collaboration. If these new objectives move individual partners in different directions, the partnership may no longer serve its intended purpose. It is critical for institutions to keep their fingers on the pulse of the partnership as it grows and develops while remaining sensitive to shifts in partner objectives and capacities.

Lesson 4:
Build in mutually acceptable ways to help the partnership to capitalize on the capacities that are built during the partnership.

Recommendations:

- Anticipate that the partners' objectives for the partnership may shift as their capacities change.
- Anticipate the need to renegotiate partner agreements and MoUs as capacities change.
- Consider each partner's newly developed capacities in planning partnership changes, and consider ways that this may affect the next phases of the partnership.

Notes

1. That is, training in agronomy, soil science, food science, agribusiness, natural resource economics, animal science, or plant pathology.

2. VEDCO staff level as of December 2013.

3. These collaborative programs have been funded by various donors including: McKnight Foundation (promoting production and consumption of grain amaranth); ILRI (development of the smallholder pig value chain); Biodiversity International (integration of small ruminants in farming systems); International Institute of Tropical Agriculture (IITA, promotion of bananas and tuber production); and USAID (strengthening nutrition and marketing of beans, and beans and soil management using biological nitrogen fixation).

4. Overhead is an accounting term referring to the costs of doing business with a customer, or for the implementation of a contract (e.g., an additional 10–75 percent of the total costs). The early contracts with VEDCO included the addition of a 10 percent administrative cost or overhead; this was soon increased to 15 percent.

5. World Bank, "Implementation Completion and Results Report (IDA-3624) on a Credit in the Amount of SDR 4.0 Million (US$5.0 million equivalent) to the Republic of Uganda for the Decentralized Services Delivery: A Makerere University Training Pilot Project," Report No: ICR0000136 (Washington, DC: December 1, 2006).

6. These factors include the heavy concentration of social scientists and faculty with extension experience in the original ISU management group; the support that ISU's management team received from several members of this department with the early connections to Ugandan NGOs; and the CSRL program's reliance on junior faculty from this department for the execution of the first baseline studies.

7. As part of the CRSP, which was funded by USAID, various faculty in the Department of Food Technology and Nutrition served as co–principal investigators and have directed graduate student research in bean processing for value addition, formulation of nutritious meals, and iron availability. These areas of investigation are all important to the goals of CSRL, and they have increased human capabilities. These studies have been conducted by Ugandan students while attending ISU, and in cooperation with the Department of Food

Science and Technology at MAK. These projects have been part of larger studies coupling increased agricultural production of common beans with improved household nutrition.

8. Ten of forty-one service-learning students who have graduated from MAK by January 2013 have applied for and received scholarships for graduate school at ISU (24 percent). Another eleven have been admitted to graduate programs in Uganda or Europe (27 percent) (total 51 percent).

9. Between 1946 and 1995, ISU CALS's trajectory was similar to colleges at other land grant universities. ISU formally began its international development and outreach activities in 1945 with the founding of the ISU Tropical Research Center in Guatemala. In 1961, an office responsible for overseeing international activities was opened, but it was not until July 1973 that an international office was officially established in CALS. ISU was active in USAID projects in the 1970s and 1980s. Since then, the Global Programs Office, along with ISU departments and centers, has been engaged in international research and development activities in over forty countries throughout the world.

10. Approximately thirty-five CALS faculty members, representing ten of the fifteen academic units within the college. Another five senior administrators—including the current and previous CALS deans, two university presidents, one vice president, and one department chair—also visited the field program. In addition, five accountants and administrative personnel who are involved in the financial management of the college's international programs visited several times for audits and training sessions with the VEDCO staff.

11. Initially, only the CEOs of the Uganda partners visited ISU. Before long, the visits expanded to include student interns, technical staff, accountants, and administrators.

12. Margaret Smith and Linda Naeve, *Strengthening Value Chains for Maize for Soybeans for Uganda Women Farmers,* Final Report, Feed the Future (FTF) Niche Project No. 1071-20-505-1 (Ames: Iowa State University Extension and Outreach, 2012).

13. "ISU Dining Hall to Open Global Café as Part of Curtiss Hall Renovations," *Iowa State Daily,* September 3, 2013, http://www.iowastatedaily.com/news/article_60e6b2e8-1320-11e3-b9b1-001a4bcf887a.html.

Epilogue:
The Partnership Today and Looking Toward the Future

Lorna Michael Butler and David G. Acker

Capacity development is an investment in the future. Iowa State University (ISU), Makerere University (MAK), and Volunteer Efforts for Development Concerns (VEDCO) built capacity at many levels—among primary school students, community-based trainers, local staff, university students, university faculty and staff, local leaders, volunteers, community residents, and donors. Perhaps most significant, the partners themselves—MAK, VEDCO, ISU, Kamuli communities, and donors—grew in ways they had not anticipated. Learning the way forward, together, has been essential to an inclusive development process. Everyone who participated in the Center for Sustainable Rural Livelihoods (CSRL) program has been touched in some way by the experience.

This chapter provides an overview of where the partnership and the community-based program is today, and some of the challenges that lie ahead for each in order to move the Kamuli communities closer to achieving the central goal of the program—achieving sustainable livelihoods.

The Partnership Today

CSRL has evolved far beyond anything anticipated in 2004. All of the partners, including the Kamuli communities, have benefited from the partnership. MAK now has a group of young faculty who are more highly trained and whose department has become greatly respected. MAK's student internship program is being transformed, and students' attitudes are more positive about agriculture as a career. VEDCO has adopted many of the Kamuli advances to improve their organization in other Ugandan districts. ISU has become more globally focused through a university-wide strategic plan that elevates the importance of ISU being engaged as a global land grant university. Many Kamuli community members have grown in their leadership capabilities, local farmers have become more knowledgeable and are more willing to adopt improved practices, and many families have improved their personal livelihoods.

The CSRL program would have been difficult to organize without the transformative impact of private funding that allowed for a carefully designed approach and a long-term commitment. What a rare opportunity it was, for all those who participated, to begin to think about a development program with an open-ended time frame. Another factor that may be rather rare at universities was the link between the university's foundation and faculty members who became part of CSRL. Faculty and foundation officers collaborated, and this made all the difference when it came to connecting groundbreaking ideas to interested benefactors, keeping donors engaged, and expanding the donor base. Enthusiasm for CSRL spread from faculty members and donors to other faculty, staff, students, family members, alumni, and friends—an extra bonus for development education at home.

A diverse partnership opens up unanticipated opportunities. One way this happens is through the blending of different competencies. For example, VEDCO, an organization with over twenty years of grassroots experience, had a level of local knowledge that neither of the universities possessed. It had local networks, and its personnel knew how to train and support community leaders. MAK had experience with monitoring and evaluation, and with student internships. Both of these strengths fit well with CSRL's goals. Being a member of the implementing team contributed to the desire by MAK's College of Agricultural and Environmental Sciences for an improved internship model patterned after the service-learning model. ISU's College of Agriculture and Life Sciences (CALS) had deep disciplinary knowledge of crop and livestock systems and social change. It also placed a high priority on student education but, without CSRL, ISU would have lacked opportunities for faculty and students with an interest in real-world global learning experiences.

Becoming involved with CSRL and Uganda has had a major impact on CALS at ISU. Global engagement will be a primary focus for the college for the foreseeable future. Even across the university, there are indications that faculty and students from several other colleges who have been involved with CSRL have brought this influence home. ISU's commitment to CSRL has deepened as illustrated by the registration in Uganda of the ISU-Ugandan program as a nongovernmental organization (NGO), and the decision to hire a full-time campus-based director for the program.

Perhaps some of the most important elements of the partnership are the relationships that have been forged and the increased level of communication and trust that now exists. All of the partners know that CSRL is in Uganda for the long run, and with this come continual opportunities to innovate.

Future Challenges

Expanding the Partnership. The next phase of CSRL may demand a closer examination of what "partnership" means. Partners' roles could become more focused, depending on their strengths, and new partners could be added. There could be different types of partnerships, for example, to address program gaps within the lifelong learning model[1] that are not well suited to any of the current partners.

Growing the Numbers of Young Participants. Young people are the key to the future—the next generation's parents, farmers, and businesspeople. Based on ten years of experience, it is apparent that CSRL will need to give more attention to young people. Some will be students at the primary, secondary, and university levels; however, there also are many young people in Kamuli communities who need to acquire skills and knowledge outside of the formal school setting to guarantee a bright future for their families and communities. A recent pilot program in training youth in agricultural entrepreneurship looks promising and may be a model for the future.

Advancing Donor Stewardship. CSRL donors range in age from ten to eighty years old. One challenge is to find the right communication channels to keep all of the donors informed and engaged. Newsletters, a website, regular donor trips to Uganda, and annual reports have been used to date. CSRL's cost of administering its program remains low. This tradition will need to be maintained to ensure donors that their funds are carefully administered. Moreover, new donors are the lifeblood of any charitable endeavor and CSRL is no different. CSRL has correctly chosen to develop a successful model and an impactful program before investing in a major fund-raising campaign for its programs. When this is launched, it will need to consider the potential that new donors offer to the long-term health and future growth of the program.

Improving Communication. As more and different partners are added to CSRL, regular and open communications will become even more important. Increased attention will need to be devoted to finding the best ways of keeping everyone apprised of changes and to soliciting continual input on decisions and policies that impact the program as well as the partnership.

The Program Today

Today's CSRL program is more focused, with better-integrated activities that respond to beneficiaries' needs. Program planning and implementation is more interdisciplinary. Team building has helped to bring different approaches together, as has regular communication between and among partners and staff members. A greater understanding of local knowledge about child malnutrition, anemia among women, and the ever present need for income helped to link the livestock and nutrition subprograms together. School gardens and livestock rearing have enhanced learning for primary school students; the gardens have become an important source of nutritious food for school lunch programs. More highly skilled community-based trainers have replaced the original cadre of community volunteers. Many program needs were not obvious in the planning phase. In many cases, their value to the beneficiaries could not have been anticipated.

Future Challenges

Empowering Communities. The partnership will have to seek alliances with local institutions and organizations to sustain important program elements. Could a blended model be devised that includes greater involvement of government health and agricultural extension workers, local schools, and farmers' associations? Links to permanent Kamuli institutions, as well as to capable and willing local leaders, will be the key to a successful planned disengagement. Perhaps it is reasonable to expect that any individual who "graduates" from a CSRL training module also has an obligation to pass on their knowledge to others. Support for this expectation will be needed.

Strengthening Learning Strategies. Diversifying learning methods and messages could increase impact, and involve a wider variety of trainers to teach and support future trainers. Messages could be segmented for beginning farmers compared to advanced levels of farmers. Farmers' own knowledge could become a greater part of the learning models.

Mobile learning may also help broaden the reach. The growth in the mobile phone market in Africa and the wide availability of this tool suggest increased opportunities for peer-to-peer learning, remote tutoring, and information sharing and access.

CSRL found it challenging to narrow the types of beneficiaries to which the program was directed. Why? Members of communities are intimately linked—infants with young parents, preschool children with primary school pupils, primary school pupils with secondary school pupils, grandparents with young children, and so on. Capacity development and learning opportunities at every stage of the life cycle are important to a functioning and sustainable community and to improving the livelihoods within it.[2]

Sustaining Vulnerable Households. Regardless of the community, there will always be families that need special assistance. Many communities have informal ways of supporting people in need; however, if they do not, CSRL needs to work with community leaders to ensure that there is a mechanism in place to support households that have limited resources or other serious challenges.

Promoting Small-Scale Commercialization. There are now substantial numbers of Kamuli farmers with whom CSRL has worked, who are food secure each year, whose children are healthy and attending school, and whose livelihoods have generally improved. CSRL would like to give more attention to this group of households and assist them with entrepreneurial skills and activities, perhaps in partnership with local companies and farmers' associations that have marketing experience. Training and advisory services are needed in value-chain development, value-added processing, transportation, accessing credit, and other business-related functions.

Conclusions and Future Directions

How might CSRL facilitate an acceptable level of sustainability in the Kamuli communities where it works in five or ten years? This was precisely the focus of a 2014 symposium that marked ten years of CSRL operation. The conversation and goal setting will continue with the beneficiary communities, local staff, and regional experts regarding improved links and strategies as well as potential roles. This planning process will lead to an exit strategy that can be documented in a collaborative pact.

CSRL started with a broad open agenda so as to respond to the many aspects of improving livelihoods in Kamuli communities. The team that designed the initial program had a lot of mutual respect, and they enjoyed working together. Quite likely, the same situation will lead the program into another phase that is different, but appropriate to the situation. This time, there will probably be a more targeted approach, perhaps with more inventive learning strategies to increase impact.

Another of CSRL's future commitments is to take donor support to a new level. Not only will it be important to identify new financial support for CSRL, but it will be equally important to show current donors that CSRL is delivering value for their investment. Improved communication will be essential, along with CSRL's ability to engage Kamuli communities in developing their own community foundations, in cultivating local volunteerism, and in identifying more local resources to support the communities' development priorities.

To achieve sustainability for both the partnership and the local program, it may be helpful to consider the meaning of philanthropy. When CRSL began, philanthropy was associated with the giving of funds by private individuals to launch and support the program. However, over time it has become evident that, in addition to financial gifts, many of CSRL's donors also give of themselves—mentoring young people, assisting them with their education, providing labor for local school improvements, working in school gardens, visiting Kamuli communities, producing videos about the program, serving on boards with similar goals, and encouraging friends and family to give to the program.

In the long term, CSRL's goal is to redefine philanthropy more in terms of the classical meaning of *philanthropy* as depicted in *Webster's* 1928 dictionary, "Love to mankind; benevolence toward the whole human family; universal good will; desire and readiness to do good to all men."[3] In the more contemporary sense, philanthropy may be seen as "voluntary action for the public good."[4] Yet the classical Greek meaning of *philanthropia*, going back for almost a thousand years, recognized the centrality of humanity, kindness, and charity between two persons.[5] Early scholars in the sixteenth and seventeenth centuries, such as Sir Francis Bacon, had already employed the word "philanthropy," but it did not enter common usage until the nineteenth century.[6]

With the broader definitions of philanthropy in mind, CSRL's future will involve working with partners and beneficiaries to make philanthropy a community endeavor, much like VEDCO's early model. Somehow, perhaps with greater public recognition, improved training, and greater peer support, it will be possible to return to the concept of neighbor-to-neighbor and farmer-to-farmer volunteerism for continuity of some of the most important development initiatives. CSRL will have accomplished a major part of its goals when community members feel sufficiently empowered to share their knowledge, skills, and humanity with their neighbors—and their neighbors do likewise—thereby carrying on CSRL's development activities.

This will be part of CSRL's exit strategy in the future. How can some of the competent and knowledgeable community members and organizations be encouraged and rewarded to voluntarily share their talents and skills with others? There are many kinds of philanthropy. Ultimately, the CSRL team will have to identify the best way to motivate philanthropy at the local level.

Notes

1. Today lifelong learning is viewed as the means of transforming economic systems in order to promote sustainable development. The globalization of society has redefined the nature of education and information. Learning opportunities must be available throughout individuals' lives, rather than being confined to formal education in the early part of life. The promotion of formal, nonformal, and continuing education, and making it accessible to all, is a means of developing the capabilities of individuals everywhere to overcome poverty and inequality, thereby leading to their participation in the building of a democratic society. Mazoor Ahmed, "Economic Dimensions of Sustainable Development: The Fight Against Poverty and Educational Responses," *International Review of Education* 56, no. 2/3 (2010): 235–253.

2. Food and Agriculture Organization (FAO) and United Nations Educational, Scientific and Cultural Organization–International Institute for Education Planning (UNESCO-IIEP), *Education for Rural Development: Towards New Policy Responses—A Joint Study Conducted by FAO and UNESCO* (Rome: FAO; Paris: UNESCO-IIEP, 2003).

3. Quoted in Marty Sulek, "On the Modern Meaning of Philanthropy," *Nonprofit and Voluntary Sector Quarterly* 39, no. 2 (2010): 193–212, at 197.

4. Robert Payton, *Philanthropy: Voluntary Action for the Public Good*, Macmillan Series on Higher Education (New York: American Council on Education, 1988).

5. Sulek, "On the Modern Meaning of Philanthropy."

6. Ibid.

Acronyms

ACDI/VOCA	Agricultural Cooperative Development International/Volunteers in Overseas Cooperative Assistance (NGO)
BS	Bachelor of Science
CAEC	Continuing Agricultural Education Center (Makerere University)
CAES	College of Agricultural and Environmental Sciences (Makerere University)
CALS	College of Agriculture and Life Sciences (Iowa State University)
CARE	Cooperative for Assistance and Relief Everywhere (NGO)
CEO	chief executive officer
CHF	Canadian Hunger Foundation (NGO)
CIAT	International Center for Tropical Agriculture
CREEC	Center for Research in Energy and Energy Conservation (Makerere University)
CRSP	Collaborative Research Support Program
CSRL	Center for Sustainable Rural Livelihoods
DFID	Department for International Development
DVM	Doctor of Veterinary Medicine
FANTA	Food Aid and Nutrition Technical Assistance
FAO	Food and Agriculture Organization of the United Nations
FTBIC	Food Technology and Business Incubation Center (Makerere University)
HDDS	Household Dietary Diversity Score
HDI	Human Development Index
HFIAS	Household Food Insecurity Access Scale
HFSS	Household Food Security Scale
HIV/AIDS	human immunodeficiency virus/acquired immunodeficiency syndrome
I@MAK	Innovations at Makerere
ICRAF	World Agroforestry Centre
ICT	information and telecommunication technologies

IDA	International Development Association
IDS	Institute of Development Studies
IGA	income-generating activity
IITA	International Institute of Tropical Agriculture
ILRI	International Livestock Research Institute
IMAM	Integrated Management of Acute Malnutrition
IPTT	indicator performance tracking table
ISU	Iowa State University (Ames, Iowa)
MAK	Makerere University (Kampala, Uganda)
M&E	monitoring and evaluation
MBA	Master of Business Administration
MoU	Memorandum of Understanding
MS	Master of Science
MUARIK	Makerere University Agricultural Research Institute Kabanyoro
MUBFS	Makerere University Biological Field Station
NAADS	National Agricultural Advisory Services
NACRRI	National Crop Resources Research Institute
NARO	National Agricultural Research Organisation
NASULGC	National Association of State Universities and Land Grant Colleges
NDP	National Development Plan
NEC	Nutrition Education Center
NGO	nongovernmental organization
Oxfam	Oxfam International (NGO)
PDA	personal digital assistant
PhD	Doctor of Philosophy
PM&E	participatory monitoring and evaluation
PPAB	Partner Planning and Advisory Board
PRA	participatory rural appraisal
QS	Quacquarelli Symonds
SANREM	Sustainable Agriculture and Natural Resource Management
SL	sustainable livelihoods
SLF	sustainable livelihoods framework
SO	strategic objective
SO1	Strategic Objective One
SO2	Strategic Objective Two
SO3	Strategic Objective Three
SO4	Strategic Objective Four
SPH	School of Public Health (Makerere University)
SRL	Sustainable Rural Livelihoods
SWOT	strengths, weaknesses, opportunities, and threats
UGX	Ugandan shilling
UNDP	United Nations Development Programme
USAID	United States Agency for International Development
USDA	United States Department of Agriculture
VEDCO	Volunteer Efforts for Development Concerns
WAN	wide area network
WFP	World Food Programme of the United Nations

Major Institutional Partners in the CSRL Program

Iowa State University

Iowa State University (ISU) is a land grant university, a special class of university created by the Morrill Act passed by the US Congress in 1862. Iowa was the first state to accept the law's provisions. Subsequently, ISU pioneered the idea of extension—extending the university's knowledge throughout the state. Iowa State's founders believed that higher education should be accessible to all, and that the university should teach liberal and practical subjects to prepare productive citizens from all walks of life. Early courses in agriculture focused on animal husbandry, agronomy, and horticulture, with the addition of the nation's first forestry course in 1874, dairying in 1880, and the world's first agricultural engineering program in 1905.

ISU's 2010-2015 strategic plan intentionally endorses the university's global commitment.[1] According to the plan, ISU's mission is to "create, share, and apply knowledge to make Iowa and the world a better place." Priorities stress the preparation of students who will "make a difference in the world" and who will succeed as "global citizens"; internationally recognized faculty, staff, and students; and strong "outreach and global partnerships to promote scientific advances, economic growth, creative thinking, and improvement of the human condition." ISU places priority on being a treasured state, national, and global resource through the involvement of the "citizens of Iowa and the world in collaborative interactions through extension, outreach, and engagement."

Iowa State is a public university, specializing in science and technology, with more than 33,000 students, 6,300 faculty and staff, and 277,000 alumni. In 2013, there were 3,797 international students from over 100 countries. The university's overall budget is approximately $1.2 billion.

The College of Agriculture and Life Sciences (CALS) is one of the world's leading institutions of agriculture, ranked fifth in the world in 2014 by Quacquarelli Symonds (QS) World University Rankings among universities offering programs in agriculture and forestry.[2] The mission is to educate future leaders, conduct mission-oriented basic and applied research, and share new knowledge for the betterment of Iowa and the world. The college provides leadership in science, education, and research in areas vital to the future of Iowa, the nation, and the world. CALS, one of seven colleges at ISU, is recognized for its strengths in crop and animal sciences, agricultural economics, agricultural engineering, environmental science, statistics, and the life sciences that support agriculture. The college aspires to lead the world in "science with practice" that shapes the future and improves lives and livelihoods.

The college has over 5,000 students as of 2014, with an annual budget of approximately $70 million plus competitively awarded research funding. During a period of flat or declining budgets spanning the past twelve years, CALS has increased its investment in international programs. This is evidence of the growing priority of global engagement.

Globalization is prominent in the CALS strategic plan. Among other items, this includes the engagement of faculty, staff, and students in global issues; students who will make a difference in the world; and being globally recognized for addressing twenty-first-century global challenges like food security, food safety, climate change, environmental stewardship, renewable energy, and human health.

Makerere University

Makerere University (MAK), one of Africa's oldest and most respected universities, was first established as the Uganda Technical College in 1922. Today, it is the largest of nine public universities in Uganda (there are over thirty private universities). Makerere, well known as a center for higher education in East Africa, has a long and impressive history. In 1949, it became a University College affiliated with the University of London. By 1963, it became the University of East Africa, which offered general degrees in cooperation with the University of London. In 1970, it became an independent national university offering its own undergraduate and graduate degrees. MAK offers day, evening, and long-distance education to approximately 35,000 undergraduate students and 3,000 graduate students, many of whom are from other countries. Makerere is also a major research institution with a research agenda that emphasizes six different themes and five cross-cutting areas, each linked to Uganda's National Development Plan (NDP). It is also the home of a number of unique centers as a result of its many partnerships such as the Food Technology and Business Incubation Center (FTBIC) and the Center for Research in Energy and Energy Conservation (CREEC).

In 2011, MAK became a collegiate university. It has nine constituent colleges—Agricultural and Environmental Sciences; Business and Management Sciences; Engineering, Design, Art and Technology; Education and External Studies; Health Sciences; Humanities and Social Sciences; Computing and Information Sciences; Natural Sciences; Veterinary Medicine, Animal Resources and Bio-Security—and one school (School of Law), each operating autonomously within the university.

Makerere's College of Agricultural and Environmental Sciences (CAES) has extensive resources associated with its three schools and eight departments. There are two institutes, one of which is the Makerere University Agricultural Research Institute Kabanyoro (MUARIK). This institute links to the national agricultural research system and serves as a training and research center for public and private sector learning. Makerere University Biological Field Station (MUBFS) is located in Kibale National Park at Fort Portal (Western Uganda). The institute involves many collaborating institutions, and focuses on ecological, behavioral sciences, and socioeconomics research as well as hosting international short courses. In addition, there is a college-wide student internship program to ensure that every undergraduate student participates in a supervised field internship before graduation. CAES has about 189 academic staff and 145 support staff.

Volunteer Efforts for Development Concerns

Volunteer Efforts for Development Concerns (VEDCO), an independent voluntary organization in Uganda, was founded in 1986 by a group of young Makerere University students hailing from the Luwero Triangle (area north of Kampala where Yoweri Museveni and his rebels started a guerrilla war in 1981). They volunteered their time to help communities displaced by the 1970s and 1980s civil war, known as the Ugandan Bush War or the Luwero War. The conflict, which destroyed the entire community's production system, gave birth to voluntary initiatives like VEDCO. This period of upheaval was a continuation of the turbulent political history in Uganda during which an army officer, General Idi Amin, deposed his boss and mentor President Milton Obote in January 1971. Idi Amin himself unleashed a reign of terror and a dictatorship between 1971 and 1979, which was notorious for human rights abuses and mass killings. Amin's "economic war" saw the expulsion of Asians and the collapse of the Ugandan economy. In

1978, a combined force of Tanzanian soldiers and Ugandan exiles, including Yoweri Museveni, ousted Amin from power and paved the way for Obote's return to the presidency in December 1980.

Museveni, upset over a fraudulent election, took his National Resistance Army to the bush and waged a guerrilla war lasting five years. In 1985, a coup d'etat against Obote ended his rule and, in 1986, Museveni became president of Uganda. A period of relative peace and transformation ensued, and the country gained the trust of the international donor community. The outcome was a thriving civil society that worked with the government to reduce poverty among the population.

This turbulent history explains the birth, survival, and eventual growth of VEDCO, whose community programs transformed from a relief focus to emphasizing sustainable livelihood improvements. These new directions appealed to donors. The organization devised a community-based extension system that eventually formed the foundation of community outreach and knowledge management in other spheres of human survival such as nutrition and health and market access.

By 2011, VEDCO's annual operating budget reached over 5 million Ugandan shillings (US$1.9 million). VEDCO's mandate is now focused on the equitable empowerment of small- and medium-sized farmers through programs that emphasize food and nutrition security, agricultural trade, and organizational development.

VEDCO uses a farmer-to-farmer approach for training farmer groups in improved agricultural technologies, family nutrition, household sanitation, marketing, and entrepreneurship. Community-based trainers are taught to engage small groups of farmers in their own communities in the use of improved technologies for increasing the production of maize, bananas, cassava, sweet potatoes, pulses (common beans, soybeans), grain amaranth, and other crops as well as in methods of animal improvement and management. They use demonstration farms, multiplication gardens, field days, and other participatory methods for farmer and group training. VEDCO is coordinated through its office in Bukesa, Kampala, with other offices in Kamuli (Buyende and Kamuli Districts), Apac (Apac and Kole Districts), Lira (Alebtong and Lira Districts), Luwero (Wakiso, Luwero, Nakasongola, and Nakaseke Districts), Mukono (Mukono and Buikwe Districts), Moyo, Yumbe, Pader, Amuria, Kanungu, Ibanda, Kabale, and Kisoro.

Notes

1. Iowa State University, 2010, *Strategic Plan 2010–2015*, Ames, Office of the President, http://www.president.iastate.edu/sp.

2. Quacquarelli Symonds (QS) World University Rankings, 2014, http://www.topuniversities.com/university-rankings/world-university-rankings.

Bibliography

Acker, David, Grace Marquis, Dorothy Masinde, and Gail Nonnecke. 2005. "Key Elements of a School Gardening and Feeding Program: Kamuli District School Gardens Plans Resulting from Participatory Visit." Unpublished Report. Ames: Center for Sustainable Rural Livelihoods, Iowa State University.

Africare. 2005. "How to Measure the Months of Adequate Household Food Provisioning." Unpublished Document. Washington, DC: Africare.

Africare. 2007. "Guidance: How to Measure the Number of Months of Adequate Household Food Provisioning (MAHFP) Based on Participatory Rural Appraisals in Food Security Interventions." *Africare Food Security Review* 2 (September).

Ahmed, Mazoor. 2010. "Economic Dimensions of Sustainable Development: The Fight Against Poverty and Educational Responses." *International Review of Education* 56: 235–253.

Ashby, Jacqueline A. 1986. "Methodology for the Participation of Small Farmers in the Design of On-Farm Trials." *Agricultural Administration* 22, no. 1: 1–19.

Bashaasha, Bernard. 1992. *Soybean Research in Uganda.* Paper prepared for USAID Manpower for Agriculture Development (MFAD). Washington, DC: USAID, Manpower for Agriculture Development (June): 1–14. http://pdf.usaid .gov/pdf_docs/PNAB&271.pdf.

Biggs, S. D. 1989. "Resource-Poor Farmers Participation in Research: A Synthesis of Experiences from Nine National Agricultural Research Systems." On-Farm Client-Oriented Research Comparative Study Paper No. 3. The Hague, the Netherlands: International Service for National Agricultural Research.

Blodget, Henry. 2006. "Grant Away: Why Venture Philanthropy Is Important, Even if It Sounds Ridiculous." *Slate Magazine,* November 13, www.slate.com /articles/life/philanthropy/ 2006/11/grant_away.html.

Bouverini, Luisa C. 2005. "When Venture Philanthropy Rocks the Ivory Tower: An Examination of High Impact Donors and Their Potential for Higher Education Development." PhD diss., University of Pennsylvania. http://repository.upenn .edu/dissertations/AAI3168014.

Brainard, Leal, and Derek Chollet. 2008. *Global Development 2.0: Can Philanthropists, the Public, and the Poor Make Poverty History?* Washington, DC: Brookings Institution.

Brilliant, L., J. Wales, and J. Rodin. 2007. "The Changing Face of Philanthropy." Paper presented at the Sixth Annual Global Philanthropy Forum Conference, "Financing Social Change: Leveraging Markets and Entrepreneurship," Mountain View, CA, April.

Brinkerhoff, David W., and Jennifer M. Brinkerhoff. 2005. *Working for Change: Making a Career in International Public Service.* Bloomfield, CT: Kumarian Press.

Brinkerhoff, Jennifer M. 2002. *Partnership for International Development: Rhetoric or Results?* Bloomfield, CT: Kumarian Press.

Butler, Lorna Michael. 1995. *The "Sondeo": A Rapid Reconnaissance Approach for Situational Assessment.* Western Regional Extension Publications, WREP0127. Pullman: Washington State University. http://cru.cahe.wsu.edu/CEPublications/wrep0127/wrep0127.html.

———. 2003. "SRL Think Tank Forum: Summary of Highlights." Sustainable Rural Livelihoods Internal Document. Ames: Center for Sustainable Rural Livelihoods, Iowa State University.

Canadian Hunger Foundation (CHF) Partners in Rural Development. 2005. *Sustainable Livelihoods Approach Guidelines.* Ottawa, Ontario: CHF Partners in Progress. http://www.shf.ca/documents/Manuals_and_Guidelines/SLA_Guidelines.pdf.

Carnegie Foundation for the Advancement of Teaching. 2010. Classification Description, Community Engagement Elective Classification. http://classifications.carnegiefoundation.org/ descriptions/communityengagement.php.

Case, D'Arcy Davis. 1990. *The Community's Toolbox: The Idea, Methods and Tools for Participatory Assessment, Monitoring and Evaluation in Community Forestry.* Volume 2 of Community Forestry Field Manual. Bangkok, Thailand: FAO Regional Wood Energy Development Programme in Asia, Food and Agriculture Organization of the United Nations, 1990.

Chambers, Robert. 1983. *Rural Development: Putting the Last First.* London: Longmans.

———. 1997. *Whose Reality Counts?: Putting the First Last.* London: Immediate Technology.

Chambers, Robert, and B. P. Ghildyal. 1985. "Agricultural Research for Resource-Poor Farmers: The Farmer-First-and-Last Model." *Agricultural Administration* 20, no. 1: 1–30.

Coates, Jennifer, Anne Swindale, and Paula Bilinsky. 2007. *Household Food Insecurity Access Scale (HFIAS) for Measurement of Food Access: Indicator Guide,* Version 3. Washington, DC: Food and Agriculture Technical Assistance (FANTA) Project.

Department of Open and Distance Learning, School of Distance and Lifelong Learning, Makerere University. "Distance Education." http://www.distance.mak.ac.ug/distance-education.html.

Eddy, Pamela L. 2010. *Partnerships and Collaborations in Higher Education.* ASHE (Association for the Study of Higher Education) Higher Education Report. Hoboken, NJ: Wiley.

Eyler, Janet, and Dwight E. Giles. 1999. *Where's the Learning in Service Learning?* San Francisco: Jossey-Bass.

Fleishman, Joel L. 2007. *The Foundation: How Private Wealth Is Changing the World*. New York: Public Affairs Books.

Food and Agriculture Organization (FAO) and United Nations Educational, Scientific and Cultural Organization–International Institute for Education Planning (UNESCO-IIEP). 2003. *Education for Rural Development: Towards New Policy Responses—A Joint Study Conducted by FAO and UNESCO*. Rome: UNESCO-IIEP; Paris: FAO.

Friedman, Eric. 2013. *Reinventing Philanthropy: A Framework for More Effective Giving*. Washington, DC: Potomac Books.

Iowa State University. 2010. *Strategic Plan 2010–2015*. Ames, Office of the President. http://www.president.iastate.edu/sp.

Iowa State University, News Service. 2004. "Gifts of $10 Million Will Endow ISU Program That Helps Developing Nations." November 1. http://www.public.iastate.edu/~nscentral/news/04/nov/srl.shtml.

Isubikalu, Prossy. 2009. *Evaluation Report: Sustainable Rural Livelihood Improvement Program in Kamuli District, Uganda*. Kampala: Makerere University; Ames: Center for Sustainable Rural Livelihoods, Iowa State University.

"ISU Dining Hall to Open Global Café as Part of Curtiss Hall Renovations." 2013. *Iowa State Daily*, September 3. http://www.iowastatedaily.com/news/article_60e6b2e8-1320-11e3-b9b1-001a4bcf887a.html.

Johnson-Pynn, Julie S. 2005. Success and Challenges in East African Conservation Education. *Journal of Environmental Education* 36, no. 2: 25–39.

Kamuli District Planning Unit. 2011. "District Development Plan for 2010/11–2014/15." Kamuli, Uganda: Kamuli District Local Government, May.

Katunguka, Samwiri. 2005. "The Learning Innovations Loan Funding Towards Capacity Building for Decentralization in Uganda." Paper presented at a World Bank workshop on the organization and management of innovation funds, Maputo, Mozambique, October 11–13, 2005. http://siteresources.worldbank.org/INTAFRREGTOPTEIA/Resources/Uganda_lif.pdf.

Klein, Kim. 1999. "Donor Cultivation: What It Is and What It Is Not." *Grassroots Fundraising Journal* 18, no. 5: 1–3.

Kurauchi, Yuko, and Sarah Anyoti. 2013. "Enhanced Resilience of Drought Prone Communities Through Conservation Agriculture: The Case of Uganda." Forum for Agricultural Risk Management in Development (FARMD). Washington, DC: FARMD.

Letts, Christine W., William Ryan, and Allen Grossman. 1997. "Virtuous Capital: What Foundations Can Learn from Venture Capitalists." *Harvard Business Review* 75, no. 2: 36–44.

Lowenstein, Ralph. 1997. *Pragmatic Fundraising for College Administrators and Development Officers*. Gainesville: University of Florida Press.

Magezi, Robert Winx. 2012. *VEDCO/CSRL Nutrition and Health Survey Report 2011–2012*. Kampala: VEDCO.

Makerere University. 2007. *Makerere University Annual Report (2007)*. Kampala: Makerere University, http://pdd.mak.ac.ug/sites/default/files/archive/makerere%20university%20%20report2007_final_0.pdf.

Makerere University College of Agricultural and Environmental Sciences (CAES). 2014. "Vision and Mission." Kampala: Makerere University. http://caes.mak.ac.ug/about-us/vision-and-mission.html

Masinde, Dorothy. 2004. "Minutes of Meeting with Makerere University Staff." Unpublished Document. Kampala, SRL office, November 19.

————. 2004. "Minutes of the First Technical Committee (TC) Meeting of the SRL Program Held at VEDCO Boardroom." Unpublished Document. Kampala, December 3.

Masinde, Dorothy, Lorna Michael Butler, and Mary Nyasimi. 2014. *Livelihood Improvement Through Training and Experience: An Analysis of Uganda Volunteer Trainers*. Draft Report. Ames: Center for Sustainable Rural Livelihoods, Iowa State University.

Masinde, Dorothy, Robert Mazur, and Lorna M. Butler. 2004. "Technical Committee." Unpublished Document. Kampala, SRL office, October.

Matama, Esther, Benon Musaasizi, and Laura Byaruhanga. 2012. "Strategic Objective Three (SO3): Reduce Malnutrition Levels Among Women of Reproductive Age and Children." In Della E. McMillan, ed., *Sustainable Rural Livelihoods Program: Summative Monitoring and Evaluation (M&E) Report: 2005–2012*. Draft Report. Ames: Center for Sustainable Rural Livelihoods, Iowa State University.

McMillan, Della E., ed. 2012. *Sustainable Rural Livelihoods Program Summative Monitoring and Evaluation (M&E) Report: 2005–2012*. Draft Report. Ames: Center for Sustainable Rural Livelihoods, Iowa State University.

McMillan, Della E., and Alice Willard. 2008. *Preparing for an Evaluation*. M&E Module Series. Washington, DC: American Red Cross; Baltimore: Catholic Relief Services.

McMillan, Della E., Alice Willard, and Guy Sharrock. 2008. *IPTT Guidance: Guidelines and Tools for the Preparation and Use of Indicator Performance Tracking Tables*. M & E Module Series. Washington, DC: American Red Cross; Baltimore: Catholic Relief Services.

Mercy Corps. 2005. *Design, Monitoring and Evaluation Guidebook*. Portland, OR: Mercy Corps.

Morino, Mario, and Bill Shore. 2004. *High Engagement Philanthropy: A Bridge to a More Effective Social Sector*. Report No. 4. Washington, DC: Venture Philanthropy Partners and Community Wealth Ventures.

National Association of State Universities and Land Grant Colleges (NASULGC) Task Force on International Education. 2004. *A Call to Leadership. The Presidential Role in Internationalizing the University*. http://www.aplu.org/Net Community/Document.Doc?id=340.

Payton, Robert. 1988. *Philanthropy: Voluntary Action for the Public Good*. Macmillan Series on Higher Education. New York: American Council on Education.

Quacquarelli Symonds (QS) World University Rankings. 2014. http://www.top universities.com/university-rankings/world-university-rankings.

Rapando, Nancy, Stephen Kato, Ronnie Balibuzani, and Henry Kizito Musoke. 2012. "Strategic Objective Four (SO4): Strengthen the Organizational Capacity of Farmer Organizations and Their Linkages to the Private- and Public-Sector Institutions that They Need to Build and Maintain Sustainable Livelihoods." In Della E. McMillan, ed., *Sustainable Rural Livelihoods Program: Summative Monitoring and Evaluation (M&E) Report: 2005–2012*. Draft Report. Ames: Center for Sustainable Rural Livelihoods, Iowa State University.

Republic of Uganda. 2008. "Kamuli District Local Government Five Year Strategic Plan, Orphans and Other Vulnerable Children Programme, Fiscal Year 2008/09–2012/13." Kamuli, Uganda, April.

Rhoades, R. E., and R. H. Booth. 1982. "A Model for Generating Acceptable Agricultural Technology." *Agricultural Administration* 11, no. 2: 127–137.

Sangi, Patrick, Jane Nakiranda, Nadiope Gideon, Charles Kategere, and Mark West-gate. 2013. "Strategic Objective One (SO1): Promote Resilient Climate-Smart Agricultural Technologies to Increase Food Availability." In Della E. McMillan, ed., *Sustainable Rural Livelihoods Program: Summative Monitoring and Evaluation (M&E) Report: 2005–2012*. Draft Report. Ames: Center for Sustainable Rural Livelihoods, Iowa State University.

SANREM Innovation Lab. 2014. "History: Phase IV." http://www.oired.vt.edu/sanremcrsp/public/about.

Sembera, John, Ronnie Balibuzani, and Jane Sempa. 2012. "Strategic Objective Two (SO2): Build Diversified Livelihoods and More Resilient Markets to Improve Food Access." In Della E. McMillan, ed., *Sustainable Rural Livelihoods Program: Summative Monitoring and Evaluation (M&E) Report: 2005–2012*. Draft Report. Ames: Center for Sustainable Rural Livelihoods, Iowa State University.

Senge, Peter. 1990. *The Fifth Discipline: The Art and Practice of the Learning Organization*. New York: Doubleday.

Smith, Margaret, and Linda Naeve. 2012. *Strengthening Value Chains for Maize and Soybeans for Ugandan Women Farmers*. Final Report, Feed the Future (FTF) Niche Project No. 1071-20-505-1. Ames: Iowa State University Extension and Outreach.

Social Innovator. 2010. "Venture Philanthropy." London, England: Social Innovation eXchange [SIX], 2010.

Sseguya, Haroon. 2006. *Annual Evaluation of the Livelihoods Improvement Program*. Ames: Center for Sustainable Rural Livelihoods, Iowa State University.

———. 2007. *Annual Evaluation of the Livelihoods Improvement Program*. Ames: Center for Sustainable Rural Livelihoods, Iowa State University.

———. 2011. *Evaluation of the Sustainable Rural Livelihoods Program in Kamuli District, Uganda. Summary Report*. Ames: Center for Sustainable Rural Livelihoods, Iowa State University.

Sseguya, Haroon, and Dorothy Masinde. 2005. *Towards Achievement of Sustainable Rural Livelihoods in Kamuli District, Uganda: A Baseline Assessment*. Ames: Center for Sustainable Rural Livelihoods, Iowa State University.

Sseguya, Haroon, Robert Mazur, and Dorothy Masinde. 2012. *Evidence of Impact and Transformation in Kamuli*. Ames: Center for Sustainable Rural Livelihoods, Iowa State University.

Sulek, Marty. 2010. "On the Modern Meaning of Philanthropy." *Nonprofit and Voluntary Sector Quarterly*, no. 2: 193–212.

Swindale, Anne, and Paula Bilinsky. 2006. *Household Dietary Diversity Score (HDDS) for Measurement of Household Food Access: Indicator Guide*, Version 2. Washington, DC: Food and Agriculture Technical Assistance Project.

Theroux, Karen. 2006. "Makerere at the Crossroads," *Carnegie Reporter* 4, no. 1. http://carnegie.org/publications/carnegie-reporter/single/view/article/item/164/.

Tierney, Thomas J., and Joel L. Fleishman. 2011. *Give Smart: Philanthropy That Gets Results*. New York: Public Affairs Books.

Tukamuhabwa, Phinehas, R. Kawuki, D. Nanfumba, T. Obus, and B. Bashaasha. 2012. "Overview of Impact Indicators of Soybean Rust Resistant Varieties on Uganda's Economy." Research application summary presented at the biennial meeting of the Regional Universities Forum for Capacity Building in Agriculture (RUFORUM), Entebbe, Uganda (September): 2155–2160.

United Nations Development Programme (UNDP). 2014. "Human Development Reports, Frequently Asked Questions—Human Development Index (HDI)." http://hdrstats.undp.org/en/countries/profiles/UGA.html.

———. 2014. "Human Development Reports. Table 2: Human Development Index Trends, 1980–2013." http://hdr.undp.org/en/content/table-2-human -development-index-trends-1980-2013.

Volunteer Efforts for Development Concerns (VEDCO). 2009. *VEDCO Strategic Plan Period 2009–2014.* Kampala: VEDCO.

Weiss, Tara, and Hannah Clark. 2006. "'Venture Philanthropy' Is New Buzz in Business." Forbes.com, June 26. http://www.nbcnews.com/id/13556127/ns/business -forbes_com/t/venture-philanthropy-new-buzz-business/#.VGptP1fF-Qw.

Wettasinha, C., L. van Veldhuizen, and A. Waters-Bayer, eds. 2003. *Advancing Participatory Technology Development: Case Studies on Integration into Agricultural Research, Extension and Education.* Silang, Cavite, Philippines: International Institute of Rural Reconstruction (IIRR), ETC Ecoculture, ACP-EU Technical Centre for Agricultural and Rural Cooperation.

World Bank. 2006. "Implementation Completion and Results Report (IDA-3624) on a Credit in the Amount of SDR 4.0 Million to the Republic of Uganda for the Decentralized Services Delivery." A Makerere University Training Pilot Project. Report No: ICR0000136. Washington, DC: The World Bank.

———. 2013. Participation and Civic Engagement. Washington, DC: World Bank.

———. 2013. Social Funds, "Social Analysis." Washington, DC: World Bank.

The Contributors

David G. Acker is associate dean for academic and global programs in the College of Agriculture and Life Sciences at Iowa State University, where he also holds the Raymond and Mary Baker Chair for Global Agriculture. He was a founding member of the Center for Sustainable Rural Livelihoods (CSRL) management team. He has directed agricultural and natural resource programs in Tanzania, Malawi, and Senegal and has been a Fulbright fellow in Greece. He is coauthor of (with Lavinia Gasperini) *Education for Rural People*.

Mateete Bekunda is chief scientist for the Africa RISING–East and Southern Africa Project and a farming systems agronomist for the International Institute of Tropical Agriculture (IITA), Arusha, Tanzania. In 2004, when CSRL's management team visited Uganda, he was dean of the Faculty of Agriculture at Makerere University. His collaboration helped establish the tripartite partnership that launched CSRL in Uganda. In 2008, he was named World Professor by Iowa State University's College of Agriculture and Life Sciences.

O. Richard Bundy III, inaugural president and chief executive officer of the University of Vermont Foundation, has extensive experience in fundraising for public higher education. As a founding member of the CSRL management team, he was chief liaison between CSRL and the Iowa State University Foundation in 2000–2010, during which time he held several positions with the Iowa State University Foundation.

Lorna Michael Butler, the first Henry A. Wallace Endowed Chair for Sustainable Agriculture at Iowa State University (2000–2007), was a founding member of the CSRL management team and Agriculture and Life Sciences Global Fellow (2009–2012). She chairs the CSRL Advisory Board and is an international consultant to the dean of the College of Agriculture and Life Sciences. She was previously professor and extension anthropologist at Washington State University. Her expertise is in rural development, sustainable agriculture, and livelihoods improvement in developing countries.

Lynn Hurtak is an independent editor and technical writer based in Saint Petersburg, Florida, specializing in food security and resettlement programs in Africa. Since 2009, she has edited and coedited technical papers, grants, and reports for dozens of projects throughout Africa as well as in Russia, Afghanistan, and Iraq.

Gerald A. Kolschowsky, along with his wife Karen, has devoted much of his philanthropy and volunteer service to the alleviation of hunger and poverty. He is former chairman of the board and co–chief executive officer of Aurora, Illinois–based OSI Industries, LLC, the predecessor to OSI Group, LLC, a global company that supplies products to many of the world's leading food brands. He and his wife are the founding benefactors of the Sustainable Rural Livelihoods Program at Iowa State University and the Tanzania Partnership Program at Michigan State University, both of which are working to establish partnerships between the United States and developing countries to address hunger and poverty.

Karen A. Kolschowsky is a recipient of the Iowa State University honorary alumni award and a lifetime member of the Iowa State University alumni association. She established the largest multicultural scholarship in the College of Agriculture and Life Sciences. She is best known for her enthusiasm and support for CSRL, the product of a founding gift from her husband and herself.

Donald Kugonza is lecturer in the Department of Agricultural Production at Makerere University, with an emphasis in animal agriculture. He serves as Makerere University's service-learning faculty leader and works extensively with Ugandan students as they complete their internships in CSRL's programs in Kamuli. His area of expertise is in the conservation and improvement of indigenous animal genetic resources.

Samuel Kyamanywa is professor of agricultural entomology, with over twenty-five years of expertise in agricultural entomology and integrated pest management. He was principal of the College of Agricultural and Environmental Sciences at Makerere University (2011–2013) and dean of the Faculty of Agriculture at Makerere University (2009–2011).

Dorothy Masinde, the first CSRL field program manager in Uganda (2004–2011), is lecturer in global resource systems in the College of Agriculture and Life Sciences at Iowa State University. In addition to her teaching role, she coordinates the global resource systems internships for Africa and serves as associate director for nutrition education for the CSRL program.

Robert Mazur, the founding director of CSRL (2003–2008), is professor in the Department of Sociology at Iowa State University and CSRL's associate director for socioeconomics. He is principal investigator in a Feed the Future Innovation Lab project, funded by the United States Agency for International Development (USAID), that addresses farmer decisionmaking in soil fertility management in maize-bean production systems in Uganda and Mozambique. His research interests are innovation and diversification in rural livelihood strategies, food security, and health.

Della E. McMillan, associate research scientist in the Department of Anthropology at the University of Florida, has worked as an independent consultant for over twenty nongovernmental organizations and international bilateral and international agencies, including the World Bank, United Nations Development Programme (UNDP), and USAID, in twenty-nine African countries. In 2012, she led an interactive training process that summarized CSRL's program assessment data to document program progress and lessons learned based on ten years of experience in Uganda.

Henry Kizito Musoke, a private entrepreneur who assists smallholder Ugandan farmers to improve soybean value-added opportunities, was chief executive officer of Volunteer Efforts for Development Concerns (VEDCO) when the CSRL program started operations in Uganda. He was one of the founding volunteers who helped establish VEDCO.

Gail Nonnecke is professor and Morrill Professor in the Department of Horticulture and founding faculty coordinator for global resource systems at Iowa State University. She initiated and manages CSRL's student service-learning and school garden program in Uganda, and she is CSRL's associate director for education. She conducts research on sustainable small fruit systems.

Max Rothschild is C. F. Curtis Distinguished Professor and M. E. Ensminger Chair in International Animal Science at Iowa State University. He is associate director for livestock production and health for CSRL, and coleads Iowa State University's research initiative on global food security. His interests are in genetic improvements for disease resistance and heat stress resilience in livestock, drought tolerance in livestock, and improving smallholder livestock production.

Haroon Sseguya is lecturer in the Department of Extension and Innovation Studies at Makerere University and CSRL's associate director for program evaluation. His areas of expertise include program planning, monitoring and evaluation, and rural development.

Mark E. Westgate is director of Iowa State University's CSRL (2009 to present) and professor of crop production and physiology in the Department of Agronomy. His research centers on understanding physiological mechanisms controlling seed formation and development of major agricultural crops. He recently led an international team working to improve yield of common beans in sub-Saharan Africa. He is a fellow of the American Society of Agronomy, Crop Science Society of America, and Australian National University.

Index

About the Book

In telling the story of an innovative program based at Iowa State University, Lorna Michael Butler, Della E. McMillan, and their colleagues offer practical step-by-step advice critical for any organization seeking to fund and manage multifaceted public-private partnerships for development.

The story begins when the College of Agriculture and Life Sciences at Iowa State University received large gifts from alumni and friends with a strong interest in Africa. Using that transformative funding, the university established the Center for Sustainable Rural Livelihoods and entered into collaborative long-term relationships with a university and a nongovernmental organization in Uganda. *Tapping Philanthropy for Development* draws on the partners' experiences to provide a unique road map for effectively navigating the challenges involved in obtaining nontraditional funding—and in using it well.

Lorna Michael Butler is professor emeritus of sociology and anthropology and Agriculture and Life Sciences Global Fellow at Iowa State University (2009–2012). **Della E. McMillan**, associate research scientist (adjunct) in the Department of Anthropology at the University of Florida, consults extensively on issues of development in Africa.